Ulla...," "Of Fishing," "A Nota Bene," "Of Haga," "Vain Quest of Beauty," "The Bathing Children," "Longing," "The Virgin Mary," "A Vagrant," from *Anthology of Swedish Lyrics from 1750 to 1925*, Copyright 1930 by the American-Scandinavian Foundation; "Gunnel the Stewardess," from *The Charles Men* by Verner von Heidenstam, Copyright 1920 by the American-Scandinavian Foundation; "Like an April Day," "The Lotus," "The Nixie," "Bird-Notes," "Norway's Highlands," "Burnt Ships," "With a Water Lily," "Light-Shy," "The Princess," "Synnöve's Song," "I Love You, Ha! You Brown-Skin Devil," from *Anthology of Norwegian Lyrics*, Copyright 1942 by the American-Scandinavian Foundation; "At Christmas," from *Told in Norway*, edited by Hanna Astrup Larsen, Copyright 1927 by the American-Scandinavian Foundation; "Eagle's Flight," from *The American-Scandinavian Review*, Copyright 1927 by the American-Scandinavian Foundation.

Mrs. Johannè Andersen-Nexø, Copenhagen: "The Passengers of the Empty Seats," from *Muldskud* by Martin Andersen-Nexø.

Ballantine Books, Inc., New York: Copyright © 1960, by Ulla Isaksson: "The Daughter of Töre in Vänge" from *The Virgin Spring*. Excerpted by permission of the publisher, Ballantine Books, Inc.

Mrs. Stina Bergman, Stockholm: "Judith," from *Labyrinten* by Hjalmar Bergman.

Mr. Paul Bjarnason, Vancouver: "The Northern Lights," "Wave-Life," "From 'Starkad's Soliloquy'," "My Mother," "Lone Peak," "When I Was an Editor," "Millennial Hymn," and "Just Like the Tender Flower," from *Odes and Echoes* by Paul Bjarnason.

The Bodley Head Ltd., London: "The Bird's Nest," from *The Queen of Kungahälla and Other Sketches*, by Selma Lagerlöf.

J. M. Dent & Sons Ltd., London: "Wildflowers and Hothouse-Plants," and "Gone," from *Lyrics and Poems from Ibsen*, translated by Fydell Edmund Garrett.

Mr. Gunnar Gunnarsson and the Ministry of Education, Reykjavík: "Father and Son," from *Seven Icelandic Short Stories*.

Gyldendal, Copenhagen: "Did They Catch the Ferry?" from *The Waving Rye* by Johannes V. Hensen; "The Gardener, the Beast, and the Child," from *Efterslæt* by Martin A. Hansen.

Mr. Tore Hamsun, Norway: "Just an Ordinary Fly of Average Size," from *Siesta* by Knut Hamsun.

Houghton Mifflin Company, Boston: "A Dangerous Wooing," from *The Bridal March and Other Stories* by Bjørnstjerne Bjørnson.

Mrs. Jakobina Johnson, Seattle: "A Greeting," "Farewell," and "At Close of Day," from *Northern Lights*.

Mr. R. P. Keigwin, England: "Morning Song," by Kingó, from *In Denmark I Was Born*. By permission of the translator, Mr. Keigwin, and of the publisher, Høst & Søns, Forlag.

Mr. Watson Kirkconnel, Novia Scotia, for his translations of "Passion-Hymn 50" and "Drift-Ice" from *The North American Book of Icelandic Verse*.

Alfred A. Knopf, Inc., New York: "The Death of Arne," reprinted from *Kristin Lavransdatter* by Sigrid Undset, by permission of Alfred A. Knopf, Inc., Copyright 1923 by Alfred A. Knopf, Inc.

Mr. Halldór Kiljan Laxness, Iceland: "The Defeat of the Italian Air Force in Reykjavík 1933," from *Sjö töframenn*, reprinted by permission of the author, Copyright 1942 by Halldór Laxness.

Macmillan & Co. Ltd., London: "It's Perfectly True!" and "The Shirt Collar," from Hans Christian Andersen's *It's Perfectly True and Other Stories*, translated from the Danish by Paul Leyssac.

Oslo University Press, Oslo: "The Dream Poem," from *Studia Norvegica*, 1946.

Random House, Inc., New York: "The Lift that Went Down into Hell," from *The Eternal Smile and Other Stories* by Pär Lagerkvist, Copyright 1954 by Random House, Inc. Reprinted by permission. Distribution outside the United States by permission of Chatto & Windus Ltd., London, publishers of *The Marriage Feast and Other Stories* by Pär Lagerkvist.

St. Olaf College Press, Northfield, Minn.: "From 'The Trumpet of Nordland'," from *The Trumpet of Nordland*, edited by Theodore Jorgenson.

Mr. Thórbergur Thórdarson, Reykjavík: "The Brindled Monster," from *Bréf til Láru*.

Mr. Arnulf Øverland, Oslo: "Thirty Dollars," from *Noveller i utvalg*.

TO MAY

without whose loving help
and encouragement
this book would never
have been attempted

CONTENTS

ICELAND

SWEDEN

PREFACE

For many readers, the world of Scandinavian literature remains a world untraveled. Although some of the highest peaks—Hans Christian Andersen's fairy tales, the philosophy of Søren Kierkegaard, the plays of Ibsen and Strindberg, and a few others—have been repeatedly scaled, the remainder of the landscape has gone nearly unnoted. Those who have made any incursions at all into the larger Scandinavian world have generally visited areas other than literature: films, for instance—those especially of Ingmar Bergman—and modern Scandinavian design, whose graceful simplicity has won many admirers. But literary regions have been explored by comparatively few outsiders. Yet these are anything but forbidding and one can hardly call them inaccessible; most major areas have, indeed, been fairly well mapped out. Besides the writers mentioned, there have been old and new editions of the works of Undset and Hamsun, Lagerkvist, Laxness, and many others. Hardly a year passes, either, without some new publications of Icelandic sagas, other Old Icelandic literature, or of scholarly works about it.

For all this, however, crossings between the Scandinavian and English-speaking worlds have been pretty much one-way. Scandinavians, both writers and readers, are acquainted with Anglo-American literature in the original as well as in translation, and are influenced by it. Contrarily, Americans seldom pick up a book of Scandinavian origin. This is one of the hard facts of life small nations must face. Because their writers are confined to languages spoken and understood by few, they remain overshadowed by their colleagues in larger nations, although they may be second to none as literary craftsmen. Scandinavia is part of Europe and Scandinavian literature has, broadly speaking, developed along much the same lines as European literature. With a few well-known exceptions, however, Scandinavian writers have, as it were, subsisted in a twilight of recognition while their French, German, Italian, and Russian colleagues have basked in the sun of fame. Even the lesser prophets of larger nations are familiar to American readers, but writers like Gustaf Fröding, Eyvind Johnson, Martin A. Hansen, William Heinesen, Olav Duun, Gunnar Gunnarsson, and Stephan G. Stephansson, to name but a few at random, go practically or entirely unheard here.

Hopefully, this state of affairs will change in time to come and there are, indeed, some signs to justify that hope. Of course, the immense popularity of Scandinavian goods in recent years may be a passing trend; similarly, people may grow tired or simply have their fill of Swedish movies. But the fact that these have found a public in America has important implications. It has contributed to a growing awareness of the Scandinavian world in general and—most important—indicates that Americans respond warmly to artistic expression from that area. Moreover, the range and depth of Scandinavian studies in American schools have increased steadily in recent years, and are likely to expand even more in years to come. Despite conflicts and hostilities in many parts of the world, nations continue to grow closer to one another. International cooperation in various areas progresses year by year, and even political leaders have come to be aware of the need for cultural exchange and free intercourse between nations. The literature of all countries—large and small—is of course one of the primary and most effective means of such mutual exchange and understanding.

As for the contents of this volume, those already acquainted with Scandinavian literature will inevitably find certain favorite authors missing; or they may feel that there is too much of one thing while too little of another. Space has been an obvious limitation; permissions and available translations have in some instances imposed further restrictions. Still, it is hoped that the experienced traveler will find here a rewarding balance of old landmarks and new vistas—and that the uninitiated will discover a whole area of fresh experience that will lead him to further exploration of the many-faceted domain of Scandinavian literature.

✳ ✳ ✳ ✳ ✳

Several people have given me valuable aid in the course of compiling this volume. I should very much like to thank all the individuals, firms, and institutions that have granted me permissions to use copyrighted material, as well as those of my friends, most notably Mr. William Akins, who have read and criticized my translations and introductions. I am grateful to Professor Charles W. Dunn of Harvard University for his encouragement during the early stages of my work. Thanks are also due to Professor C. A. Bodelsen of Copenhagen and Mrs. Lydia Cranfield of Orpington, Kent, England, whose gracious assistance has considerably enriched the book. I am indebted to my friend Professor Thórhallur Vilmundarson of the University of Iceland and Librarian Erling Grønland of Oslo University Library for their quick responses to my appeals for help. The American-Scandinavian Foundation and its Literary Secretary, Mr. Erik J. Friis, have also rendered generous assistance for which I am deeply grateful. Most of all, however, I owe a debt of gratitude to my wife, who has been not only my good adviser and critic, but virtually the second editor of my entire manuscript. It is befitting, therefore, that this book should be dedicated to her.

H. H.

DENMARK

INTRODUCTION

It is recorded that shortly before 800 the northward march of Charlemagne's armies was halted. Thirty years of campaigning against the Saxons of northern Germany had ended in the conversion of these heathens and in the extension of the Frankish kingdom all the way to the river Eider in southern Schleswig. The plan was to push even farther north. But this time the mighty conqueror failed.

On the northern bank of the river he was confronted by another heathen nation whose determination and valor in battle he could not overcome. For the first time, the Danes stepped into the spotlight of history. A few decades later, these same people repaid Charlemagne's visit and even stormed and plundered his old capital of Aix-la-Chapelle (Aachen). Nor did they stop there. By the end of the Viking age (c. 1000), they had established permanent rule over Normandy, conquered the whole of England, and penetrated as far as Sicily in the south.

Yet, in spite of all these accomplishments, the Danish realm was unstable. They did not have the power to follow up their conquests by colonization. Internal feuds and infiltration of German farmers and traders from the south further weakened their kingdom. Before the middle of the 11th century, England was lost, and the subsequent annexations of Baltic lands proved only temporary.

For the young warrior nation these were, nevertheless, glorious times and there surely were poets at hand to sing the praise of the heroes and laud their valiant deeds. Unfortunately, however, this early literature is now lost. Still, with the help of Old Icelandic verse, we can fairly well imagine the form of Danish poetry, while the Latin versions recorded by Saxo Grammaticus in his *Deeds of the Danes* (see p. 7) tell us that it was heroic in content.

Due to the influence of their German neighbors, the Danes adopted Christianity in the late 10th century, and with the new

3

religion came learning. Latin was the language of the Church and, consequently, the earliest records of Danish literature, written toward the end of the 12th century, are in that language. At that time, the long struggle for a centralized power vested in the king had proved, temporarily at least, successful. The realm could be called fairly well consolidated, and the Danes once again felt sure of themselves. Both these factors—patriotic pride in the stabilized prosperity of the country and the impact of the common European culture—are reflected in Saxo's writings.

This encounter with the more advanced civilization of Europe brought to the Danish nobility a certain refinement together with new forms of entertainment. Histrionics, clowns, jugglers, and singers made their way to the north and performed their arts to grateful audiences. During the 12th century, too, dancing became popular, and this, combined with the influence of German minnesingers and French troubadours, stimulated the growth of the Danish ballad.

Unlike the sacred poetry of the time, ballads were composed in the vernacular and sung, originally, as an accompaniment to the dance. They dealt mostly with love and chivalry and were written in the simplest of meters. Because they were easily understood by the common people, the ballads soon became more pleasing to Northern ears than the obscure and ornate skaldic praise poetry (see p. 183). Ballads were popular from about 1200 to the end of the Middle Ages (and beyond) and are considered the most important genre of Danish medieval literature.

With the economic and political growth of the Hanseatic League in the 14th century, Danish culture was further subjected to German influence. This became even more pronounced in the following century when German princes occasionally sat on the Danish throne. The marks left upon the Danish language are still visible. On the other hand, these circumstances had little immediate effect on the literature, for Latin remained the written language of the learned classes.

By the 16th century the vernacular had replaced Latin, but the energies of the Lutheran reformers and humanists were mainly devoted to translations and study of the past. Consequently, little new literature was created. It was not until the following century that some original writers emerged (see Kingo,

p. 21). The best of these baroque poets managed to make the Danish language a flexible instrument for their thoughts and moods, and for a time, poetry flourished in Denmark.

After the devastation of the Thirty Years' War, Germany—and its influence in Denmark—was considerably weakened. The trend of the time was toward despotism modeled after that of Louis XIV of France, and in 1660 Denmark became an absolute monarchy. By the beginning of the 18th century German influence had been replaced by that of the French Enlightenment. The growing prosperity of the bourgeois middle class—the principal supporters of absolutism—created a demand for new literature. While lyrical poetry declined, satire became popular. Danish drama, which had been practically nonexistent, became a flourishing genre (see Holberg, p. 24).

Then, in the second half of the 18th century, Danish writers were caught up by the German Renaissance and the literature of the *Sturm und Drang* poets. Like their neighbors to the south, the Danes turned their attention to lyrical poetry. At the same time, they cultivated serious drama, for which they frequently borrowed material from the heroic age (see Ewald, p. 41). From the literary ideals of these writers to those of the Romanticists it was only a short way.

The Romantic movement in Denmark not only nurtured gifted writers (see Oehlenschläger, p. 46); it also gave new impetus to the scholarly study of Scandinavian antiquity. The early Romanticists found most of their readers among the educated classes, but later writers of the movement made a conscious effort to reach every layer of society. The result was a literature which was at once more realistic and more sophisticated.

When the century was well past the halfway mark, it became apparent that a change of course was due in Danish literature. The spectacular defeat in the Dano-Prussian War of 1864 came as a shock and surprise. At the same time, Darwin was busily shattering man's belief in his divine origin. It was little wonder that young writers, impatient with the romantic dreamings of their elders, began to call for a new and more direct view of reality. Known alternately as Naturalists and Realists, they demanded the truth, however sordid, and ardently debated the social problems of the day. Nevertheless, many of those who set out under the banner of the new movement later defected (see Pontoppidan, p. 70), for in the long run naturalistic methods of observation did not satisfy them. By the 1900's they had, for the most part, either aligned themselves with the Neo-Romanticists or developed their own blend of subjective realism.

There was, among those writers reacting against Naturalism, a trend toward regional literature. In spite of a certain social consciousness, they frequently adopted a conservative view, while those who were more outspoken in their social criticism rallied to an essentially leftist outlook and later leaned toward Communism (see Andersen Nexø, p. 75). Still others attempted a counterreaction, enthusiastically hailing the new century of technological progress. The latter were materialistic in their views (see Jensen, p. 81).

As in so many other countries, the period after World War I produced a generation of disillusioned and, in many ways, confused writers. While faltering between Left and Right, they concerned themselves mainly with social problems, often depicting drab pictures of everyday life. Later, in the thirties, the rise of Nazism in neighboring Germany and the fall of the Spanish republic resulted in deep anxiety for the future of Europe, whose imminent doom was already visible.

SAXO GRAMMATICUS

(fl. c. 1200)

Although Saxo ranks among the great medieval historians, his life is obscure. However, the title Grammaticus, accorded him in the 14th century, indicates that he was considered a man of great learning.

Saxo's fame rests exclusively on his *Gesta Danorum* ("The Deeds of the Danes"), a history of Denmark from the earliest times to his own age. The work consists of sixteen books, the first nine of which deal with legendary times (before 800). His sources for this period were old myths and ancient heroic poetry.

Like most scholars of the Middle Ages, Saxo wrote in Latin, but the pervading spirit of his work is truly Danish. In fact, it is the first important Danish contribution to world literature.

"The Story of Amleth," the first part of which appears below in a slightly abridged form, is the earliest recorded version of the tale which Shakespeare later developed into his famous tragedy, *Hamlet*. Saxo flourished around 1200. His book dates from the same time.

The Story of Amleth

Horwendil and Feng, whose father Gerwendil had been governor of the Jutes, were appointed by Rorik[1] to defend Jutland. But Horwendil held the monarchy for three years, and then, to win the height of glory, devoted himself to roving. He passed three years in valiant deeds of war; and, in order to win higher

---

[1] More commonly spelled Rurik. Founder of the Kievan state which later became the nucleus of the Russian empire (see Sweden, Introduction, p. 271). Some confusion exists regarding his original nationality. While Saxo makes him king of the Jutes, other historians hold the view that he was a Swedish chieftain. According to old Russian chronicles he was from "beyond the sea."

rank in Rorik's favor, he assigned to him the best trophies and the pick of the plunder. His friendship with Rorik enabled him to woo and win in marriage his daughter Gerutha, who bore him a son Amleth.

Such great good fortune stung Feng with jealousy, so that he resolved treacherously to waylay his brother, thus showing that goodness is not safe even from those of a man's own house. And behold, when a chance came to murder him, his bloody hand sated the deadly passion of his soul. Then he took the wife of the brother he had butchered, capping unnatural murder with incest. Gerutha, said he, though so gentle that she would do no man the slightest hurt, had been visited with her husband's extremest hate; and it was all to save her that he had slain his brother; for he thought it shameful that a lady so meek and unrancorous should suffer the heavy disdain of her husband. Nor did his smooth words fail in their intent; for at courts, where fools are sometimes favored and backbiters preferred, a lie lacks not credit. Nor did Feng keep from shameful embraces the hand that had slain a brother; pursuing with equal guilt both of his wicked and impious deeds.

Amleth beheld all this, but feared lest too shrewd a behavior might make his uncle suspect him. So he chose to feign dullness, and pretended an utter lack of wits. This cunning course not only concealed his intelligence but ensured his safety. Every day he remained in his mother's house utterly listless and unclean, flinging himself on the ground and bespattering his person with foul and filthy dirt. His discolored face and visage smutched with slime denoted foolish and grotesque madness. All he said was of a piece with these follies; all he did savored of utter lethargy. In a word, you would not have thought him a man at all, but some absurd abortion due to a mad fit of destiny. He used at times to sit over the fire, and, raking up the embers with his hands, to fashion wooden crooks, and harden them in the fire, shaping at their tips certain barbs, to make them hold more tightly to their fastenings. When asked what he was about, he said that he was preparing sharp javelins to avenge his father. This answer was not a little scoffed at, all men deriding his idle and ridiculous pursuit; but the thing helped his purpose afterwards. Now it was his craft in this matter that first awakened in the deeper observers a suspicion of his cunning. For his skill in a trifling art betokened the hidden talent of the craftsman; nor could they believe the spirit dull where the hand had acquired so cunning a workmanship. Lastly, he always watched with the most punctual care over his pile of stakes that he had pointed in the fire. Some people, therefore, declared that his mind was quick enough, and fancied that he only played the simpleton in order to hide his understanding, and veiled some deep purpose under a cunning feint. His wiliness (said these) would be most readily detected if a fair woman were put in his way in some secluded place, who should provoke his mind to the temptations of love. So men were commissioned to draw the young man in his rides into a remote part of the forest, and there assail him with a temptation of this nature. Among these chanced to be a foster brother of Amleth, who had not ceased to have regard to their common nurture. He attended Amleth among his appointed train, being anxious not to entrap, but to warn him; and was persuaded that he would suffer the worst if he showed the slightest glimpse of sound reason, and above all if he did the act of love openly. This was also plain enough to Amleth himself. For when he was bidden mount his horse, he deliberately set himself in such a fashion that he turned his back to the neck and faced about, fronting the tail; which he proceeded to encompass with the reins, just as if on that side he would check the horse in its furious pace. By this cunning thought he eluded the trick, and overcame the treachery of his uncle. The reinless steed galloping on, with rider detecting its tail, was ludicrous enough to behold.

Then his companions purposely left him, that he might pick up more courage to practice wantonness. The woman whom his uncle had dispatched met him in a dark spot, as though she had crossed him by chance; and he took her and would have ravished her, had not his foster brother, by a secret device, given him an inkling of the trap. For this man, while pondering the fittest way to play privily the prompter's part, and forestall the young man's hazardous lewdness, found a straw on the ground and fastened it underneath the tail of a gadfly that was flying past; which he then drove toward the particular quarter where he knew Amleth to be: an act which served the unwary prince exceedingly well. The token was interpreted as shrewdly as it had been sent. For

Amleth saw the gadfly, espied with curiosity the straw which it wore embedded in its tail, and perceived that it was a secret warning to beware of treachery. Alarmed, scenting a trap, and fain to possess his desire in greater safety, he caught up the woman in his arms and dragged her off to a distant and impenetrable fen. Moreover, when they had lain together, he conjured her earnestly to disclose the matter to none, and the promise of silence was accorded as heartily as it was asked. For both of them had been under the same fostering in their childhood; and this early rearing in common had brought Amleth and the girl into great intimacy.

Thus all were worsted, and none could open the secret lock of the young man's wisdom. But a friend of Feng, gifted more with assurance than judgment, declared that the unfathomable cunning of such a mind could not be detected by any vulgar plot, for the man's obstinacy was so great that it ought not to be assailed with any mild measures; there were many sides to his wiliness, and it ought not to be entrapped by any one method. Accordingly, said he, his own profounder acuteness had hit on a more delicate way, which would effectually discover what they desired to know. Feng was purposely to absent himself, pretending affairs of great import. Amleth should be closeted alone with his mother in her chamber; but a man should first be commissioned to place himself in a concealed part of the room and listen heedfully to what they talked about. For if the son had any wits at all he would not hesitate to speak out in the hearing of his mother, or fear to trust himself to the fidelity of her who bore him. The speaker, loath to seem readier to devise than to carry out the plot, zealously proffered himself as the agent of the eavesdropping. Feng rejoiced at the scheme, and departed on pretense of a long journey. Now he who had given his counsel repaired privily to the room where Amleth was shut up with his mother, and lay down skulking in the straw. But Amleth had his antidote for the treachery. Afraid of being overheard by some eavesdropper, he at first resorted to his usual imbecile ways, and crowed like a noisy cock, beating his arms together to mimic the flapping of wings. Then he mounted the straw and began to swing his body and jump again and again, wishing to try if aught lurked there in hiding. Feeling a lump beneath his feet, he drove his sword into the spot, and impaled him who lay hid. Then he dragged him from his concealment and slew him. Then, cutting his body into morsels, he seethed it in boiling water, and flung it through the mouth of an open sewer for the swine to eat, bestrewing the stinking mire with his hapless limbs. Having in this wise eluded the snare, he went back to the room. Then his mother set up a great wailing, and began to lament her son's folly to his face; but he said: "Most infamous of women; dost thou seek with such lying lamentations to hide thy most heavy guilt? Wantoning like a harlot, thou hast entered a wicked and abominable state of wedlock, embracing with incestuous bosom thy husband's slayer, and wheedling with filthy lures of blandishment him who had slain the father of thy son. This, forsooth, is the way that the mares couple with the vanquishers of their mates; for brute beasts are naturally incited to pair indiscriminately; and it would seem that thou, like them, hast clean forgot thy first husband. As for me, not idly do I wear the mask of folly; for I doubt not that he who destroyed his brother will riot as ruthlessly in the blood of his kindred. Therefore it is better to choose the garb of dullness than that of sense, and to borrow some protection from a show of utter frenzy. Yet the passion to avenge my father still burns in my heart; but I am watching the chances, I await the fitting hour. There is a place for all things; against so merciless and dark spirit must be used the deeper devices of the mind. And thou, who hadst been better employed in lamenting thine own disgrace, know it is superfluity to bewail my witlessness; thou shouldst weep for the blemish in thine own mind, not for that in another's. On the rest see thou keep silence." With such reproaches he rent the heart of his mother and redeemed her to walk in the ways of virtue; teaching her to set the fires of the past above the seductions of the present.

When Feng returned, nowhere could he find the man who had suggested the treacherous espial; he searched for him long and carefully, but none said they had seen him anywhere. Amleth, among others, was asked in jest if he had come on any trace of him, and replied that the man had gone to the sewer, but had fallen through its bottom and been stifled by the floods of filth, and that he had then been devoured by the swine that came up all about that place. This speech was flouted by those who heard; for it seemed senseless, though really it expressly avowed the truth.

Feng now suspected that his stepson was certainly full of guile, and desired to make away with him, but durst not do the deed for fear of the displeasure, not only of Amleth's grandsire Rorik, but also of his own wife. So he thought that the King of Britain should be employed to slay him, so that another could do the deed, and he be able to feign innocence. Thus, desirous to hide his cruelty, he chose rather to besmirch his friend than bring disgrace on his own head. Amleth, on departing, gave secret orders to his mother to hang the hall with woven knots, and to perform pretended obsequies for him a year thence; promising that he would then return. Two retainers of Feng then accompanied him, bearing a letter graven on wood—a kind of writing material frequent in old times; this letter enjoined the king of the Britons to put to death the youth who was sent over to him. While they were reposing, Amleth searched their coffers, found the letter, and read the instructions therein. Whereupon he erased all the writing on the surface, substituted fresh characters, and so, changing the purport of the instructions, shifted his own doom upon his companions. Nor was he satisfied with removing from himself the sentence of death and passing the peril on to others, but added an entreaty that the King of Britain would grant his daughter in marriage to a youth of great judgment whom he was sending to him. Under this was falsely marked the signature of Feng.

Now when they had reached Britain, the envoys went to the king, and proffered him the letter which they supposed was an implement of destruction to another, but which really betokened death to themselves. The king dissembled the truth, and entreated them hospitably and kindly. Then Amleth scouted all the splendor of the royal banquet like vulgar viands, and abstaining very strangely, rejected that plenteous feast, refraining from the drink even as from the banquet. All marveled that a youth and a foreigner should disdain the carefully cooked dainties of the royal board and the luxurious banquet provided, as if it were some peasant's relish. So, when the revel broke up, and the king was dismissing his friends to rest, he had a man sent into the sleeping room to listen secretly, in order that he might hear the midnight conversation of his guests. Now, when Amleth's companions asked him why he had refrained from the feast of yester-eve, as if it were poison, he answered that the bread was flecked with blood and tainted; that there was a tang of iron in the liquor; while the meats of the feast reeked of the stench of a human carcass, and were infected by a kind of smack of the odor of the charnel. He further said that the king had the eyes of a slave, and that the queen had in three ways shown the behavior of a bondmaid. Thus he reviled with insulting invective not so much the feast as its givers. And presently his companions, taunting him with his old defect of wits, began to flout him with many saucy jeers, because he blamed and caviled at seemly and worthy things, and because he attacked thus ignobly an illustrious king and a lady of so refined a behavior, bespattering with the shamefulest abuse those who merited all praise.

All this the king heard from his retainer; and declared that he who could say such things had either more than mortal wisdom or more than mortal folly; in these few words fathoming the full depth of Amleth's penetration. Then he summoned his steward and asked him whence he had procured the bread. The steward declared that it had been made by the king's own baker. The king asked where the corn had grown of which it was made, and whether any sign was to be found there of human carnage? The other answered, that not far off was a field, covered with the ancient bones of slaughtered men, and still bearing plainly all the signs of ancient carnage; and that he had himself planted this field with grain in springtide, thinking it more fruitful than the rest, and hoping for plenteous abundance; and so, for aught he knew, the bread had caught some evil savor from this bloodshed. The king, on hearing this, surmised that Amleth had spoken truly, and took the pains to learn also what had been the source of the lard. The other declared that his hogs had, through negligence, strayed from keeping, and battened on the rotten carcass of a robber, and that perchance their pork had thus come to have something of a corrupt smack. The king, finding that Amleth's judgment was right in this thing also, asked of what liquor the steward had mixed the drink? Hearing that it had been brewed of water and meal, he had the spot of the spring pointed out to him, and set to digging deep down; and there he found, rusted away, several swords, the tang whereof it was thought had tainted the waters. The king, seeing that Amleth had rightly given the causes of the taste he had found so faulty, and learning that the ignoble eyes wherewith Amleth had reproached him concerned some stain upon his birth, had a secret interview with his mother, and asked her who his father had really been. She said she had submitted to no man but the king. But when he threatened that he would have the truth out of her by a trial, he was told that he was the offspring of a slave. Abashed as he was with shame for his low estate, he was so ravished with the young man's cleverness that he asked him why he had aspersed the queen with the reproach that she had demeaned herself like a slave. But while resenting that the courtliness of his wife had been accused in the midnight gossip of a guest, he found that her mother had been a bondmaid. For Amleth said he had noted in her three blemishes showing the demeanor of a slave; first, that she had muffled her head in her mantle as bondmaids do; next, that she had gathered up her gown for walking; and thirdly, that she had first picked out with a splinter, and then chewed up, the remnant of food that stuck in the crevices between her teeth. Further, he mentioned that the queen's mother had been brought into slavery from captivity, lest she should seem servile only in her habits, yet not in her birth.

Then the king adored the wisdom of Amleth as though it were inspired, and gave him his daughter to wife; accepting his bare word as though it were a witness from the skies. Moreover, in order to fulfill the bidding of his friend, he hanged Amleth's companions on the morrow. Amleth, feigning offense, treated this piece of kindness as a grievance, and received from the king, as compensation, some gold, which he afterward melted in the fire, and secretly caused to be poured into some hollowed sticks.

When he had passed a whole year with the king he obtained leave to make a journey, and returned to his own land, carrying away of all his princely wealth and state only the sticks which held the gold. On reaching Jutland, he exchanged his present attire for his ancient demeanor, which he had adopted for righteous ends, purposely assuming an aspect of absurdity. Covered with filth, he entered the banquet room where his own obsequies were being held, and struck all men utterly aghast, rumor having falsely noised abroad his death. At last terror melted into mirth, and the guests jeered and taunted one another, that he whose last rites they were celebrating as though he were dead should appear in the flesh. When he was asked concerning his comrades, he pointed to the sticks he was carrying, and said: "Here is both the one and the other." This he observed with equal truth and pleasantry; for his speech, though most thought it idle, yet departed not from the truth; for it pointed at the weregild of the slain as though it were themselves. Thereon, wishing to bring the company into a gayer mood, he joined the cupbearers, and diligently did the office of plying the drink. Then, to prevent his loose dress hampering his walk, he girdled his sword upon his side, and purposely drawing it several times, pricked his fingers with its point. The bystanders accordingly had both sword and scabbard riveted across with an iron nail. Then, to smooth the way more safely to his plot, he went to the lords and plied them heavily with draught upon draught, and drenched them all so deep in wine that their feet were made feeble with drunkenness, and they turned to rest within the palace, making their bed where they had reveled. Then he saw they were in a fit state for his plots, and thought here was a chance offered to do his purpose. So he took out of his bosom the stakes he had long ago prepared, and went into the building, where the ground lay covered with the bodies of the nobles wheezing off their sleep and their debauch. Then, cutting away its support, he brought down the hanging his mother had knitted, which covered the inner as well as the outer walls of the hall. This he flung upon the snorers, and then applying all the crooked stakes, he knotted and bound them up in such insoluble intricacy, that not one of the men beneath, however hard he might struggle, could contrive to rise. After this he set fire to the palace. The flames spread, scattering the conflagration far and wide. It enveloped the whole dwelling, destroyed the palace, and burnt them all while they were either buried in deep sleep or vainly striving to arise. Then he went to the chamber of Feng, who had before this been conducted by his train into his pavilion; plucked up a sword that chanced to be hanging to the bed, and planted his own in its place. Then, awakening his uncle, he told him that his nobles were perishing in the flames, and that Amleth was here, armed with his crooks to help him, and thirsting to exact the vengeance, now long overdue, for his father's murder. Feng, on hearing this, leapt from his couch, but was cut down while deprived of his own sword, and as he strove in vain to draw the strange one. O valiant Amleth, and worthy of immortal fame, who, being shrewdly armed with a feint of folly, covered a wisdom too high for human wit under a marvelous disguise of silliness! and not only found in his subtlety means to protect his own safety, but also by its guidance found opportunity to avenge his father. By this skillful defense of himself, and strenuous revenge for his parent, he has left it doubtful whether we are to think more of his wit or his bravery.

Translated by Oliver Elton

FOLK BALLADS

One of Denmark's greatest literary treasures is her vast number of medieval folk ballads. No other country, with the possible exception of Scotland, can compare with Denmark in the richness and variety of this genre. Ballads grew out of a mating of short lyrical songs, used as dance poems, with narrative verse. They became popular in Denmark about 1200, displacing the skaldic poetry, which by this time had already lost much of its audience (see Iceland, Introduction, p. 183). Though chiefly prominent during the 13th and 14th centuries, they were still fashionable as late as 1600 and even today the best of the medieval ballads hold a romantic fascination for many readers.

The characters alluded to in "Song of the Falcon" are not fictitious; they actually lived in the 14th century. "Lovel and John" probably dates from that century, too, although it appears first in written form three centuries later.

Song of the Falcon

I know where stands a linden
With many a flower,
That sheltereth all from frost and snow
In wintry hour.
That causeth she alone I bear within my heart.

Therein the throstle and nightingale
Do sing their lay
And therein singeth the little bird
Sweeter than they.

But still I know the falcon gray
Buildeth beside,
The little birds to scare away
In all his pride.

And were it not for the falcon's rage
(Trust what I tell)
All in the linden I'd build my nest
Ever to dwell.

It is no linden tree so green
Whereof ye hear,
It is the courteous maiden
I love so dear.

Translated by E. M. Smith-Dampier

Lovel and John

Lo now I bid ye, my merry men all,
Put your armor on,
Bind on your helms of the burning gold,
And follow Sir John!

Sir Peter home from the Thing[1] did fare,
(Put your armor on)
Little Kirsteen came forth to greet him there,
And ask after John.

"Welcome, dear father, home from the Thing!
(Put your armor on)
Tell me what tidings hast thou to bring?"
What tidings of John?

"These are the tidings I have for thee,
(Put your armor on)
That young Sir Lovel thy bridegroom shall be."
And not Sir John.

"And must young Sir Lovel my bridegroom be,
(Put your armor on)
Sorrow and care shall he have with me!"
While liveth Sir John.

[1] An assembly, legislative or judicial, held at regular intervals in a fixed place. The word is still a common one in Icelandic, for example in Althing, the Icelandic parliament.

Sir Lovel to bridal feast doth speed,
(Put your armor on)
Sir John hath bidden them shoe his steed.
"I go also," says John.

Sir John he rode to the blithe bridale,
(Put your armor on)
High on his horse in his coat of mail.
"I come!" said John.

When dew fell fast and eve was sped
(Put your armor on)
The bride must go to the bridal bed.
"I go with her!" said John.

The bride they led to the bridal bower,
(Put your armor on)
Sir John himself bore the torch before.
"I'm first!" says John.

Sir John he locked the door aright,
(Put your armor on)
"Now bid Sir Lovel a gay good night!"
All from Sir John.

Straight to Sir Lovel the news they cried:
(Put your armor on)
"Sir John doth sleep with thy fair young bride!"
That did Sir John.

All in the morning when dawn was gray,
(Put your armor on)
To the King Sir Lovel did hasten away.
"I go with thee," said John.

"My Liege, my Liege, now hark and hear!
(Put your armor on)
I've a tale of woe for thy gracious ear."
"Of me!" said John.

"A fair young maid I thought to wed,
(Put your armor on)
But another knight took the bride to bed!"
" 'Twas I," said John.

"Now since the maid to ye both is so dear,
(Put your armor on)
For her sweet sake ye shall break a spear."
"I shall win!" says John.

When the first course they rode so free,
(Put your armor on)
Sir Lovel's charger fell on his knee.
"Hold up!" said John.

But when they rode the course again,
(Put your armor on)
Sir Lovel's neck was broken in twain.
"Lie there!" said John.

She clapped her hands, did the dainty dame:
(Put your armor on)
"Ne'er did I see so gladsome a game!"
So he won, Sir John.
Bind on your helms of the burning gold,
And follow Sir John!

Translated by E. M. Smith-Dampier

THOMAS KINGO
(1634–1703)

Despite the fact that Thomas Kingo attained the rank of bishop at a comparatively early age, he was a worldly man who did not reject material pleasures. An avaricious and belligerent character, he was married three times (once for money alone) and was constantly engaged in lawsuits and quarrels with the secular authorities of his diocese. Paradoxically, he was painfully aware of the vanity of earthly values, and the deeply religious tone of his poetry rings true and sincere. Although he mastered every literary genre of his times, he is primarily remembered for his hymns, some of which are the very finest in the Danish language.

The selections below are from Kingo's two hymn collections, 1674 and 1681.

Sorrow and Gladness Together Go Wending

Sorrow and gladness together go wending;
  Evil and good come in quick interchange;
Fair and foul fortune forever are blending;
  Sunshine and cloud have the skies for their range.
    Gold of earth's day
    Is but splendid clay,
Alone heaven's happiness lasteth for aye.

Scepters and crowns shine with diamonds resplendent,
  Yet 'tis no pastime the garb of a King;
Sorrows a thousand on crowns are attendant;
  Scepters a thousand anxieties bring.
    Palaces fair
    Are but gilded care;
Only in heaven is joy not a snare.

Everything here has the germ of decay in it;
　　Everyone findeth some grief in his breast;
And soon is the bosom, though jewels blaze on it,
　　Filled full of sorrow and secret unrest.
　　　　Each has his own,
　　　　Known or unknown;
Heaven from woe is exempted alone.

Honor external and wisdom and station,
　　Youth's strength and beauty, the pride of life's May,
Oft fill the spirit with boastful elation,
　　Yet there all must perish as time wears away.
　　　　Everything must
　　　　Pass into dust;
In the sure bliss of heaven alone can we trust.

Sharp thorns guard the rose in which most thou delightest,
　　And the deadlier the poison, the fairer the flower.
The heart may be crushed while the cheek is the brightest,
　　For fortune oft changes her tide in an hour.
　　　　'Mid many woes
　　　　The stream of time flows;
Heaven alone steadfast happiness knows.

Go to, then! Henceforth it no longer shall vex me,
　　Because as I wish the world goes not alway.
The turmoils of life shall no longer perplex me,
　　Nor my heart be worn out with the grief of today.
　　　　Woe is time's blight;
　　　　The seed of delight
Shall spring up and bloom in heaven's island of light.

The pain shall inherit a rich overpayment;
　　Then tears shall be wiped from all sorrowing eyes;
The poor be clothed then in the fairest of raiment,
　　And the sick with the vigor of health shall arise.
　　　　Hatred shall cease;
　　　　All shall be peace;
For in heaven alone doth good ever increase.

Oh! let then my lot and my life be appointed
　　Just as my God and my Lord seeth meet.

Let the wicked go on still for evil anointed,
And the world have its way till the end is complete:
Time's tree will cast
Its leaves on the blast,
And heaven make everything right at the last.

Translated by William and Mary Howitt

Morning Song

Up, up the sun doth glide
in eastern glory,
regilding mountainside
and promontory.
Rejoice, my soul, thy voice in song ascending;
rise, leave the earth behind,
in thankful trust thy mind
to Heaven bending.

Like sand upon the shore
beyond assessing,
deep as the ocean floor,
is Heaven's blessing
that God doth every day upon me scatter—
each morning of the year
a boon beyond compare
pours in my platter.

Last night His angel-hosts
my home invested,
all watchful at their post
that unmolested
myself and mine should be by foe or stranger;
my body safe and free
from mortal jeopardy,
my soul from danger.

Translated by R. P. Keigwin

LUDVIG HOLBERG
(1684-1754)

When a permanent theater was cpened in Copenhagen in 1722, its directors were confronted with the painful fact that a native drama scarcely existed. Determined to secure Danish material for the new theater, they set out to find themselves a playwright. Their choice was Ludvig Holberg, a Norwegian-born professor of history who was already known for his humorous poetry.

Holberg had never before written for the stage. Yet, during the following year and a half, he turned out no less than fifteen full-length comedies in which he unsparingly ridiculed his fellow men for their hypocrisy, pedantry, and vanity, much as Molière had done in France.

Influenced by the French master as well as by the Italian *commedia dell'arte*, Holberg has sometimes been called "the Molière of the North." Abounding in wit and gay intrigues, his plays rank among the masterpieces of European theater. They remain, even in the 20th century, among the favorite presentations of the Danish stage.

The Christmas Party was first printed in 1731.

The Christmas Party
A comedy in one act

DRAMATIS PERSONAE

JERONIMUS, *an elderly townsman*
LEONORA, *his wife*
MAGDELONE, *his sister*
PERNILLE, *the maid*
ARV, *the manservant*
A SCHOOLMASTER

CHILDREN
LEANDER, *a young gentleman*
LEANDER'S LANDLORD AND
    LANDLADY
STRANGERS
THE WATCH

LEONORA. Oh, today has seemed like two days. But love is an overpowering passion; it's like a raging ocean—the more you check it and confine it the more violent it becomes. Oh, Leander, it was sad for me when you came to live in this place and I could see every day in front of me the man whose society I cannot enjoy because of my old husband's suspicions. My only comfort is that I can get a few nice letters from him, in which he pours out his protestations, but they are only like oil that adds to the fire and makes me despair. We've plotted to get together a few times, but so far all has been in vain. If there's to be a chance to enjoy the happiness I've waited for so long and to have a private talk with him, it will be at the Christmas party we're holding this evening. Pernille, who knows about my love, is standing in the doorway to tell me when he passes—he usually does so about this time, as we've arranged it by letter, so that we can see each other through the window. I daren't even open the window because I'm so afraid my husband may come along all of a sudden. But this fear and restraint, so far from cooling my love, just adds fuel to the flames. But there they are.

PERNILLE (*enters*). Get ready, Madame, Monsieur Leander is just coming; the signal is three loud coughs. Then you can take him into the hall and come to some agreement.

LEONORA. Oh, Pernille, I'm mortally afraid to do that. Suppose my husband happened to come along?

PERNILLE. Leave that to me. As soon as he comes I'll run in and keep talking nonsense to the old man. I've thought up a whole lot of stories to keep him as long as you need the time to speak to Leander.

LEONORA. But sometimes he won't listen to any talk.

PERNILLE. I don't want to hear any talk from you either. Do you think, Madame, that I haven't thought everything over? I know what sort of talk that fellow will listen to. Do you think I'm going to tell him what's in the papers: that the French regent is dead, that Mir-Vais has taken a beating in Turkey, that the Spanish silver-fleet has come in, that Prince Eudemius has won a victory over the Duke of Vendôme? No, I'll tell him some old wives' tale that he'll take in eagerly. I'll tell him that a calf's been born with a crest on its head and flounces on its

legs, and then he'll start at once to moralize and preach about
the wickedness of the age, and about finery and showing-off——
But I hear Monsieur Leander coughing outside; run out and
bring him in; I'll go off to the old man. (*Exeunt.*)

(*Leonora enters leading Leander. They both stop in the hall.*)

LEANDER (*kneeling*). Oh, my sweetest Leonora, is it possible
that after all this long waiting I shall have the happiness to——
LEONORA. Oh, my dearest Leander, get up, we haven't much time
for preliminaries. I feel sure of your love. Let's think of how
we can arrange matters this evening at the Christmas party.
I know your landlord and landlady are invited, but I'm not
sure you will be.
LEANDER. If I'm not, I'll invite myself and take no notice of any
sour looks. My landlord and landlady will take me along and
make the excuse that they couldn't leave me alone at home.
LEONORA. That will do. But do they know anything about our
arrangements?
LEANDER. I've never spoken about them. But my landlady must
have noticed something about it. She said the other day: "We'll
soon be going to the Christmas party at our neighbor's Jeronimus, and then you'll be lucky enough to kiss the beautiful
Leonora's hand." That made me silent, but my silence was
caused by excessive joy. Then she smiled and said: "My husband and I have both suspected something; if we can help you,
we'll do so with the greatest pleasure." I thanked her and took
her into my confidence, for they are people who would give
their lives for me and love me more than their own brother.
LEONORA. Well, dear Leander, it's a good thing they are loyal to
you and we have them as accomplices. But how can we manage to get together in private?
LEANDER. We must put our heads together and think of a Christmas game that will give us a chance.
LEONORA. But now I hear my husband coming. We must part.
LEANDER. Then I must say good-bye for just now, much against
my will. Good-bye, dearest Leonora. You can be sure that——
LEONORA. Oh, Monsieur, I *am* sure. Good-bye. (*Exit Leander.*)
PERNILLE (*enters*). Well, Madame, did you manage to talk to
him?

LEONORA. Yes, of course, Pernille. But why did you come back so quickly? I made him go as soon as I heard the door open; I thought it was my husband.

PERNILLE. If I'd thought of it, I'd have waited a little longer. But I'm afraid, Madame, I've made a devil of a mistake.

LEONORA. How?

PERNILLE. The old man became so pious when I told him the story of the calf that had been born that I'm afraid the Christmas game will be called off.

LEONORA. If that's so, you played your part very badly. You often cheat yourself when you try to cheat others. But you can soon put it right; just say it was not true.

PERNILLE. I'faith that won't do. I swore I saw the calf with the crest and the flounces with my own eyes.

LEONORA. That certainly was a bad mistake and we're in a devil of a mess. But did he say there would be no Christmas game?

PERNILLE. No, he didn't say so definitely, but he began to talk about parties and pranks that should be abolished. If he's got that bee in his bonnet, you must persuade him all over again to have some merrymaking.

LEONORA. Yes, that's just the right way to spoil the game. No, if he speaks about it, I must pretend to agree with him; when an old man has a young wife, the more retiring he thinks she is, the more liberty he gives her. But I don't think there's any danger; if we had no Christmas game, our old aunt would be beside herself. She sticks to all those ceremonies as if they were her creed. You couldn't get her to eat unless you had the Epiphany lights on the table. But there's my husband; you run off and talk to Auntie. (*Exit Pernille.*)

JERONIMUS (*enters*). Easter is coming, and I give you my word that those women's headdresses, flounces, and hanging curls are the invention of Lucifer.

LEONORA. What's the matter, darling?

JERONIMUS. They see one sign after another and yet they're just as crazy.

LEONORA. Has something bad happened?

JERONIMUS. Heark'ee, darling. You'll be doing me a favor if from now on you wear a round hat and have your clothes made the same way as my old sister Magdelone.

LEONORA. But, dearest, if you compare my clothes and Auntie's, you'll find hers cost more.

JERONIMUS. That's not the question, poppet. It's not the cost; but those new ideas, those headdresses, those flounces, those curls that our honest forefathers knew nothing about, that's a sinful way of dressing that causes all the world's misfortunes.

LEONORA. If I'd known it was a sin, darling, I'd have given them all up.

JERONIMUS. We don't want to believe it a sin till we are warned by a sign, and then it's too late. D'you know a calf has just been born here with a crest, curls and flounces?

LEONORA. But can you believe that's true?

JERONIMUS. Bad cess to me if it isn't true. Pernille and other decent folk here in Aebeltoft have seen the calf. Heark'ee, darling, I don't feel at all like having the Christmas party tonight.

LEONORA. Has the story about the calf frightened you?

JERONIMUS. No, not at all; it isn't the first story I've heard. But I've thought it over carefully and find that these Christmas parties and games don't do any good.

LEONORA. It's all the same to me. You know yourself how little I go out into the world. You won't find many young wives like me; I'd be quite happy if there wasn't such a thing as games or dancing. I enjoy sitting at home with my work and looking after my old man.

JERONIMUS. Of course I know that, poppet. You set an example to all the young wives in Aebeltoft. The best thing I ever did was to choose such a virtuous person as my wife.

LEONORA. I can't understand how sensible people can find any pleasure in Christmas games. They are all right for children but they ought to disgust grown-ups.

JERONIMUS. And sometimes these Christmas games have bad results.

LEONORA. Both Christmas games and other big parties, darling. I don't like them at all. If it wasn't just to please you, I'd never go out any more.

JERONIMUS. But, poppet, you mustn't cut yourself off from the world altogether; you must have some pleasure now and then. Otherwise young folk may become melancholy.

LEONORA. I'faith I'm always sad at a party and I get better when I'm alone again.

JERONIMUS. Yes, quite right, my dear, but there's reason in everything. But I'm really glad you don't want this Christmas party tonight. I'll go out for a minute and see what my sister says about it. (*To himself as he goes out.*) What a lucky man I am to have a wife like that! I can celebrate my wedding anniversary each year as a festival.

LEONORA (*alone*). What bad luck Pernille has brought on us by being such a busybody! But I hope that Auntie makes him change his mind. If I'd argued with him, he would have got worse and had a hundred suspicious ideas, but now I'll play my cards so that he'll beg me himself to go to the Christmas party, and it'll look as if I'm doing it just to please him. (*Exit.*)

JERONIMUS (*enters with Magdelone*). It's no use talking, sister. I won't hear of any Christmas party. It only means a lot of expense and brings undesirable results.

MAGDELONE. Oh, my dear brother, surely you're not in earnest.

JERONIMUS. Of course I'm in earnest. I've seen too many examples of such folly. I wish I had a dollar for every girl that has lost her virginity on those occasions.

MAGDELONE. But it's a good old custom.

JERONIMUS. It's an old custom, sister, but not a good one.

MAGDELONE. I've always heard that things were better in the old days than now. Why shouldn't we follow in our forefathers' footsteps? My dear brother, you should have seen the Christmas party they had at the miller's yesterday. Aren't we as good as he is?

JERONIMUS. We're just as good, but we're more sensible. Besides, we can't follow the miller's example, he has more resources than we, he can eat his Christmas cakes all the year round.

MAGDELONE. I'faith I'm not saying all this for my own pleasure but for the sake of your dear children.

JERONIMUS. Yes, there we have it. Just blame the children.

MAGDELONE. But, my dear brother, what will our neighbors think of us if we have no Christmas party this year? They'll say we've lost our faith and look on us as Turks or heathens. (*She cries.*)

JERONIMUS. What silly talk! Do you change your faith because you stop being crazy?

MAGDELONE. You call it craziness, my dear Jeronimus. I know a lot of people who despised those good old customs, but they came to a bad end.

JERONIMUS. And I know a lot who despised them and did well.

MAGDELONE. Look what happened to Christopher von Bremen, who always laughed when his wife put the Epiphany lights on the table. That man was as healthy as any of us, but just as he was fastening the suspenders on his trousers he dropped down dead.

JERONIMUS. I suppose he *never* would have died if he had been willing to burn the Epiphany lights.

MAGDELONE. Look at Jeremiah the tobacconist, who wouldn't make a difference between the Christmas evenings and other evenings by having as much as a dish of milk-porridge and lived like a heathen all through Christmas time. In his old age he had great troubles; three of his sons failed their degree examinations one after the other.

JERONIMUS. If those rascals had studied a little more they would have passed. I've known those who got *laudabilem* and yet never ate milk-porridge. D'you think a person has to eat porridge before he goes up for an examination?

MAGDELONE. Look at what happened to Hendrik Buttercup's daughters.

JERONIMUS. Yes, and look what happened to the daughters of Hendrik Daffodil, Hendrik Buttercake, Hendrik Sauerkraut. What confounded nonsense, what silly stories! Perhaps Hendrik Buttercup's daughters lost their virginity at a Christmas party. I'm crazy to go on talking like this.

MAGDELONE. Look at what happened to Christopher Oldfox.

JERONIMUS. I'faith I don't know what happened to Christopher Oldfox or Youngfox, but I do know there'll be no Christmas party this year, for besides what I've said I have other reasons. (*Exit.*)

MAGDELONE (*crying bitterly*). Oh, what a wretched creature I am! I wish I were dead. I've lived for forty-five years, and I've never had such a poor Christmas. Why should you drudge away in this world if you never have any pleasure? All our neighbors make such a noise you can hear them all night long and we have to live as if it's always Lent. (*She continues to cry.*)

PERNILLE (*enters*). Why are you crying, Madame?

MAGDELONE. Oh, Pernille, I have good reason to cry. Anyone who has such a difficult brother as mine must——

PERNILLE. I can't believe the old man has been so rash as to hit his sister.

MAGDELONE. No, it's worse than that. He won't have any Christmas party tonight.

PERNILLE. No Christmas party? (*They both cry.*) Deuce take it if I work any longer in a house like this! I'd rather go without my wages.

MAGDELONE. I tell you, Pernille, I felt as if someone had stuck a knife in my heart when I heard it. Everyone in Aebeltoft will despise our house.

PERNILLE. I was so sure we'd have a Christmas party that I'd already invited the miller's daughter.

MAGDELONE. Yes, it will be an everlasting disgrace to our whole house. The one who put the idea in Father's head should be ashamed of himself.

PERNILLE. When Arv hears about it, he won't like it any more than the others. Poor fellow, he's been practicing all morning to be a hobgoblin.

MAGDELONE. Poor fellow, he'll be quite downhearted.

PERNILLE. You'd never believe, Madame, how perfectly he can imitate a hobgoblin; you'd almost think you saw a real one.

MAGDELONE. Oh, don't talk about it any more, my heart breaks when I think of it.

PERNILLE. But would you try again to persuade the old man, Auntie?

MAGDELONE. It's no good, Pernille, even if I went down on my knees. (*They both cry. Arv enters, wrapped in a white sheet and with two horns on his head, tries to frighten the others. They continue to cry.*)

ARV. Don't be afraid, Madame. Don't cry, it's me. Don't you know me now? (*Removes his disguise.*)

PERNILLE. Yes, we knew you all right. We're crying about something else. You're not going to dress up at the Christmas games tonight.

ARV. Why?

PERNILLE. We're not having any Christmas party.

ARV. The devil take such talk! Who will stop us?

PERNILLE. The old man has got ideas in his head and has sworn—— Oh! (*All three start to cry.*)

ARV. The devil split me if I'm not going to ask the old man whose servants he thinks we are, Turks' or heathens'!

MAGDELONE. You'll only get a good thrashing, Arv.

PERNILLE. I've just thought of something, Madame. Suppose we get the children to worry him.

MAGDELONE. If anything could help, that would.

PERNILLE. I'faith I'll go along to the school and tackle the school-master.

ARV. You can promise him a hug.

PERNILLE. Shut up, you, the schoolmaster and I know each other pretty well.

ARV. It would be a poor maid who didn't know the schoolmaster. (*Exit Pernille.*)

JERONIMUS (*enters*). What's this all about?

ARV. I'm a hobgoblin, master.

JERONIMUS (*giving him a box on the ears*). You're a hobgoblin, eh?

ARV (*falling over*). No, master, I'm not a hobgoblin.

JERONIMUS. What does all this mean?

ARV. I only want to be a hobgoblin.

JERONIMUS (*giving him another box on the ears*). You only want to be a hobgoblin?

ARV. No, I don't want to be a hobgoblin.

MAGDELONE. Oh, Jeronimus, it's a shame to hit the poor boy on a holiday.

JERONIMUS. Get out, you rogue, and take a book and read it, that's the best thing for you to do.

ARV (*going off in tears*). There's no one in the whole street that's reading a single word this holiday night.

JERONIMUS. You should have spared me that job and given him a couple of boxes on the ear before I came.

MAGDELONE. My dear brother, I don't see why our folks shouldn't have some fun as well as the others.

JERONIMUS. You ought to be a Christmas goat too. It wouldn't look bad for an old lady like you.

MAGDELONE. I don't see why we should be considered the scum of the town.

JERONIMUS. Have you seen any of the upper classes having a Christmas party?

MAGDELONE. If we follow the whims of the upper classes all we'll give people will be snuff and good wishes.

JERONIMUS. No one holds Christmas parties in Copenhagen.

MAGDELONE. Are you talking about Copenhagen? I've heard from the schoolmaster that people there don't have much faith. There's a fellow just come from Copenhagen who has no faith at all. He doesn't even believe that Doctor Martin Luther ordered us to eat goose on Martinmas Eve and he even says the world is as round as an egg, which is the worst lie I've ever heard.

JERONIMUS. It's no use arguing. Let's stop talking about it. Call the schoolmaster and the children in; I want to hear if they've learned something nice for the holiday. (*Exit Magdelone.*)

JERONIMUS (*sitting at the table with a basket of toys*). It's an art to hand out toys to children so that they are all pleased. Christopher must have this horse with the whistle inside it. What about the cart? I'll give that to Henning. Peer must have the fiddle, as I think he's going to be a musician. Else must get the cradle with the child in it; as soon as girls are old enough to talk they think about marriage and cradles. Marie, you must be satisfied with the whistle. Oh, I almost forgot little Anne; she'll have the dangling toy with the little bells on. But there they are coming along with the schoolmaster.

(*Enter Magdelone, Leonora, Pernille, and the schoolmaster with the children. The children walk on in pairs, the schoolmaster arranging the ranks with a cane in one hand and a book in the other. He places the children in a row, makes a pedantic bow and utters the following congratulatory verses.*)

> Misfortune's black cloud, go! Black-winged mist, away!
> Come, Dawn! Shine, Sun! You certainly must stay.
> Prosperity, pour over us just like the Nile in foam,
> Besprinkle us like dew and settle in our home.
> O Fortune, let thy strength flow o'er us like a brook,
> Like the birds on the branch . . . (*He repeats this and feels in his pocket.*)

JERONIMUS. Can't you find a rhyme? What about . . . Our porridge we must cook?

SCHOOLMASTER. Now I have to start again from the beginning. (*He repeats his previous lines.*)

How happy we all look!
May all go well forever with Father and Mother dear,
And may their house produce a plant with every single year.
May their big cellar hold all the ale and gin they can use,
And fish and meat and butter their dainty kitchen choose.
May grain in heaps around their farm its bounty raise aloft,
As long as there's a single soul in our good old Aebeltoft.

JERONIMUS (*touching his hat*). Thank you, Mr. Schoolmaster. That was a beautiful poem. You must have taken a lot of trouble over it.

PERNILLE. Anyone else would have had to rack his brain over it, but the schoolmaster can do anything.

JERONIMUS. But what interesting things have the children learned for the holiday? Last year they knew so many strange proverbs. Do they know any this year?

SCHOOLMASTER. Yes, will you have proverbs or riddles?

JERONIMUS. They're both good. Let Arv come in, so he can hear how the small children can show him up. (*Pernille runs for Arv, who enters and stands with his hands folded, listening.*)

JERONIMUS. Mr. Schoolmaster, first ask Arv, and then let one of the children tell him so that he's ashamed.

SCHOOLMASTER. Arv, who was it that shouted so loud that he was heard over the whole world?

ARV (*scratching his head*). It was a . . . a hobgoblin.

JERONIMUS. He's still got that hobgoblin in his head.

SCHOOLMASTER. Christopher, Henning, Peer, Else, Marie, Anne, who was it that shouted so loud that he was heard all over the world?

ALL. A donkey in the ark, because the whole world was inside there.

JERONIMUS. Shame on you, you big rascal! The children can teach you.

SCHOOLMASTER. Arv, how far is it from here to the glass heaven?

ARV. It's fifty miles to Mariager.

SCHOOLMASTER. Christopher, Henning, Peer, Else, Marie, Anne, how far is it from here to the glass heaven?

ALL. As far as it is from the glass heaven to the crystal heaven.

JERONIMUS. Now, children, everyone point your finger at Arv.

(*They all point their fingers at him.*)

SCHOOLMASTER. Arv, how many heavens are there?

ARV. There's a heaven on every bed, so there are as many heavens as beds.

SCHOOLMASTER. Christopher, Henning, Peer, Else, Marie, Anne, how many heavens are there?

ALL. There are seven heavens; one above the other.

JERONIMUS. Point your fingers at him again.

CHILDREN. Oh, oh, oh . . .

SCHOOLMASTER. Christopher, the first heaven?

CHRISTOPHER. The blue heaven.

SCHOOLMASTER. Henning, the second heaven?

HENNING. The milky heaven.

SCHOOLMASTER. Peer, the third heaven?

PEER. The glass heaven.

SCHOOLMASTER. Fold your hands nicely when you are being questioned. (*They fold their hands.*) Else, the fourth heaven?

ELSE. The crystal heaven.

SCHOOLMASTER. Marie, the fifth heaven?

MARIE. The diamond heaven.

SCHOOLMASTER. Anne, the sixth heaven?

ANNE. The pearly heaven.

JERONIMUS. There's still one left.

SCHOOLMASTER. Arv, the seventh heaven?

ARV. It's the one next to the eighth.

JERONIMUS. He's a regular idiot. He never looks at a book the whole year round and so he doesn't know any more than a Turk or a heathen. Can they answer any more questions, Mr. Schoolmaster?

SCHOOLMASTER. Yes. Arv, what is as round as an egg and as long as a church wall?

ARV (*aside*). The devil split him and his questions. (*Aloud.*) It's a pipe; the head is round and the tail is long.

SCHOOLMASTER. Christopher, Henning, Peer, Else, Marie, Anne, what is as round as an egg and as long as the church wall?

ALL. A ball of thread. When you unwind it, it's as long as a church wall.

JERONIMUS. Point your fingers at Arv again, children.

CHILDREN. Oh, oh, oh . . .

JERONIMUS. Thank you, Mr. Schoolmaster, on behalf of my children. I see you work hard with them; you'll get a nice New Year's present. (*Jeronimus hands out the toys to the children.*) Now go into the nursery and behave yourselves nicely. I had thought of having a Christmas party, but for various reasons I've changed my mind. (*The children cry.*) Well, it can't be helped, children. I won't have such craziness in my house any more; I'm against it, and your mother is even more so. (*He turns his back at them.*)

PERNILLE. Go and torment him. (*The children hang on to him and shout for a Christmas party.*)

JERONIMUS. That's enough, children. You've got your toys to play with. (*The children hold him tight and shout again for a Christmas party.*)

JERONIMUS. Just ask your teacher if it's any use. What do you say, Mr. Schoolmaster?

SCHOOLMASTER. Pliny, a wise and clever Roman nobleman, talks very elegantly about games and sports as follows: *Anima fulturis corporis nititur,* and in another place: *Graves seriosque mores lusibus jocisque distinguere identidem soleo.* That means: At times for the sake of my bodily health I set aside my serious habits and modesty and go in for childish games.

PERNILLE. That man spoke like an angel.

SCHOOLMASTER. Now if a modest gentleman in Rome found this necessary and decent, how much more necessary and decent it is for us in Aebeltoft. I myself will add this: that as hobgoblins and subterranean folk spoil the big festivals with their weeping and wailing because they have no share in them, then we should be happy and enjoy ourselves so as to show that we do take part in them. For just as the phoenix, that lives in Arabia, lives a thousand years alone and sets fire to himself as soon as he produces his offspring, because he will not live together with others of his kind, so we human beings, on the other hand, should get together and have fun so as to show we are not related to such a brute beast. *Anthropos,* says Aristotle, *esti zoon politikon, id est: homo est animal sociable,* and so, just as the bird of paradise——

JERONIMUS. That's enough, Mr. Schoolmaster. I see I must give in. That comparison with the phoenix was so striking. I agree that we should have a Christmas party. Now, little ones, enjoy yourselves and thank your teacher for the party. (*The children jump and shout for joy.*)

JERONIMUS (*to Leonora*). Darling, I know you don't care much for parties. If you don't want it, I'll stick to my first decision.

LEONORA. To tell you the truth, I'd rather not have it, but as we've already invited our neighbors, I'll put up with it because of that.

PERNILLE. Oh, that nice phoenix! The other birds are just no good in comparison.

JERONIMUS. Get ready and bring in the Epiphany lights.

LEONORA. All right, it's about time; we'll have the neighbors here before we know it.

(*Everything is arranged, and Arv enters and places the Epiphany lights on the table. The visitors enter one after the other and pay their compliments. Some of them are disguised in strange costumes. Finally Leander's landlord and landlady enter, with Leander, who is well dressed.*)

LANDLORD. We hope that you, Mr. Jeronimus, and Madame will not mind us bringing a good friend of ours along. He's like a brother in the house and is a stranger here, so we want him to have a little fun.

JERONIMUS. He's very welcome.

LEANDER. Monsieur and Madame, I ask most humbly that you forgive my boldness. My landlord and landlady assured me that you, Mr. Jeronimus, were much too kind to take any offense. I'm a stranger in this place and have no pleasures except what these good people arrange for me. (*As he pays these compliments Leonora turns her back to him.*)

JERONIMUS. Don't turn your back to the visitor. My poor wife is very shy with strange men.

LEANDER. Fair lady, I think you are lucky to have such a reasonable husband who, so far from being suspicious because of your beauty, takes pleasure in seeing you associate with young men.

JERONIMUS. Just this once, Monsieur, just this once.

LEANDER. For, beautiful Leonora——

JERONIMUS. That word "beautiful" is not suitable for my wife, Monsieur; she doesn't pretend to be beautiful. It's enough for her to please me.

LEANDER. For, I say, if——

JERONIMUS. That's enough. We're simple folk, Monsieur, and don't understand compliments. Please sit down here by my sister.

LEONORA. Darling, I can't stand that man.

JERONIMUS. It doesn't matter; you must be polite.

LEONORA. No one asked him to come here.

JERONIMUS. But we must treat him politely because of our neighbors, as he is lodging in their house.

LEONORA. I hate these young whippersnappers like the plague. Did you notice how offended he was when you took him away from me and asked him to sit with old Auntie?

JERONIMUS. I should be sorry to cause him any displeasure.

LEONORA. The more displeased he is the happier I am.

JERONIMUS. No, that's no way to talk. We must show him we know how to live. Now I want you to sit together, to show him he's welcome.

LEONORA. Darling husband, please don't make me sit by him.

JERONIMUS. Now, do me that favor. I have my reasons.

LEONORA. But, dear husband, I'll be in bad humor all evening.

JERONIMUS. Well, if it's going to put you in a bad humor, poppet, I'll not persuade you.

LEONORA. Very well, for the sake of his landlord and landlady I'll sit by him, but it's against my will.

JERONIMUS. That's right, poppet. That's the proper thing to do. (*She sits down next to Leander.*)

JERONIMUS (*aside*). I don't believe there's another wife like her in the whole town. The poor woman's sitting as if she has an armor on and is doing it all for my sake. Ha, ha!

(*They begin the Christmas games with forfeits. The schoolmaster has to sing a song. Arv has to be polite and then rude to Jeronimus, so he pays him a compliment first face to face and then with his back turned. Pernille has to go out with a man she chooses and count the stars. She picks her partner, who leads her to the front of the stage and says:*) My sweet Pernille, let's go up into the hayloft; the higher we are the better we can see the stars.

PERNILLE. Of course.

(*They go off together. Meanwhile the games continue. Arv comes in, his face blackened; in his mouth he has a stick with two candles on it; he is riding on two men with their backs to each other. The children are afraid and begin to cry. Jeronimus tells them to be quiet, that it is only Arv. After this is over Pernille comes in again with her partner.*)

JERONIMUS. You good people took a long time to count the stars.

PERNILLE (*rubbing her mouth*). Yes, master, there's a heap of stars in the sky.

LEONORA (*taking Jeronimus aside*). Listen, dearest, don't let's play these forfeit games any more. It might happen that this horrid fellow who is sitting with me will have to kiss me, and that would be a pity, as it's something I could not stand at all.

JERONIMUS. I wouldn't like that either, to tell you the truth. But what shall we play?

LEONORA. Let's play blindman's buff. It's a decent game and amusing as well.

JERONIMUS. Well, just as you like. Heark'ee, my friends, we're going to play blindman's buff.

PERNILLE. I'faith I think it's the best game. Let me be blind-folded first. (*Leonora brings Pernille downstage and bandages her eyes.*)

PERNILLE. You're tying the bandage too tight, Madame; if I can't see anything, I won't be able to get hold of the old man, as we arranged with Leander. That's better; now I can see as much as I need.

(*She goes round a little, groping, and at last gets hold of Jeronimus, who won't play until the whole company compel him to. While Jeronimus is blindfolded Leonora and Leander move downstage.*)

LEANDER. Oh, most gracious Leonora, now's the time we've had so much trouble to arrange.

LEONORA. Go out into the passage at once; I'll come out another way and meet you.

(*Leander goes off at one side and Leonora a little later at another. Meanwhile Jeronimus is the blind man and Pernille arranges it so that he cannot catch anyone, for whenever he is near another person, Pernille shouts to him to turn round. In the end he gets annoyed, as it goes on so long, and loosens the bandage. He misses his wife and Leander, runs out, and comes back dragging them in.*)

JERONIMUS (*shouting*). Oh, you chaste Lucretia! Was that why I had to play blindman's buff? And you, Monsieur Jean de France, you'll pay for this. I'll teach you to go down on your knees to a decent man's wife.

(*He seizes him by the throat. Leander's landlord and landlady catch Jeronimus by the hair. Everyone takes sides, so that the whole company get into an altercation. The children cry. Jeronimus lies on the floor calling for the police, and so do the others. The schoolmaster creeps under the table. The watch are heard whistling outside and then enter.*)

THE WATCH (*enter, shouting*). Come along to the town hall, you dogs, all of you! Is this the way to keep the Christmas season holy? Don't you know what the magistrates announced a little while ago?

JERONIMUS. They're trying to murder me in my own house.

LEANDER'S LANDLORD. We thought an honest man lived here, but he's a murderer.

THE WATCH. Quick, quick, all of you to the town hall! Tomorrow we'll hear what it was all about. Come along, you old bandit!

(*They drag them all away. The women and children follow.*)

SCHOOLMASTER (*who has remained under the table, peeps out, finally gets up, and says to the audience*). Please accept this Christmas party. If the confounded watch had not come, it would have lasted longer and it would not have stopped with this, but—— Well, you can imagine what I mean.

Curtain

JOHANNES EWALD

(1743–81)

Early disappointment in love and broken health, resulting
from an attempt in adolescence to win fame as a soldier in
the Seven Years' War, set the stage for Ewald's tragic life.
Determined to "saunter through life," he devoted himself
wholly and passionately to poetry and alcohol. He soon won
renown for his poetry, which has a genuine, lyrical, and at
times inspired, quality. A forerunner of Romanticism, Ewald
was the first to make use of the many treasures of old Scandinavian literature. His poetic output was both rich and
varied: verse tragedies, odes, philosophical poetry, and an
autobiography in lively and charming prose.

All the pieces below are taken from his tragedies: "The
Lament Over the Dead Balder" from *The Death of Balder*
(1773); "King Christian," which has become Denmark's
royal anthem, and "Little Gunver" from *The Fishermen*
(1780).

King Christian

King Christian[1] stood by the lofty mast
    In mist and smoke;
His sword was hammering so fast,
Through Gothic helm and brain it passed;
Then sank each hostile hulk and mast,
    In mist and smoke.
"Fly!" shouted they, "fly he who can!
Who braves of Denmark's Christian
    The stroke?"

Nils Juel[2] gave heed to the tempest's roar,
    Now is the hour!

[1] Christian IV of Denmark reigned 1588–1648.
[2] Danish admiral of the 17th century, the country's greatest sea hero.

He hoisted his blood-red flag once more,
And smote upon the foe full sore,
And shouted loud through the tempest's roar,
"Now is the hour!"
"Fly!" shouted they, "for shelter fly!
Of Denmark's Juel who can defy
The power?"

North Sea! a glimpse of Wessel³ rent
Thy murky sky!
Then champions to thine arms were sent;
Terror and Death glared where he went;
From the waves was heard a wail, that rent
Thy murky sky!
From Denmark thunders Tordenskjol',
Let each to Heaven commend his soul,
And fly!

Path of the Dane to fame and might!
Dark-rolling wave!
Receive thy friend, who, scorning flight,
Goes to meet danger with despite,
Proudly as thou the tempest's might,
Dark-rolling wave!
And amid pleasures and alarms,
And war and victory, be thine arms
My grave!

Translated by H. W. Longfellow

Lament Over the Dead Balder

CHORUS: Thunders, burst your cloudy portals!
             Heaven, earth, and ocean rave!
             Weep ye gods, and mourn ye mortals,
             Over the mighty Balder's⁴ grave!

³ Norwegian-born naval commander of the early 18th century. He distinguished himself in the service of Denmark and was knighted under the name of Tordenskjold, i.e., "Thundershield."

⁴ Old Icelandic: Baldr. In Scandinavian mythology the fair god of innocence and piety. The son of Odin and Frigg (see note 10, p. 190), he was slain unintentionally by his blind brother Hother (or Hod) at the instigation of Loki.

THOR:[5] Gods of battle stern and gory,
Weep ye over the hero slain!
Balder, thou the Aser's[6] glory!
Love, base love, has proved thy bane.

CHORUS: Balder, thou the Aser's glory!
Love, base love, has proved thy bane.

ROTA:[7] I of slaughter swift purveyor,
Sorrow over the hero slain!
Balder, thou the Jotun-slayer,
Loke's[8] falsehood was thy bane.

CHORUS: Balder, thou the Jotun-slayer,
Loke's falsehood was thy bane.

HOTHER: Hother's burning tears are flowing
Over the mighty Balder slain.
Ah, thy heart with virtue glowing,
Noble Balder, was thy bane.

CHORUS: Ah, thy heart with virtue glowing,
Noble Balder, was thy bane.

NANNA:[9] Nanna weeps with pallid feature
Over the mighty Balder slain:
Friend of gods and every creature!
Fate alone has proved thy bane.

CHORUS: Friend of gods and every creature!
Fate alone has proved thy bane.

CONCLUDING CHORUS: Thunders, burst your cloudy portals!
Heaven, earth, and ocean rave!
Weep and howl, ye gods and mortals,
Over the mighty Balder's grave.

Translated by George Borrow

---

[5] The chief warrior against the Giants and guardian of men. He was the son of Odin and Earth (or Jord) and lived in Thrudvang. His weapon was the hammer Mjolnir, and he possessed a chariot drawn by two goats.

[6] Old Icelandic: Æsir. Collective designation of the gods. Another race of gods were the Wanes (or Vanir).

[7] One of the Valkyries.

[8] More commonly Loki. The evil force among the gods and the foster brother of Odin. He belonged to the race of Giants but lived with the gods in Asgard (see note 4, p. 188). Artful and sly, he was the cause of nearly every calamity among the gods, though he was occasionally forced to use his cunning for good purposes.

[9] One of the goddesses and the wife of Balder. She loved him so much that her heart broke at his death.

Little Gunver

Little Gunver wandered at evenfall,
Sunk deep in thought.
Her heart was of wax, her spirit all
Of fine gold wrought.
　　Beware, my child, of the false menfolk!

Little Gunver fished with a silken thread
On the sea strand;
The billows reared, the water sped
Far up the sand.
　　Beware, my child, of the false menfolk!

Then in green attire a merman fleet
Came from the sea.
Tender his glance, and a voice as sweet
As a harp had he.

"Little Gunver, you torture me night and day
With love's hot anguish.
My soul is faint and my heart alway
Doth pine and languish.

"Oh, trust and give me your snow-white arm
To ease my pain,
And I'll hold it close to my breast so warm
And have peace again.

"Little Gunver, my heart in its scaly sheath
Is soft and mild.
Fear not in a simple merman's faith
To be beguiled!"

"If my arms can give thee delight in sooth
And thy longing slake,
O beautiful merman, I give thee both.
Come here and take!"

Glad in his wiles the merman swept
Her away and fled.
Like a storm was his laugh; but the fishermen wept
Over Gunver dead.
　Beware, my child, of the false menfolk!

Translated by Charles Wharton Stork

ADAM OEHLENSCHLÄGER
(1779–1850)

At a ceremony in Lund, Sweden, in 1829, Oehlenschläger was crowned with laurels by Esaias Tegnér (see p. 291), who called him "the Nordic king of singers and heir apparent to the world of poetry . . ."

This Danish prince of poets wrote his first important poem, "The Golden Horns," in 1802, and many regard it as the manifesto of Danish Romanticism. Later, following in the footsteps of Ewald (see p. 41), he wrote many verse tragedies on old Scandinavian themes, some of which are among his best-known works.

To the end of his life, Oehlenschläger was recognized as the leader and the greatest exponent of the Romantic movement in Denmark. The beauty of his language and style, his lyrical splendor, and the rich art of his metrics are, however, all qualities which can scarcely be translated. This fact, as in the case of so many other Scandinavian poets, has often tended to obscure to the rest of the world the real nature and power of his literary genius.

The Golden Horns were two actual drinking horns, made of gold, and thought to date from the 5th century. They were found separately in 1639 and 1734 near Gallehus, a village in southern Jutland. The horns were decorated with illustrations of Nordic legends, and one of them also bore a runic inscription. The immediate pretext for this poem was the theft of the horns, in 1802, from the royal cabinet in Copenhagen. They were never found again, and copies that had been made of them were later lost at sea. They are now known only from two drawings which are, however, not entirely accurate.

The Golden Horns

They pry in pages
Of ancient sages,
They search in the glooms
Of mounded tombs,
On swords and shields
In ruined fields,
On runic stones
Among crumbled bones.

A fugitive glance
Of the past enchants
The inquisitive mind;
But the dark flows over
And shadows cover
The dusty screeds,
The heroic deeds,
Till the eyes are blind
And the thoughts go out
In a mist of doubt.
"You old, old
Ages of gold,
Flaming forth
Light of the North,
When heaven was on earth;
Out of the black
Where the years mingle,
Give us a single
Glimpse back."

Night hurries
In cloudy flurries;
Tumuli awaken,
The rose is shaken,
A voice through the skies
Profoundly sighs.
Over the storms
The gods arise,
War-crimsoned forms,
Star-flashing eyes.

"O you who fumble blind
Shall find
A timeless trace
Of the vanished race.
A while you shall hold it,
Then darkness shall fold it.
The graven mark
Of the years that are dark
Is stamped on its sides—
There your secret abides.
To honor us, lift
Devout hearts for the gift.
The fairest of mortals,
A maid,
Is destined to find it."
So they sing, and the shade
Surges over the throng;
Night captures their song
And closes the portals
Behind it.

Hrymfaxe[1] the black
Snorts, and plunges
Into the tide.
Delling[2] flings back
The bolts of dawn.
The gate swings wide.
Skinfaxe[3] lunges
Up from the dark
On the heavenly arc.

And the birds are singing
In the pearled showers
Of the dew on the flowers
Where the winds are swinging.

[1] Old Icelandic: Hrímfaxi. In Scandinavian mythology the horse driven
by Night in her journey over the heavens. Its name means "the one with
the mane of rime." The froth dripping from its bit bedews the earth during
the night.
[2] The father of Day.
[3] Old Icelandic: Skinfaxi, i.e., "the one of the shining mane." The horse
which pulls Day's chariot across the heavens.

And the winds breathe her
Over the day,
The maid who dances
To fields away.
Violets wreathe her,
Cheeks aglow,
Hands like snow,
Light as a hind,
Gainly and gay,
Carefree mind,
Smile that humbles
The smiling land;
Sprightly wandering,
Love pondering—
She stumbles.
She starts to behold
Flames of gold,
And lifts from under
The black mold
With her white hand
The red gold.

The zenith shakes
With thunder.
All the North wakes
In wonder.

Then come the crowds
In busy clouds,
Dig and measure
To find more treasure.
There is no more gold,
Their hopes are shaken,
They see only the mold
Whence it was taken.

A century passes.

Over the masses
Of shadowy peaks
The sluice of the storm
Tremendously breaks.
The turbulent swarm,

The warrior legion,
Across the Norwegian
Mountain, calls;
Over the wold
And the Danish plain
To the cloud-built halls
Where the radiant Old
Gather again.

"The few who know
The gifts we bestow,
Who never surrender
To earthly bond;
Who scale the splendor
Of eternity,
And through Nature see
The light beyond,
Who trembling divine
God's fires that shine
In flowers, in suns,
In west, in east,
In greatest, in least;
Whose thirst burns
For the Life of life;
Who—O Great Spirit
Of the vanished days!—
Who see thy rays
In radiance, rife
On the holy form
Of the ancient relic;
Over the storm,
Through the gathered night,
Surely they hear
Again thy clear
'Let there be Light!'
The son of Nature,
Unsought, obscure,
In whom endure
The heroic stature,
The honest face
Of his father's race;
Whose fruitful soil

Is rich with his toil—
It shall be our pleasure
To honor him.
He shall find again
Our hidden treasure!"
The light is gray,
The forms grow dim,
Over rock and plain
They vanish away.

Hrymfaxe the black
Snorts, and plunges
Into the tide.
Delling flings back
The bolts of dawn.
The gate swings wide.
Skinfaxe lunges
Up from the dark
On the heavenly arc.

Where trees and bushes
Spread their shadow,
The plough pushes
Through the black meadow.

Abruptly the plough
Stops, and the rush
Shudders of wonder
Through every bough.
The clouds sunder,
Bird-notes cease,
All voices fall
In a holy hush.
Profound peace
Consecrates all.

Then clinks in the mold
The timeless gold.

Glimpses from the days of yore
Sparkle down the aisles of time;
Strangely they appear once more,
Riddles shining through the grime.

Aureoles of mystery hover
Over every secret mark;
Flames of deity discover
Beauty working through the dark

Hallow them, for Fate's undaunted
Hand shall sweep away the trove.
Christ's blood fill them, like the wonted
Blood beneath the sacred grove.

Yet, you only see the graven
Gold, and not the light above it;
Common riches shown for craven
Eyes to estimate and covet.

The hour strikes; the gods have given;
Now the gods have taken back;
Storms crash; the clouds are riven;
The relics vanish in the black.

Translated by Robert Silliman Hillyer

Song

Behind black woods the pale
Moonlight is sifting.
To God the nightingale
Her song is lifting.
The low tones float and linger,
Blend and expire,
And I hear the brook's white finger
Plucking her lyre.

In the wood there is one flower
Death has chosen;
(Soon, soon, perhaps, my hour!)
Its heart is frozen.
Let the last flower die.
From clouds that smother
Its seeds, toward a fairer sky
Rises another.

O Darkness! perhaps soon
Here in the deathless
Path of thy summer moon,
I shall lie breathless.
Though the shadow of death is blue,
Smile, thou immortal!
And bear my last sigh through
Dawn's scarlet portal.

Translated by Robert Silliman Hillyer

The Rose of Roses

Behold them all, dew-sprinkled, standing there!
 Out of the dusk each smiling blossom peeps,
 While, pouring chill across the crimson heaps,
The silver moonlight makes them doubly fair.
Under the trees their fragrance fills the air,
 Eros in them his arrows nightly steeps;
 And, though each flower in glowing rapture sleeps,
They charm the soul no less with beauty rare.

Yet, in the house within this happy grove,
 Sheltered beneath its quiet canopy,
 A rose is blushing that is far more bright.
Sleep, gentle rosebud, sleep! Oh, could my love
 Bear with the message but a kiss to thee,
 I were the happiest among men tonight.

Translated by Charles Wharton Stork

HANS CHRISTIAN ANDERSEN
(1805-75)

"First one suffers so terribly much, and then one becomes famous."

This, in his own words, is the story of Hans Christian Andersen's life. For more than a century now, the poor shoemaker's son from Odense has enjoyed more fame and more love than any other Scandinavian writer of any age. Yet, from the time he went out into the world, at the age of fourteen, until the end of his life, this great master of the fairy tale was a lonely and, in many ways, unhappy man. Physically homely, he was never able to forget an early disappointment in love. Even after he became financially comfortable, and the emotional sufferings of his youth were far in the past, his sensitive, vain, and egocentric mind was constantly plagued by insecurity. His novels, overshadowed by his beautiful fairy tales, never won the acclaim he hoped they would receive. Loved though his fairy tales are, they have, in a way, also suffered a sad fate, restricted as they usually are to the nursery, although they belong, in no lesser degree, on the bookshelves of adults.

The following selections were both written about 1850.

It's Perfectly True!

"It's a dreadful business," said a hen, and she said it in a part of the town where the incident had not taken place.

"It's a dreadful business to happen in a henhouse. I wouldn't dare sleep alone tonight. Thank goodness there are so many of us on the perch!"

And then she told her story in such a way that the feathers of the other hens stood on end, and even the rooster's comb drooped. It's perfectly true!

But let's begin at the beginning.

It happened in a henhouse at the other end of the town. The sun went down and the hens flew up. One of them was a white-feathered, short-legged, nice little thing who laid her eggs regularly—a most respectable hen in every way. She settled herself on the perch, preening herself with her beak. One tiny feather fluttered down.

"There's that feather gone!" said the hen. "Well, well, the more I preen myself, the more handsome I shall become, no doubt!"

She said it only in fun, you know. She was the life and soul of the crowd, but otherwise, as we've said, most respectable. Then she fell asleep.

All was dark. There sat the hens, packed closely together. But the white hen's neighbor wasn't asleep; she had heard and not heard, as one must do in this world for the sake of peace and quiet. But she couldn't resist telling it to her neighbor on the other side.

"Did you hear? Well, my dear, I won't mention any names, but there's one hen I know who is going to pluck out all her feathers just to make herself look smart! Humph! If I were a rooster I should simply treat her with contempt."

Up above the hens lived Mother Owl, with Father Owl, and all the little Owls. They were a sharp-eared family and they heard every word; they rolled their eyes, and old Mother Owl flapped her wings. "Don't take any notice—you heard what she said, of course. I heard it with my own ears. Upon my word, I don't know what the world is coming to! One of the hens, so utterly lost to all sense of henly decency, is sitting there plucking out her feathers with the rooster looking on the whole time!"

"Prenez garde aux enfants!" said Father Owl. "Be careful what you're saying!"

"Oh, but I shall have to tell the owl across the road," said Mother Owl. "She is somebody, and worth associating with, you know." And off she flew.

"Tu-whit, tu-whoo, tu-whit, tu-whoo," they hooted together outside the pigeon house over the way. "Have you heard the news? Have you heard the news? There is a hen who has pulled out all her feathers just to please the rooster. She is freezing to death, if she isn't dead already, tu-whit, tu-whoo, tu-whit, tu-whoo. . . ."

"Where? Where?" asked the pigeons.

"In the yard opposite; I saw it, so to speak, with my own eyes! It's not at all a nice story to tell, but it's perfectly true!"

"Trrrue, too trrrue—trrrue, too trrrue," cooed the pigeons, and they flew down to tell the story in the chicken run below. "There's a hen—in fact, some say there are two hens who have plucked out all their feathers to be different from the rest, and to attract the attention of the rooster. A dreadful thing to do, what with the risk of chills and fever; and they caught cold and died, both of them!"

"Cock-a-doodle-doo! Wake up! Wake up!" crowed the rooster, flying up on to the fence. He was still half-asleep, but he crowed all the same. "Three hens have died of a broken heart, all for the sake of the rooster; they've plucked out all their feathers, and now they are dead! It's a dreadful business, but it's no use trying to keep it quiet. Tell anyone you please!"

"We'll tell, we'll tell!" squeaked the bats; and the rooster crowed and the hens clucked, "Tell, tell, tell, tell," and so the story flew from one henhouse to another, until at last it came to the place where it had really started.

"Five hens"—that's how it was told—"five hens have plucked out all their feathers to show which one has lost most weight for love of the rooster; then they pecked at one another till they bled, and all five dropped down dead—a shame and a disgrace to their relations, and a serious loss to their owner!"

The hen who had dropped the little loose feather naturally didn't recognize her own story, and as she was a respectable hen, she exclaimed, "I despise such hens! But there are many others just as bad! Things like that ought not to be hushed up; I must do what I can to get the story into the papers, then it will soon be known all over the country, and serve the wretches right, and their relations too!"

It was put into the papers, all clear in plain print. And it's perfectly true—one little feather can easily become five hens!

Translated by Paul Leyssac

The Shirt Collar

Once upon a time there was an elegant gentleman whose whole outfit consisted of a bootjack and a comb, but he also had the most wonderful shirt collar in the world, and it's about this shirt collar that we're to hear a story.

The collar had now arrived at an age when he began to think of getting married and it so happened that in the wash he found himself next to a garter.

"My word!" exclaimed the collar. "I've never seen anyone so slender, so fine, so soft and so dainty as you. May I ask your name?"

"I won't tell you," said the garter.

"Where do you live?" asked the collar.

But the garter was overcome with shyness and found it rather embarrassing to answer such a question.

"I should imagine that you're a belt," said the collar. "I mean a sort of inner belt. I realize that you're useful as well as ornamental, my pretty one."

"I forbid you to speak to me," said the garter. "I can't see that I've given you any encouragement."

"The mere fact of being so beautiful is encouragement enough," said the collar.

"Please don't come any nearer," said the garter. "You look so masculine."

"Well, after all, I'm an elegant gentleman," said the collar. "I own a bootjack and a comb." Now that was not true at all, for it was his master who owned them, but he was boasting.

"Keep your distance," said the garter. "I'm not accustomed to such familiarity."

"Prude!" said the collar.

At that very moment he was taken out of the washtub, starched, hung over a chair in the sun and laid on the ironing board. Then the hot iron appeared on the scene.

"Honored Madam," said the collar, "fascinating little widow, my blood is stirring within me. I shall never be the same again. You're taking the crease out of me! You're burning a hole in me! Oh!—will you be my wife?"

"Rag!" said the iron, and she passed haughtily over the collar, for she fancied she was a steam engine running on a railway track, pulling carriages behind her.

"Rag!" she said again.

The collar was a bit frayed at the edges, so the cutting-out scissors arrived to snip off the ends.

"Oh!" said the collar, "I can see you're a Première Danseuse. How magnificently you point your toes! I've never seen anything more fascinating. No one in the world can do that like you."

"I know," said the scissors.

"You really ought to be a countess," said the collar. "All I possess is an elegant gentleman, a bootjack, and a comb. Oh, if I only possessed an earldom!"

"As I live and breathe, he is proposing to me!" said the infuriated scissors, and gave him such a snip that he had to be scrapped.

"Now I shall have to propose to the comb," said the collar. "It's very remarkable how you keep all your teeth, my pretty one. Have you never thought of getting married?"

"Of course I have," said the comb. "Didn't you know that I'm engaged to the bootjack?"

"Engaged!" exclaimed the collar.

There was nobody left to propose to, and so he disdainfully turned his back on lovemaking.

A long time passed, and the collar found himself at the paper mill in a box where there was a social gathering of rags; the upper ten on one side, and the ragtag and bobtail on the other, which is just as it should be.

Everyone had a great deal to tell, but the collar had the most, for he was a consummate braggart.

"You've no idea how many sweethearts I've had," he said. "They would never give me a moment's peace. After all, I was a stiff and starched gentleman once. I had a bootjack and a comb that I never used. You should have seen me then—you should have seen me when I had a day off! Never shall I forget my first love. She was a belt, so lovely, so soft and charming! She threw herself into a washtub for my sake. There was also a widow; she was red-hot for me, but I gave her the slip and she turned black again. Then there was a Première Danseuse. She gave me the cut which you can still see—a fiery minx she was! Even my own comb was mad about me, and lost all her teeth from unrequited love. Oh yes, I've had plenty of experiences like that. But the gart . . . I mean the belt who threw herself into the washtub is the one I feel most sorry for. I've a great deal on my conscience; it's about time I was made into a white paper."

And that is what actually happened. All the rags were made into white paper, but the collar became that very piece of white paper we see here, the very one on which this story is printed. And that was because he boasted so dreadfully of what he had never been. So let us remember not to behave like that, for who knows? One day we might land in the ragbag, be made into a piece of white paper, and have our whole life's history, even the most intimate details, printed on the front, and so publish it abroad ourselves—just like the collar.

Translated by Paul Leyssac

J. P. JACOBSEN

(1847–85)

One of Denmark's first Darwinists and a translator of two of Darwin's major works, Jens Peter Jacobsen could probably have pursued a brilliant career as a natural scientist. In fact, he was awarded a gold medal by the University of Copenhagen for one of his many scientific essays. Consequently, when his literary interests finally gained the upper hand, it was inevitable that he join the ranks of the exponents of that "new" theory of art called Naturalism.

Jacobsen's novels have been compared with those of Flaubert and, indeed, the two writers have much in common. But Jacobsen was also an accomplished lyrical poet, a fact which is clearly reflected in his novels. Hence, his emphasis as a Naturalist upon scientific observation in the treatment of character is tempered by his compassion.

The following selection is an excerpt from Chapter 5 of *Marie Grubbe* (1876), one of Jacobsen's best-known works. It is set in the 17th century. Ulrik Christian Gyldenlöve, the principal character of the piece, was a son of King Christian IV and a half-brother of Frederick III. He distinguished himself as a general during the defense of Copenhagen against the Swedes in 1658.

The Last Hours of Ulrik Christian

Toward the end of November Ulrik Christian fell dangerously ill. His health, long undermined by debauchery of every conceivable kind, had perhaps been unable to endure the continued strain of nightwatches and hard work in connection with his post. Or possibly fresh dissipations had strung the bow too tightly. A wasting disease, marked by intense pain, wild fever dreams, and constant restlessness, attacked him, and soon took such a turn that none could doubt the name of the sickness was death.

On the eleventh of December, Pastor Hans Didrichsen Bartskjær, chaplain to the royal family, was walking uneasily up and down over the fine straw mattings that covered the floor in the large leather-brown room outside of Ulrik Christian's sickchamber. He stopped absentmindedly before the paintings on the walls, and seemed to examine with intense interest the fat, naked nymphs, outstretched under the trees, the bathing Susannas, and the simpering Judith with bare, muscular arms. They could not hold his attention long, however, and he went to the window, letting his gaze roam from the gray-white sky to the wet, glistening copper roofs and the long mounds of dirty, melting snow in the castle park below. Then he resumed his nervous pacing, murmuring, and gesticulating.

Was that the door opening? He stopped short to listen. No! He drew a deep breath and sank down into a chair, where he sat, sighing and rubbing the palms of his hands together, until the door really opened. A middle-aged woman wearing a huge flounced cap of red-dotted stuff appeared and beckoned cautiously to him. The pastor pulled himself together, stuck his prayer book under his arm, smoothed his cassock, and entered the sick-chamber.

The large oval room was wainscoted in dark wood from floor to ceiling. From the central panel, depressed below the surface of the wall, grinned a row of hideous white-toothed heads of blackamoors and Turks, painted in gaudy colors. The deep, narrow lattice window was partially veiled by a sash curtain of thin, blue-gray stuff, leaving the lower part of the room in deep twilight, while the sunbeams played freely on the painted ceiling, where horses, weapons, and naked limbs mingled in an inextricable tangle, and on the canopy of the four-poster bed, from which hung draperies of yellow damask fringed with silver.

The air that met the pastor, as he entered, was warm, and so heavy with the scent of salves and nostrums that for a moment he could hardly breathe. He clutched a chair for support, his head swam, and everything seemed to be whirling around him —the table covered with flasks and phials, the window, the nurse with her cap, the sick man on the bed, the sword rack, and the door opening into the adjoining room where a fire was blazing in the grate.

"The peace of God be with you, my lord!" he greeted in a trembling voice as soon as he recovered from his momentary dizziness.

"What the devil d'ye want here?" roared the sick man, trying to lift himself in the bed.

"*Gemach, gnädigster Herr, gemach!*" Shoemaker's Anne, the nurse, hushed him, and coming close to the bed, gently stroked the coverlet. " 'Tis the venerable *Confessionarius* of his Majesty, who has been sent hither to give you the sacrament."

"Gracious Sir, noble Lord Gyldenlöve!" began the pastor, as he approached the bed. "Though 'tis known to me that you have not been among the simple wise or the wisely simple who use the Word of the Lord as their rod and staff and who dwell in His courts, and although that God whose cannon is the crashing thunderbolt likewise holds in His hand the golden palm of victory and the blood-dripping cypresses of defeat, yet men may understand, though not justify, the circumstance that you, whose duty it has been to command and set a valiant example to your people, may for a moment have forgotten that we are but as nothing, as reed in the wind, nay, as the puny grafted shoot in the hands of the mighty Creator. You may have thought foolishly: This have I done, this is a fruit that I have brought to maturity and perfection. Yet now, beloved lord, when you lie here on your bed of pain, now God who is the merciful God of love hath surely enlightened your understanding and turned your heart to Him in longing with fear and trembling to confess your uncleansed sins, that you may trustfully accept the grace and forgiveness which His loving hands are holding out to you. The sharp-toothed worm of remorse——"

"Cross me fore and cross me aft! Penitence, forgiveness of sins, and life eternal!" jeered Ulrik Christian and sat up in bed. "Do you suppose, you sour-faced baldpate, do you suppose, because my bones are rotting out of my body in stumps and slivers, that gives me more stomach for your parson-palaver?"

"Most gracious lord, you sadly misuse the privilege which your high rank and yet more your pitiable condition give you to berate a poor servant of the Church, who is but doing his duty in seeking to turn your thoughts toward that which is assuredly to you the one thing needful. Oh, honored lord, it avails but little to kick against the pricks! Has not the wasting disease that has struck your body taught you that none can escape the chastisements of the Lord God, and that the scourgings of heaven fall alike on high and low?"

Ulrik Christian interrupted him, laughing: "Hell consume me, but you talk like a witless schoolboy! This sickness that's eating my marrow I've rightfully brought on myself, and if you suppose that heaven or hell sends it, I can tell you that a man gets it by drinking and wenching and reveling at night. You may depend on't. And now take your scholastic legs out of this chamber with all speed, or else I'll——"

Another attack seized him, and as he writhed and moaned with the intense pain, his oaths and curses were so blasphemous and so appalling in their inventiveness that the scandalized pastor stood pale and aghast. He prayed God for strength and power of persuasion, if mayhap he might be vouchsafed the privilege of opening this hardened soul to the truth and glorious consolation of religion. When the patient was quiet again he began: "My lord, my lord, with tears and weeping I beg and beseech you to cease from such abominable cursing and swearing! Remember, the axe is laid unto the root of the tree, and it shall be hewn down and cast into the fire, if it continues to be unfruitful and does not in the eleventh hour bring forth flowers and good fruit! Cease your baleful resistance, and throw yourself with penitent prayers at the feet of our Saviour——"

When the pastor began his speech, Ulrik Christian sat up at the headboard of the bed. He pointed threateningly to the door and cried again and again: "Begone, parson! Begone, march! I can't abide you any longer!"

"Oh, my dear lord," continued the clergyman, "if mayhap you are hardening yourself because you misdoubt the possibility of finding grace, since the mountain of your sins is overwhelming, then hear with rejoicing that the fountain of God's grace is inexhaustible——"

"Mad dog of a parson, will you go!" hissed Ulrik Christian between clenched teeth; "one—two!"

"And if your sins were red as blood, ay, as Tyrian purple——"

"Right about face!"

"He shall make them white as Lebanon's——"

"Now by St. Satan and all his angels!" roared Ulrik Christian as he jumped out of bed, caught a rapier from the sword rack, and made a furious lunge after the pastor, who, however, escaped into the adjoining room, slamming the door after him. In his rage, Ulrik Christian flung himself at the door, but sank exhausted to the floor, and had to be lifted into bed, though he still held the sword.

The forenoon passed in a drowsy calm. He suffered no pain, and the weakness that came over him seemed a pleasant relief. He lay staring at the points of light penetrating the curtain, and counted the black rings in the iron lattice. A pleased smile flitted over his face when he thought of his onslaught on the pastor, and he grew irritable only when Shoemaker's Anne would coax him to close his eyes and try to sleep.

In the early afternoon a loud knock at the door announced the entrance of the pastor of the Trinity Church, Dr. Jens Justesen. He was a tall, rather stout man, with coarse, strong features, short black hair, and large, deep-set eyes. Stepping briskly up to the bed, he said simply: "Good day!"

As soon as Ulrik Christian became aware that another clergyman was standing before him, he began to shake with rage, and let loose a broadside of oaths and railing against the pastor, against Shoemaker's Anne, who had not guarded his peace better, against God in heaven and all holy things.

"Silence, child of man!" thundered Pastor Jens. "Is this language meet for one who has even now one foot in the grave? 'Twere better you employed the flickering spark of life that still remains to you in making your peace with the Lord, instead of picking quarrels with men. You are like those criminals and disturbers of peace who, when their judgment is fallen and they no longer can escape the red-hot pincers and the axe, then in their miserable impotence curse and revile the Lord our God with filthy and wild words. They seek thereby courage to drag themselves out of that almost brutish despair, that craven fear and slavish remorse without hope, into which such fellows generally sink toward the last, and which they fear more than death and the tortures of death."

Ulrik Christian listened quietly, until he had managed to get his sword out from under the coverlet. Then he cried: "Guard yourself, priest-belly!" and made a sudden lunge after Pastor Jens, who coolly turned the weapon aside with his broad prayer book.

"Leave such tricks to pages!" he said contemptuously. "They're scarce fitting for you and me. And now this woman"—turning to Shoemaker's Anne—"had best leave us private."

Anne quitted the room, and the pastor drew his chair up to the bed, while Ulrik Christian laid his sword on the coverlet.

Pastor Jens spoke fair words about sin and the wages of sin, about God's love for the children of men, and about the death on the cross.

Ulrik Christian lay turning his sword in his hand, letting the light play on the bright steel. He swore, hummed bits of ribald songs, and tried to interrupt with blasphemous questions, but the pastor went on speaking about the seven words of the cross, about the holy sacrament of the altar, and the bliss of heaven.

Then Ulrik Christian sat up in bed and looked the pastor straight in the face.

" 'Tis naught but lies and old wives' tales," he said.

"May the devil take me where I stand, if it isn't true!"—cried the pastor—"every blessed word!" He hit the table with his fist, till the jars and glasses slid and rattled against one another, while he rose to his feet and spoke in a stern voice: " 'Twere meet that I should shake the dust from my feet in righteous anger and leave you here alone, a sure prey to the devil and his realm, whither you are most certainly bound. You are one of those who daily nail our Lord Jesus to the gibbet of the cross, and for all such the courts of hell are prepared. Do not mock the terrible name of hell, for it is a name that contains a fire of torment and the wailing and gnashing of teeth of the damned! Alas, the anguish of hell is greater than any human mind can conceive; for if one were tortured to death and woke in hell, he would long for the wheel and the red-hot pincers as for Abraham's bosom. 'Tis true that sickness and disease are bitter to the flesh of man when they pierce like a draught, inch by inch, through every fiber of the body, and stretch the sinews till they crack, when they burn like salted fire in the vitals, and gnaw with dull teeth in the innermost marrow! But the sufferings of hell are a raging storm racking every limb and joint, a whirlwind of unthinkable woe, an eternal dance of anguish; for as one wave rolls upon another, and is followed by another and another in all eternity, so the scalding pangs and blows of hell follow one another ever and everlastingly, without end and without pause."

The sick man looked around bewildered. "I won't!" he said, "I won't! I've nothing to do with your heaven or hell. I would die, only die and nothing more!"

"You shall surely die," said the pastor, "but at the end of the dark valley of death are two doors, one leading to the bliss of heaven and one to the torments of hell. There is no other way, no other way at all."

"Yes, there is, pastor, there must be—tell me, is there not?— a deep, deep grave hard by for those who went their own way, a deep black grave leading down to nothing—to no earthly thing?"

"They who went their own way are headed for the realm of the devil. They are swarming at the gate of hell; high and low, old and young, they push and scramble to escape the yawning abyss, and cry miserably to that God whose path they would not follow, begging him to take them away. The cries of the pit are over their heads, and they writhe in fear and agony, but the gates of hell shall close over them as the waters close over the drowning."

"Is it the truth you're telling me? On your word as an honest man, is it anything but a tale?"

"It is."

"But I won't! I'll do without your God! I don't want to go to heaven, only to die!"

"Then pass on to that horrible place of torment, where those who are damned for all eternity are cast about on the boiling waves of an endless sea of sulphur, where their limbs are racked by agony, and their hot mouths gasp for air, among the flames that flicker over the surface. I see their bodies drifting like white gulls on the sea, yea, like a frothing foam in a storm, and their shrieks are like the noise of the earth when the earthquake tears it, and their anguish is without a name. Oh, would that my prayers might save thee from it, miserable man! But grace has hidden its countenance, and the sun of mercy is set forever."

"Then help me, pastor, help me!" groaned Ulrik Christian. "What are you a parson for, if you can't help me? Pray, for God's sake, pray! Are there no prayers in your mouth? Or give me your wine and bread, if there's salvation in 'em as they say! Or is it all a lie—a confounded lie? I'll crawl to the feet of your God like a whipped boy, since He's so strong—it is not fair—He's so mighty, and we're so helpless! Make Him kind, your God, make Him kind to me! I bow down—I bow down—I can do no more!"

"Pray!"

"Ay, I'll pray, I'll pray all you want—indeed!" He knelt in bed and folded his hands. "Is that right?" he asked, looking toward Pastor Jens. "Now, what shall I say?"

The pastor made no answer.

For a few moments Ulrik Christian knelt thus, his large, bright, feverish eyes turned upward. "There are no words, pastor," he whimpered. "Lord Jesus, they're all gone," and he sank down, weeping.

Suddenly he sprang up, seized his sword, broke it, and cried: "Lord Jesus Christ, see, I break my sword!" and he lifted the shining pieces of the blade. "*Pardon*, Jesus, *pardon!*"

The pastor then spoke words of consolation to him and gave him the sacrament without delay, for he seemed not to have a long time left. After that Pastor Jens called Shoemaker's Anne and departed.

The disease was believed to be contagious, hence none of those who had been close to the dying man attended him in his illness, but in the room below a few of his family and friends, the physician-in-ordinary to the King, and two or three gentlemen of the court were assembled to receive the noblemen, foreign ministers, officers, courtiers, and city councilmen who called to inquire about him. So the peace of the sick-chamber was not disturbed, and Ulrik Christian was again alone with Shoemaker's Anne.

Twilight fell. Anne threw more wood on the fire, lit two candles, took her prayer book, and settled herself comfortably.

She pulled her cap down to shade her face and very soon was asleep. A barber-surgeon and a lackey had been posted in the anteroom to be within call, but they were both squatting on the floor near the window, playing dice on the straw matting to deaden the sound. They were so absorbed in their game that they did not notice someone stealing through the room, until they heard the door of the sick-chamber close.

"It must have been the doctor," they said, looking at each other in fright.

It was Marie Grubbe. Noiselessly she stole up to the bed and bent over the patient, who was dozing quietly. In the dim, uncertain light, he looked very pale and unlike himself, the forehead had a deathly whiteness, the eyelids were unnaturally large, and the thin wax-yellow hands were groping feebly and helplessly over the dark-blue bolster.

Marie wept. "Are you so ill?" she murmured. She knelt, supporting her elbows on the edge of the bed, and gazed at his face.

"Ulrik Christian," she called, and laid her hand on his shoulder.

"Is anyone else here?" he moaned weakly.

She shook her head. "Are you very ill?" she asked.

"Yes, 'tis all over with me."

"No, no, it must not be! Whom have I if you go? No, no, how can I bear it!"

"To live? 'Tis easy to live, but I have had the bread of death and the wine of death, I must die—yes, yes—bread and wine— body and blood—d'you believe they help? No, no, in the name of Jesus Christ, in the name of Jesus Christ! Say a prayer, child, make it a strong one!"

Marie folded her hands and prayed.

"Amen, amen! Pray again! I'm such a great sinner, child, it needs so much! Pray again, a long prayer with many words— many words! Oh, no, what's that? Why is the bed turning? Hold fast, hold fast! 'Tis turning—like a whirlwind of unthinkable woe, a dance of eternal anguish, and—ha, ha, ha! Am I drunk again? What devilry is this—what have I been drinking? Wine! Ay, of course, 'twas wine I drank, ha, ha! We're gaily yet, we're gaily— Kiss me, my chick!

> Herzen und Küssen
> Ist Himmel auf Erd——

Kiss me again, sweetheart, I'm so cold, but you're round and warm. Kiss me warm! You're white and soft, white and smooth——"

He had thrown his arms around Marie, and pressed the terrified child close to him. At that moment, Shoemaker's Anne woke and saw her patient sitting up and fondling a strange woman. She lifted her prayer book threateningly and cried: "*H'raus*, thou hell-born wench! To think of the shameless thing sitting here and wantoning with the poor dying gentleman before my very eyes! *H'raus*, whoever ye are—handmaid of the wicked one, sent by the living Satan!"

"Satan!" shrieked Ulrik Christian and flung away Marie Grubbe in horror. "Get thee behind me! Go, go!" He made the sign of the cross again and again. "Oh, thou cursed devil! You would lead me to sin in my last breath, in my last hour, when one should be so careful. Begone, begone, in the blessed name of the Lord, thou demon!" His eyes wide open, fear in every feature, he stood up in bed and pointed to the door.

Speechless and beside herself with terror, Marie rushed out. The sick man threw himself down and prayed and prayed, while Shoemaker's Anne read slowly and in a loud voice prayer after prayer from her book with the large print.

Two hours later Ulrik Christian died.

Translated by Hanna Astrup Larsen

HENRIK PONTOPPIDAN

(1857–1943)

Henrik Pontoppidan originally set out to be an engineer. But the thoughts which preoccupied him could not be communicated through the medium of that profession, so he left his studies to become a writer. A restless, probing character, he probably managed to delve deeper into the souls of his countrymen than any other writer before him. And if it was not always gold that he brought to the surface, it was the truth as he saw it. Pessimistic, but objective, he castigated the Danes in no uncertain terms. In spite of his unflattering descriptions, the quality of his writings was such that he retained the love and respect of his compatriots. He was awarded the Nobel Prize for literature in 1917.

"Eagle's Flight" (1894) is a direct answer to Hans Christian Andersen's viewpoint as it appears in "The Ugly Duckling." The concluding sentence echoes Andersen's words, except the moral is reversed. While Pontoppidan's story lacks the charm of Andersen's fairy tale, its logic and irony are stunningly convincing.

Eagle's Flight

This is the story of a young eagle which in its yellow-beaked infancy was found by some boys and taken to the old parsonage, where kind people cared for it and became so attached to it that they kept it there. Like the Ugly Duckling of the fairy tale it grew up among quacking ducks and cackling hens and bleating sheep, and so well did it thrive in these surroundings that it grew large and broad and, as the minister said, "actually acquired a belly."

It was usually perched on an old fence near the pigsty, where it sat and waited for the maid to bring garbage from the kitchen.

As soon as old Dorothy came in view, it would throw itself on the pavement and waddle toward the filled trough with the burlesque sack-race stride peculiar to the kings of the ether when moving on earth.

Once in a while, especially on windy days or before a thunderstorm, a vague longing, like a dim homesickness, might awaken in the bosom of the captive prince of the air. Then it would sit for days with its beak buried in the dirty plumage of its breast, and would refuse to stir or eat. Then suddenly it would spread its wings as if embracing the air and start boldly toward the sky —but its flight was always brief. Its wings were well clipped, and after fluttering clumsily for a moment it would fall to the ground where, perplexed, it would take a few sidewise hops, and with craned neck run and hide in some dark corner, as if ashamed.

When it had lived in this way for a couple of years, it happened that the old minister was taken ill and died. In the following confusion the royal bird, which had been given the plebeian name of Claus, was for a while forgotten. As usual it waggled around peacefully and a little timidly among the other birds of the poultry yard, being used to cuffings from the minister's daughters when once in a while it resolved to assert its innate superiority over the small fry.

But when one day a fresh south wind blew spring and warmth over the country, the strange thing happened that the eagle suddenly found itself upon the ridge of the big barn, without any idea of how this had come to pass. As so often before, it had been perched on the fence, dreaming dejectedly, and then in a sudden vague yearning for liberty had spread its wings for flight. But instead of dropping down on the pavement as usual, it had been lifted into the air so swiftly that, frightened, it had hurried to the nearest foothold.

Now it was sitting there on the high roof, quite dazed by the course of events. Never before had it seen the world from such a lofty place. Eagerly it turned its head, now one way, now the other; then, irresistibly drawn by the drifting clouds and the azure of the sky, it spread its wings anew and soared upward, at first carefully and tentatively, soon with greater boldness and assurance, until at last with a wild scream of joy it swung itself high up in the air and made a great circle. In a flash it knew what it meant to be an eagle.

Villages, forests, sunny lakes passed under it. The eagle rose higher and higher toward the blue sky, dizzy from the wide horizon and the strength of its wings.

But suddenly it stopped. The empty vastness all around frightened it, and it began to search for a resting-place.

By good luck it reached a projecting rock high above the river valley. But looking around, still a little dizzy, in search of the parsonage and the ridge of the barn, it received a new shock. All around, wherever it glanced, spread a strange and unknown country. Not one familiar spot, not one refuge was there as far as the eye could see.

Above its head rose rock upon rock—steep bare stone walls without a single shelter from the wind. In the west, beyond the open country, the sun was just setting in scarlet evening clouds which boded storm and dark nights.

A crushing sense of loneliness seized the young royal bird, as the yellowish mists of the dusk enveloped the valley far beneath. Depressed, it gazed after a flock of crows which with shrill cries were passing it on the way home to their nests, down there near the cozy human dwellings. With closely folded wings, and its beak plunged into its breast feathers, it sat solitary and still on the silent, desolate rock.

Suddenly a whir of wings is heard overhead. A white-breasted female eagle is circling above it under the red evening sky.

For a while the young eagle remains where it is, craning its neck and pondering on this strange sight. But all at once its indecision is swept away. With a mighty rushing of its stretched wings it soars upward and in a moment is close to its mate.

Now begins a wild chase over the mountains, the she-eagle always ahead and above, Claus doing his best to overtake her, though heavier and panting.

Soon they are among the high mountains. The sun is still illuminating the loftiest peaks, but they sail over the mountain-tops, into the growing darkness. Far beneath is heard the somber rustling of huge forests and the hollow boom of the rivers in the deep gorges.

"Will she never sit down?" he thinks, frightened by this sinister unknown roaring. He is almost exhausted, and his wings feel tired and heavy.

Higher and higher soars his beloved, farther and farther above the crimson peaks, calling, coaxing him to follow.

They have reached a vast stone desert, a chaos of gigantic blocks tumbled upon each other like the ruins of an overthrown tower of Babel. Suddenly the view before them opens. High above the drifting clouds spreads like a vision the unearthly realm of perpetual snow, unsoiled by swarming life, the home of the eagle and the great stillness. The last rays of day seem to be resting in quiet slumber on the white snow. Behind it rises the dark-blue sky covered with calm stars.

Terrified, Claus stops his flight and settles on a rock. He sits there trembling with cold and discomfort, gazing at this white spectral land, these large stars which twinkle at him through the darkness like so many evil cat's eyes. Sadly his thoughts turn back anew to the home which he left behind. He recalls his warm place on the fence and the cozy poultry yard where his small friends are now sitting on their perches, sleeping peacefully with their heads under their wings. He thinks of the chubby little pigs which are now lying in a heap close to their mother, dreaming and sucking at the same time, and of fat old Dorothy who will come from the kitchen with the steaming food, when the church bells announce the rising of the sun.

The call of the female comes down through the frosty air. But Claus spreads his wings noiselessly and steals back, first irresolutely, fluttering from block to block, but soon swiftly, eagerly, chased by his terror, his anxiety, his sweet longing—home—home —home!

Not until next morning did the poor bird reach the parsonage after his headstrong flight. For some moments it remained hovering over its beloved home, as if wanting to make sure that everything down there was as usual.

Then it descended slowly.

But a disaster was to take place. The hired man, who happened to notice it, and had not heard of the disappearance of Claus, ran quickly to the house for his gun, and took a stand behind a tree, to give fire when the supposed poultry thief should be near enough.

The shot fell.

A few feathers fluttered through the air, and the dead eagle fell like a stone straight down on the dunghill.

It avails but little to have come from an eagle's egg, if one is raised in the poultry yard.

Translated by Lida Siboni Hanson

MARTIN ANDERSEN-NEXØ

(1869–1954)

Born in the slums of Copenhagen and brought up on the island of Bornholm, Andersen-Nexø was one of eleven children and had of necessity to make himself useful at an early age. In his youth he worked as a shepherd boy, a shoemaker's apprentice, and a bricklayer until he managed, in his early twenties, to get some formal education. At the same time he fell under the influence of Socialism and began to write. With him, the Danish proletariat had, for the first time, its own voice in the country's literature.

Though Andersen-Nexø knew the pangs of hunger and poverty from firsthand experience, he never became embittered. On the contrary, his writings are permeated with his fundamental, sometimes even naive, belief in human kindness which, combined with his wonderful humor, gives his books a personal tenderness and warmth. He was, without doubt, one of the greatest Danish novelists of the early 20th century.

The selection below is from *Muldskud* ("Molehills"), a collection of stories published in two volumes, in 1900 and 1905.

The Passengers of the Empty Seats

I am sitting in the express train and rolling out into the Danish summer. It is one of those gray, hazy days when the sun is cowering in some hidden place, shedding its silvery light over the country. It is quiet, and everything shimmers with a vague luster. The landscape, which lazily changes with the speed, lies quivering in the haze of the heat.

On such a day, when the humid air waves over woods and fields like a thick veil of porridge and the lakes have the shifting glimmer of silver and lead, Denmark should be seen. Other countries have sharp contours against a sky which rises far away to intense azure. Here, there's no gaping gulf between sky and earth, space itself moves close up to the land, softens its features and itself acquires from it a material-like aspect. Every color in the landscape is moistened by this embrace, every line looks like a soft caress of the sky. On such a day one could wish to take all one's countrymen on a tour through the Danish countryside—especially those of them who seldom or never get to see it.

There aren't many people on the train; in the long carriage where I have a seat maybe all of twenty travelers. The carriage has space for about a hundred and fifty. All the more yawning the empty seats look.

My only fellow traveler is not embarrassed by them. As soon as the train starts moving he closes the door of our compartment and draws the curtain. "Now maybe we'll be free of others in here," he says.

"What have you really got against the other seats being occupied?" I say. "I think it's more cozy to be in a full compartment than an empty one."

"That's exactly what I mean, too—more cozy! So you can neither move nor breathe, right? No, thank you, give me a compartment with as few passengers as possible—and preferably none at all." So saying he leaned back into the corner by the window and closed his eyes; shortly after he fell asleep with his hands folded over his belly.

Still, it is more cozy to be in a carriage with as many as it can hold, even though each one has to make a little room for the other. The most cheerful vehicle one can encounter is, accordingly, not the big, undulating sedan with a single clod of a man rocking between soft cushions, but the overloaded charabanc. The empty seats radiate curses; joy dies in their presence. And yet one rides along with them—in every sense. My corpulent fellow traveler's view is, at the moment, the prevailing one—one must have room to puff up!

For most travelers in this life empty seats are probably just a happy opportunity to stretch their legs; but for a few they happen to become alive—even more alive than the occupied ones—and to reveal a whole world of human longings and human needs.

Over the empty seats there rambles an eternally thronging swarm of starved human souls.

I close my eyes, tired of the passing fields out there, perhaps also of the yawning emptiness which—like an accusation—keeps staring me in the face from the empty seats of the compartment. The snoring of my fellow traveler provides the last little touch— it overpowers me.

When I open my eyes again, the compartment is full of passengers. Next to me sits an old woman, whom I think I have seen before. Yellow and scrawny she is, but she smiles! She sits erect on the edge of her seat and responds to every movement of the train, newly starched like a child on a holiday, curious to look at, like a strange bird which is ready to take off at the slightest provocation. Nor do the others settle back and relax, but sit as if there were a pin through them, stiff and staring. It is a family— a man, a woman and three children—and evidently, until just recently, of the most besieged sort. Scrawny and bluish they are, with deep-set eyes that stare almost like empty sockets. They seem in no way to belong anywhere; their clothes don't lay naturally but in stiff folds like winding sheets.

For a moment I wonder where they got aboard the train, which, according to schedule, was not yet supposed to have stopped anywhere; but it slips my mind again because of the strangeness of their appearance.

The old one at my side rests her worn hands in her lap and stares out of the window with an expression as full of humming joy as a child's the first time it sees the world. Nothing in the world is as pretty as a poor granny's drooping hands; I must take this hand, resting there so misshapen by arthritis and blue varices, in my own. It is ice-cold.

"It's probably a long time since you've been out to the country, gram?" I say.

She nods. "But how lovely the summer is nowadays."

"How long actually has it been?" I ask again.

She blinks her eyes. Then she says remotely, "I haven't been out there since I came to the capital, an eighteen-year-old lass. But now I'll stay out there—forever."

"You're going to your home district then?"

She smiles mysteriously. "They had, right enough, consigned me to a plot, but then I took myself a liberty for once. For now I've served others for eighty-two years and put my own aside. There's a high spot in the west corner of the churchyard at home; from there one can see the sun go down when the bell rings and have a view of everything. There I'd prefer to lie."

It was the old granny from the backyard of Nörrebro—now I recognized her. And began to understand.

"She's going there to die," interrupted the younger woman in a voice which sounded as if every word burnt her, "for she's quite old already. But you see, we others, we're going now because we'd rather live. Oh, excuse me for speaking so badly; that's because they took my set of teeth and sold it to pay for what was more important, I guess." Then a cough seized her—and I saw for the first time how terribly skinny she was. And as if by contagion it spread over to the man and children, a dry cough which rang hollow—as if they had no lungs.

"It's this tuberculosis," she whispered, "we all have it. But now we want to go to the seaside and get well; it's supposed to be so salutary at the seaside."

"Only, it shouldn't be too late," says the old one. "It's sometimes too late when we poor people begin such things."

"Yes, we just haven't been able to before. The man there was a brush-maker, and we all had to help in order to have food. Then it attacked our lungs."

"Isn't he any more?" I asked. Something struck my mind; perhaps they too had known how to profit, one way or the other, from the war. They were going to the seaside, the whole family; they must have made a killing, although, perhaps, in a small way.

"No," she answered lightly. "For then the war broke out—or rather the inflation that followed it—and helped us over all the difficulties. We just couldn't make both ends meet any more, not even for bread—so terribly worthless had our money become. But then we met the *Prophet from Void.*"

"The Prophet from Void?"

"Yes—and he converted us to his congregation. There they don't eat food at all—as protest against the inflation; and then it doesn't matter how expensive food is. And the clothes don't wear out either; for the set of clothes each of us receives when he enters

the congregation is of such nature that it never has to be renewed. And since, besides, all members of the congregation
travel for free, we thought we could well enough afford to go to
the seaside, all five of us."

"Don't you have any tickets, then?" I ask worriedly, thinking
what will happen when the conductor comes.

She shakes her head smiling. "What do we need tickets for?
Old Granny doesn't have any either, for she is also one of us.
Right, mom? Yes, we always know each other by the eyes!"

Just then the conductor came. He woke up the sleeping sales-
man and punched both our tickets; then he went away without
even looking at the other six.

My corpulent fellow traveler smacked his lips and went on
sleeping. And the two women began talking again—about all the
loss and suffering they had known before they discovered this
new way of life. The man and the three children sat motionless
as before; there was a monotonous rattle in his throat, and the
small ones seemed not to breathe at all. But nothing had managed to subdue the two women; an endless history of sufferings
sounded from their lips like an alternating song, a chant of a
kind that might be sung of the lives of any number of thousands
of people.

"And just think," exclaimed the old one, "how privileged we
are now. Twice before, when my homesickness was too much to
bear, I got on the train, wanting to go. I knew from the papers
that many trains went back and forth every day and there was
enough room in them. They run with far too many empty seats,
they wrote. But both times I was driven off the train. One must
go across two straits to get home, and once I had already reached
the first one; but then they stopped me and transported me back
again; there was even some talk about punishment, although I
didn't take the seat from anybody. And now I can travel for free
wherever I want."

"Yes, all the empty seats in the world belong to us," said the
other to me, "and they are many. If you have a hard time of it
you should come over to us, for with us there's no inflation, and
everybody has equally much. We don't know any difference between high and low; before the Prophet from Void all are equal."

Then the train gave a long, shrill whistle. My corpulent fellow traveler yawned and stretched—we were at the ferry. And before I could turn around the occupants of the empty seats were gone.

I saw them again out on the platform as I stepped out. There they were with uncountable others who obviously belonged to the same world. They mixed with the real group of travelers and almost swallowed them; a strange swarm of pilgrims it was that took over the ferry.

"Peculiar people that you're taking through Denmark today," I said to a conductor.

He looked at me astonished. "Do you mean that group of salesmen over there? We have them every day the whole year round!"

But I wasn't having hallucinations. Now they took possession of the uppermost deck, the broad promenade deck which was otherwise exclusively for first- and second-class travelers; they took possession of it quite naturally, as if its unused world of luxury had been reserved just for them. I saw them with my own eyes swarming up there in the sunshine, almost assimilated with it—*the passengers of the empty seats.*

Translated by Hallberg Hallmundsson

JOHANNES V. JENSEN

(1873–1950)

A native of the remote district of Himmerland, North Jutland (which he has so unforgettably described in *Tales from Himmerland*), Johannes V. Jensen came to be more of a traveler than most other Scandinavian writers, seeking material in distant places, such as Japan and the Wild West. With equal ease he traversed the boundaries of time and managed in his work to span the centuries from the Ice Age to the present.

An expounder of Darwinian philosophy, Jensen regarded mankind, nature, and evolution with a deep and almost religious veneration. Yet he had many other interests, being as complex as he was prolific. He filled nine volumes with his "myths," a genre he created from a curious mixing of journalism, poetry, and philosophy. In addition, he wrote novels, short stories, lyrical poetry, essays, and travel books.

Jensen's style was virile and unsentimental. He was awarded the Nobel Prize for literature in 1944.

The selection below is from Jensen's fourth volume of myths, *Ved Livets Bred* ("The Border of Life"), published in 1928.

Did They Catch the Ferry?

Along the main road from Middelfart to Odense a motorcycle came roaring: a powerful engine of large bore and with an open exhaust, a long piece of copper pipe in all the colors of the rainbow protruding behind with no silencer. When the machine was coasting along comfortably, the engine gave a shattering report, like a bursting shell, with each explosion, but when the throttle was opened out and the machine gathered speed, reaching sixty miles an hour, or more, the explosions fused into a steady roar from the exhaust pipe where the metal vibrated: this is a noise which causes other road-users to shake their heads in indignation, while to the motorcyclist it is the essence of life itself. We all know that there is a world of difference between having to suffer earsplitting noises and making such noise oneself.

The throttle was kept wide open all the time because the road from Middelfart to Odense is wide and straight with a smooth surface; and they had to catch the ferry at Nyborg.

The driver was Sophus Hansen, returning to Copenhagen from a short trip to Jutland; Elvira was on the pillion. They were always called Sophus and Vira by their friends, so they will be called the same here. Vira sat, her long legs pointing backward and downward from under her dustcoat, a chic small leather helmet on her head, a little above Sophus, her head held on one side behind his shoulder, enabling her to peer ahead. Sophus steered, hunched forward, short in the neck, alert for any surprises the road might bring. It was a summer morning with early morning mist and restricted visibility calling for careful driving. Funen lay bathed in dew, with gossamery gardens and hedges, the road slightly damp from the mist but not quite wet enough to lay the dust. Here and there treacherous fresh sand had been sprinkled; the back wheel skidded more than once, and it was necessary to steer and balance as on a hair.

Sophus, nevertheless, was not averse to racing anything when he had a chance. The opportunity came but seldom as he went far too fast for most of the traffic. It was not often that he met up with a motorcycle of comparable power to his own which could give him a race, and in such cases the result was decided by a combination of road conditions and slick driving, as well as by the question of what risks the opponent was prepared to run, for in such cases Sophus went flat out.

As for exceeding the speed limit, of course, it was never in the built-up areas nor the towns, where control was likely to be exercised, that Sophus went all out; and it cannot harm him now to disclose the fact of his high speeding, for as will shortly be seen, he is far removed from having to account for the readings of his speedometer.

Two or three cars had come over on the same ferry from Jutland as Sophus, and had had a short lead because they were off the ferry first; two of these Sophus had overtaken immediately outside the town, a couple of Fords they were, but the third car he had not so far seen again; it was a small red Afag which he had noticed on the ferry.

Sophus and Vira were anxious to catch the first ferry[1] from Nyborg. Counting every minute it could just be done, assuming, of course, that the machine continued to run as it was now doing. That is why the roar of the engine was so high, and the countryside so streaky. Vira sat securely behind, as close to Sophus as possible, with one knee on either side of him like a pair of tongs to assure a good grip. She was entirely and happily ignorant of the small critical situations with which Sophus dealt en route: the farm cart which pulled out without giving any sign of its intention, right across the road, to take a side turning at the very moment when Sophus was about to overtake it: it was a crime, plain murder, damn the fool! But then Sophus on principle mistrusted any horse-drawn vehicle and managed to scrape round it with a quick maneuver based entirely on instinct; there was no question of reducing speed at the decisive moment; the driver's eyes and his own met for a split second and Sophus shook his head at him, pityingly, with an expression of sorrow for the man's mental standards and morals; but afterward his heart thumped hard, and Sophus felt a passing weakness which found expression in a sigh: he had had a very narrow escape from thundering at the rate of sixty miles an hour right into the side of that damned muckcart. Vira had suspected nothing.

About eight miles before Odense they could glimpse the spire of St. Alban's Church at the end of the straight road. Sophus overtook one car after another in long sweeps. He lay behind them until by bending sideways and surveying the road for oncoming traffic he could see if there was room to overtake—then forward in a sweep with open throttle, and the occupants of the car did not suffer from his dust in their eyes for long!

Shortly before Odense he caught up with the small red Afag —one had to say this for its driver, he certainly knew how to drive. Sophus lay behind him, glancing at his own speedometer.

---

[1] At the time this story was written two ferries had to be taken to get from Jutland to Copenhagen, one over the Little Belt between Jutland and Funen, and another over the Great Belt between Funen and Zealand. The Little Belt was bridged in 1935.

You did not notice it from behind, but the man was actually going over sixty miles an hour. Sophus managed to pass him just outside the town, and in overtaking he gave the driver a glance and saw that he wore large, dark goggles and smiled almost imperceptibly when the motorcycle flashed by.

With loud blasts from his exhaust pipe Sophus drove with hypocritical caution through Odense at the few miles per hour the speed limit allows. He lost his way as one does in intricate provincial towns—and swore; when he eventually found the main road again the Afag was once more ahead. Sophus looked at his watch. By fast driving he had gained a quarter of an hour on his timetable. It was obvious that the Afag was also heading for Nyborg so there was every reason to try a race with him! But Sophus felt he was running short of petrol and swung in at the next filling station, a red pump, looking like a man in armor, standing outside a blacksmith's. While the petrol was being pumped in, he exchanged some words with the garage hand, a young, rural mechanic, and Vira could hear the two oil-smeared characters discussing the various makes of machine. Their remarks were expert and cool. Take, for instance, the machine Sophus was riding, there could be no doubt about its superiority; but there was, of course, also the little new single-cylinder job, the K.G.W., which made quite a show on the speedway . . . then, with a nod, Sophus was off.

He soon caught up with the Afag again, but only by driving very fast indeed. He hooted, and the driver, to show that he had heard, turned, presenting two large, dark eye-sockets; then Sophus accelerated and pressed forward alongside him. The road was free, wide enough and straight, and he accelerated still more until he felt that his powerful engine was running at its absolute maximum speed. The motorcycle swayed under him in a peculiar manner at the tremendous speed, and the vibrations from the engine could be felt in the whole machine. Even fairly long depressions in the road beat like hammers against the wheels. Everything rushed by until the air became streaky, but Sophus could not get past. He accelerated for all he was worth with the throttle wide open, but the driver in the car beside him smiled and bent forward a little further, a movement which showed that he too was accelerating. The car crept into the lead again with the motorcycle beside; then the man in the Afag had the nerve to smile at Vira on the pillion . . .

Suddenly Sophus felt that he could just make it, but there was a bend ahead, and he dared not risk the camber of the road at his present speed, so he slowed a fraction and let the car go ahead again. He lay behind it gathering his forces and, as it were, accumulating speed for a new forward drive, for he had been speeding for a long time now. He looked at the speedometer and saw the needle vibrating between seventy and eighty, although they were now going at well under the speed they had held when they were side by side. The car in front, however, kept pitching horribly as if at any moment it might leave the road and go skyward, the springs could be seen yielding beneath the chassis, it took the bumps in the road with small, hard thuds —it was unbelievable that he dared keep up such a speed with such a small car! Now they were going downhill, and Sophus held back wisely and let the other go ahead. His chance of overtaking the car, which was heavier, would come when they were again going uphill. The road again climbed ahead and when he had accelerated and was immediately behind the car, the driver turned and grinned; they could see his dark sockets and a wide double row of teeth, and Sophus swore—and the race continued.

By now it had become a lovely, clear summer morning. Funen displayed her green charms, the flowers were nodding in the ditches, the air was filled with white butterflies, so many that it looked like a snowfall. They stuck on to the front of Vira's dustcoat by sheer pressure of air from the speed which was so great that it would have forced one's mouth open if one hadn't the whole time done one's utmost to keep it closed. But neither Sophus nor Vira saw much of Funen—they had to keep their eyes screwed up because of the showers of dust and stones from the car in front. It was literally as if the back wheels were shooting gravel, the air was a flying mass of fine, biting dust which whipped their faces with the force of a hurricane; it was like riding in a stream of sand fired from a gun. It could not be endured for long and once more Sophus pressed forward up alongside the Afag . . .

And then occurred just what may happen when a motorcyclist ventures to race a motorcar; the car driver grinned and dropped his mask—he was Death. He veered right over in front of Sophus to the other side of the road, a dirty but by no means unknown trick by a motorist who does not wish to be overtaken, and Sophus was forced off the road toward the ditch with greensward and loose sand. He experienced the sinking feeling underneath the saddle which occurs when the back wheel is skidding, held on to the handlebars for dear life, and crashed.

He and Vira never knew. The machine hurtled straight up into the air at the insane speed, came crashing down, and Sophus and Vira rolled and rolled, down, down, down, straight down to the Underworld.

At that very moment the ferry touched against the shore with a bump—it was Charon's black barge, which is old and worn, and slimy and slithery inside. Charon had been ordered for just that moment and was on time, and as he swung alongside, the two figures rolled and rolled down the incline, down, down, down, ending up with a thud in the bottom of the ferry.

And Charon laughed, ho, ho, ho, so that it echoed from the opposite shore of the river, an echoing roar as when icebergs calve in a fiord. Then he swung his pole over and briskly pushed off from the shore carrying Sophus and Vira across.

Oh yes! They caught the ferry.

Translated by Lydia Cranfield

MARTIN A. HANSEN

(1909–55)

The son of a tenant farmer, Martin A. Hansen knew the lot of the peasants at firsthand. Influenced by the social realism of the 1930's, he wrote about them in his early novels, and though he later dealt with other subjects, his interest in the life and traditions of country people made him repeatedly return to the rural environment of his youth for the setting of his stories.

The German occupation was of crucial importance to his career. Nazi restrictions on free expression forced many writers to resort to devious means of conveying their meaning. Hansen, during this period, found a highly personal form: the fantasy- and symbol-filled narrative which was closely related to the fairy tale and the myth. Within this literary frame, he explored the secret, winding paths of human psychology, criticizing the materialism of an age which he found devoid of enduring values.

Hansen's symbolism is sometimes rather obscure, but the occasional faults in his style become unimportant when seen against the quiet dignity of his work.

The selection below is from the posthumous short story collection *Efterslæt* ("Aftermath"), 1959.

The Gardener, the Beast, and the Child

Twilight is falling; it is wet. I am busy tying up dripping roses. "Just why are you a gardener?" I'm thinking.

It's growing dark. It's been raining. The high treetops and the bushes beneath are wringing wet. The air is clammy and dead.

I tie the stems of the roses tighter to the rusty iron pipes that arch over the alley. Leaves and blossoms are covered with water, and every time I touch them the water falls over me. My hands are bleeding from the thcrns which I cannot see any more.

87

The asphalted alley is shiny. Here, in the dusk of the trees, it is bright like a river.

Nothing is to be heard except the sound of the drops dripping and the playful steps of my little boy down the alley.

"Why are you standing here? Why are you a gardener?" I whisper to myself again. "Just why are you a gardener?" It is a riddle to me. But it's not a riddle to make me meditate deeply. It lingers in my mind like an old tumor which only throbs.

"I don't care for the roses," I think. Here in the dark they look more like mushrooms than flowers, anyway. I take care of the roses as I'm supposed to; I tie them up, but they don't concern me.

"Why are you a gardener?"

"Hans, come here with me," says my little boy down there. He is calling his invisible friend, Hans.

"Why don't you take the little step aside?" I think. "Then you'd step away from the gardener, away from your age; you'd step out of your many years. Then you'd be a boy again, and yourself. Then you'd be free."

I have frequently dreamt of this. Just one step, and you are who you were before.

"Look, your face is a rose, Hans!" says Egon down the alley.

"Why are you here? Why are you tied up? Why aren't you somewhere else in the world? Would your life there also have become a quiet water with worms on the bottom?"

The dusk creeps over. I cannot distinguish the stems of the roses any more, but the clammy flowers shine pale, swollen, obscene.

And the alley is bright. Far away it fades into a dark mass of leaves. "What is down there?" I think. My sluggish memory cannot tell me.

"Hans, come here!" my little boy shouts to his invisible playmate, who is always with him. He comes mincing toward me.

I keep my arms inside the bush of roses and look toward the boy. I'm half-hidden. As he comes skipping, long shadow-like reflections run over the asphalt. The boy looks peculiar, as if his legs were tremendously long. He seems strange, and I look upon him as an alien being.

"It's little Egon," I think, "but who is Egon? Hasn't he been a

stranger all the time?" Your child, they say. I don't understand
the word. I don't understand anything. He's in the way when I
want to step aside and become who I was before.

Carefully I slip farther into the darkness behind the bush.

I don't even know him. What is he doing here? He and everything else is an alien burden which I have slaved for. My own
life has become alien and cursed to me. I don't know him.

He comes nearer.

"It's almost completely dark, Hans," he says.

"Yes, how dark it is," says Hans, the invisible one who is
always with him.

I'm still behind the thorny bushes concealed. If a spot of my
face is visible, he'll think it is a rose. My eyes are like a pair of
drops hanging on the dim leaves.

Egon has gone by. Now he stands still and looks around.

"Father, where are you?" he calls.

I keep motionless, and I don't answer.

"Father," he calls.

I don't answer but look at the stranger from my hiding place.

"Where is my father, Hans?" he says.

Then he stands quite still. I don't step forward; I don't answer.

"Father!" he shouts.

Then quietness. I myself am the quiet and the darkness which
has taken his father away from him.

"Hans, Hans, where are you?" he complains.

Whimpering he runs down the alley, away.

"Father," he gasps.

I step out from my hiding place and see him jump down the
dimly shining asphalt on his short legs.

"Egon!" I shout, not very loudly.

He doesn't hear anything; he runs. He turns out of the alley
to the left and disappears. And the alley lies open and shiny like
the inside of a gun barrel.

A shadow jumps across the alley and vanishes behind the boy.
"Egon!" I shout.

It was an evil shadow. A beast, it seemed, a large beast.

Everything is quiet.

"Egon!" I run. My muddy boots rap heavily on the asphalt.
There is a slushy sidepath leading in between the bushes where

he turned off. I see his footprints on the ground. One of them is already collecting water. And there are other footprints. Those of the beast.

"It's happened," I think. "You have no more to worry about. You're not a gardener any more. You're free."

The liberation makes me drowsy. Most of all I'd like to sleep; it doesn't matter where. In the mud, where I'm standing. Sleep and turn to earth, to mud, to a quiet, staring pool of water.

And everything is quiet. In the dusk the trees, bushes and soil are weighed down with fulfillment.

"Egon!" I call. Something begins to burn in my eyes. But my breast is frozen, it seems.

A spade is leaning against a tree. It must be mine. The white, worn steel is covered with brown soil and greasy clumps of mold. The handle is swollen with water and it feels good in my hands.

"Egon!" I roar.

I jump forward with the spade raised. I throw myself through the bushes which are closed over the pathway. The water spurts over me.

The path leads to a big open lot. I don't remember really having seen it before.

It is one of those big lots that lie unused on the outskirts of a city. At some time gardening has been pursued here, and there are still remnants of broken substructures from the hothouses. For a long time trash has been thrown on the lot—rubbish, brick debris, broken furniture, the garbage of a city. But what there is in the piled-up, fermented mass can only be seen here and there in an uncovered spot. Over the heaps thick forests of mugworts, nettles, thistles, and wormwoods are growing. In hollows between the dark, luxuriant mounds, there are hairy knolls of white, flowering silverweed.

But there are places where the all too dense forest of weeds has sunk down, washed away by a shower of rain or tumbled over in their wild urge for life. In these places the trash left by people is exposed.

Over the big lot there is a heavy, sweetish vapor from the decay and the growth. It's an air which at any moment might become dense and living, something unseen and unheard.

Around the lot, but far away, as if on the outermost edge of the earth, are blocks of light-colored houses. In the rows there are black gaps; houses have tumbled down as if struck by fire or bombs. On others the gable or the roof is missing. The windows are black, staring eyes.

I see it all but I stand still with the spade on my shoulder. I feel a heavy, sluggish interest in all things, although they are of no concern to me and far away.

"I must have seen the place before, given it a cursory glance," I think, but I'm too lazy to remember it. When I look around the lot it appears to me strange and unknown. But if I close my eyes I seem to recognize it. Or is it the place which recognizes me? This big lot wishes to close itself around me; I feel it wants to keep me.

"Egon," I say in a muffled voice, absentminded. And I smile stupidly.

"Have I perhaps played here at some time, when this place looked a little different?" I think drowsily. "Yes, perhaps now I have taken the step aside? Out of my withered life. And I'm free."

Staggering I reach in front of me and tear the top off a plant. I crush the small, soft flowers beneath my fingers and inhale a sharp and wild smell of absinthe. It's wormwood.

"I don't care," I say out loud; I'm awakening.

It is lighter here than inside the park. The sky is pale-green, washed clean by the rain, its color thin from dampness. In the vague gleam the heaps bulge over the darkening lot, the place of fulfillment.

"Egon!" I call.

If he still exists, he mustn't stay here. This is a horrible playground.

"Egon!" I roar. Then I listen. There is an answer far away. "Gon, gon!" The echo from the lifeless houses.

I run forward with the spade raised. And here his footprints appear again. There's a long distance between them in spite of his short legs; he's been leaping. The water is already shining in the small footprints.

I listen again. I hear only vague, creeping sounds round about between the shadowy mounds. I don't know if they are really creeping footsteps or just the dripping and oozing of the water.

The footprints disappear in one place where there is an old stone pavement, and chickweeds and plantains grow tight between the stones.

Reluctantly and dully I stare at a weed-grown heap. In there, in the middle of the forest of plants, the tops of the wormwoods are moving. There must be something living under them.

I jump in, wade through the luxuriant clusters which reach me to the armpits and lash the water through my clothes. My feet stumble over old bricks, decayed sacks, rusty pails which screech under my soles. I can't see anything. I must kneel and search on the ground, where the broad stems are densely grown with yellow, slimy leaves. There is nothing. I see only a beetle which, frightened, crawls farther into the darkness of the plants. There's nobody there.

Standing in the middle of the cluster, I look around in the dusk and feel a faint, wretched relief. "You don't care," I say, "you're free."

Then everything is quiet.

"Egon!" I call.

I'm free, but the freedom is poisonous. I want to be free from that also. I must make myself ready so that my self can slumber. Only oblivion makes one completely free.

Behind the mound I hear a lapping and licking sound. I sneak around. There, by a pool of water, a big beast is drinking. It must be a wolf. I'm not afraid of it but approach with the spade raised.

The beast lifts his jaw and looks at me aslant. From either corner of his mouth hang glittering threads of slime. The thin tongue quivers between glistening canine teeth. His look is treacherous and unclean.

"I want to know it," I whisper.

We look at each other, I and the beast, and I feel a deep sympathy for him, so that a savage desire goes through me, the desire to kneel down on all fours and drink with the wolf. "I would fain kill you and be killed by you," I think.

"Egon!" I shout to the beast. I raise myself and step forward with the spade in a striking position. The glance of the wolf falters but the corners of his mouth bend upward as if in a smile. On stiff forelegs the beast swings to one side, moving away through the filth—a long, skinny, torn body of a beast, not gray, but dirty yellowish. The wolf limps off and I see he has only one hind leg. I hew after him but hit only a stone. A faint blue spark springs forth, a little flash of violets.

I'm alone, and everything is quiet. I cannot endure it, and I hew around me with the spade, hew into the forest of nettles so that clusters of plants sink and open up their dead under-world.

"I don't care," I shout, "I'm free; I'm not a gardener; I'm not a man; I'm not a father; I'm nothing; I'm free!

"Egon! Egon!"

I jump forward with uncontrollable movements. I feel I can see myself. I am my own onlooker. The wildness is not real, not complete, as I wish it to be. Far inside there sits a tired and cold onlooker, filled with boredom.

"Boy!"

The madness of the body washes inward like big waves, and my self rocks in it like seaweed. "If you keep on, you'll tear yourself loose, you'll be mad, you'll have peace.

"Boy!

"Have peace. Don't think, don't remember."

I stand still. A little ahead of me there's a cement wall, battered and eroded. Up from it stick short iron barbs.

Behind the wall I see the back of the running beast. Quite another beast; a far bigger beast. Yes, I see two beasts now. They can't be wolves. They are much longer, much bigger. Their backs wave over the top of the cement wall, yes, they run on behind it like long waves.

The back of the first beast is long-haired and bristly and dark. The second and smaller beast looks naked, so tight and smooth is the light-colored fur on its body.

I run after the beasts. But although their movements seem slower, I can't keep up with them. Now the first one darts up on the cement wall and now the light-colored, slim one. They are big, lion-like, a male and a female. I pursue them panting. I see them from behind, the rippling shoulders, the rippling small of the back, and it occurs to me again how strangely small and weak the big beasts of prey look when one sees them from behind. I see the two powerful beasts run a little awry, like trotting, small dogs do.

They vanish in the wilderness of the lot, over which the dusk grows darker. I stop and listen. From inside the shadows comes a deep growl, so deep that I sense it just as clearly through my bones as through my ears.

I reach the place from before, where I met the wolf, the pool with the shining water, and the trampled, dirty banks. I see the big, dark lion bent over a body which he clasps with his forepaws, tearing at the thing with his shaking head. The slim female approaches with a protruding snout, and she is beautiful in her stealth-like movements. But the other strikes out at her and she stops, and her yellow eyes become tired.

I walk heavily toward the lion. I am aware that I cannot stop. I cannot stop myself. But I'm afraid. I don't know whether it's the lion or the thing under his paws that I'm most afraid of. The fear makes me stiff, a deathly cold creeps over me, I walk like a machine. My boots sink into the mud up over the ankles. I don't raise the spade. I bend forward to the beast and tightly grip the dark, limp thing. I get hold of wet, muddy clothes. Right next to my sinewy, dirty hands I see the powerful, rippling paw of the beast. I pull at the piece of cloth. The beast holds on to it. A big muscle of the foreleg moves under the fur. There, on the leg, the beast has a broad, inflated wound.

The fetid breath of the beast hits me in the face. It's a hot, foul vapor. Then I take a strong grip on the leg of the lion, just where the wound is. "Now it'll happen," I think, "now you'll have peace, now you shall forget."

The exhalation from the half-open jaws of the beast is hot and heavy so that for a moment I feel dizzy and unsteady. But I discern a quivering of his mighty body, and the beast moves his paw away.

I raise my head and look the beast in the eyes. It doesn't have the eyes of a lion or a cat. I look into big, irrational, faltering eyes that I know. I feel I'm looking into my own eyes.

Then my eyes smart, my glance is dazzled, there's a cramplike movement in my throat. I cannot see clearly any more, but I still see. The big, old lion has powerful horns.

"Go!" I say. "Go!"

I drop the spade; there's a splash in the water, and I push the beast with my hands. It yields. I step over the dark body which lies in the pool. I raise my hands. The big beast turns and creeps away almost crawling with its belly to the ground.

I'm alone in the quietness. I bend down and lift up the dark thing. It's heavy and the mud is dripping from it. It is a leg of a horse, entangled in an old blanket. The hoof sticks out. The shoe is broken off, and the holes from the nails gape in the gray horn. Under the hoof there's still some old, yellow dung.

I drop the heavy, smelling leg. Mud splashes up over me.

Then I stand and look around. It is evening. The sky is above me like a dome of steel. The houses are light and dead.

At last I know what the terrible thing will be. In this place there must be other beasts. I'm not afraid to meet them any more. I'm anxious about one thing only.

"Egon!" I say.

There's thaw in my frozen breast. Fear freezes, but anxiety is warm.

Yes, something will happen on the evil trash lot which is my world, something which is judgment itself. If I want, I shall meet still one more being. Out of the dark and the quietness a being will come against me, walking on short legs, on small feet; someone who is just like he, looks like he, is he. His face, his eyes, it is he. But I know that in these eyes I shall meet with a deep and painful knowledge, a wonder of death, which I can't bear to see and yet must see—which I never shall forget. For I shall never forget anything.

"Leave off calling," I think, "then you're free."

Sharp stars pierce the sky of steel.

"Don't call, don't call!" I think.

The quietness is waiting.

"Egon!" I call.

Translated by Hallberg Hallmundsson

NORWAY

INTRODUCTION

The peaceful life of Lindisfarne came to an abrupt end on a summer's day in 793.

Moving swiftly, the horde of helmeted, red-bearded Norsemen invaded the monastery, looted and plundered its rich treasury, and left it in ashes. It was all over in a matter of hours. Many of the good monks who were not instantly slain or drowned were dragged away and enslaved. A few managed to escape to northern England, there to relate the terrifying news of the Vikings' attack.

The story was the same everywhere: the Danes were ravaging southern England and France, the Swedes were engaged in similar ventures in Russia, while the Norsemen, in time to come, would strike again and again, conquering the Orkneys and other Scottish islands and settling their own kingdoms both in Scotland and Ireland. For two centuries, no part of the long shoreline of the British Isles would be safe from their pillaging.

But if the raids in foreign countries brought the Vikings rich reward in gold and slaves, it also weakened their position at home. There, even as in the lands they had conquered, the Norsemen were divided into numerous petty kingdoms, each with an individual warrior-ruler and a number of noble-born farmers. When a ruler was away his realm at home was frequently ill-defended, and he sometimes returned to find a usurper on his throne. Consequently, when Harald the Fairhaired (d. 933) conceived the ambitious idea of unifying all Norway under his own rule, he found the other kingdoms a relatively easy prey. Unification was achieved in the last quarter of the 9th century.

At that time, having emerged from an unknown past, poetry was a highly developed art in Norway. From Old Icelandic books we know the names as well as the works of several Norse poets of this period. Many scholars believe that some of the mythological and heroic poetry preserved in Iceland was also composed in Norway. However, it seems that the outflow of

99

emigrants to Iceland, precipitated by King Harald's subjugation of the nobles, depleted Norway of her poetic resources, so that as far as we know Norse poetry ceased to be cultivated except in Iceland. Even after Christianity was introduced (c. 1000), Norway's writers remained curiously silent. Thus, during the golden age of medieval Icelandic literature, the history of Norway and her kings was written by Icelandic historiographers.

Norwegian energy was, however, spent in other ways, for the country, in the meanwhile, became a well-established state, and during the latter half of the 13th century reached a zenith of power and sophistication. Iceland was added to the realm in 1262 and, along with it, the colony of Greenland. Life at court followed the common European fashion. Foreign, especially French, romances were translated, and ballads grew out of the need for accompaniment to dancing. Individual works of poetry and prose reached a high literary level (see "The Dream Poem," p. 103); nevertheless, the literature as a whole was meager.

The 14th century was one of political and economic decline in Norway. As a result of a royal marriage the country was united with Denmark in 1380 and ceased to be an independent state. Norwegian literature came to an end, for Danish became the written language of the nation and in time also the spoken one, especially in urban centers. By the middle of the 16th century, it had completely replaced the native tongue, except in some rural areas. Consequently, when, shortly after the Reformation, a new literature arose in Norway, it was written in Danish.

At first, writers were concerned primarily with history and humanistic studies. The 17th century did produce some good poets (see Dass, p. 109), but the first truly influential representatives of Norwegian letters did not appear until the 18th century. In fact, Norwegian writers in Copenhagen (see Holberg, p. 24) contributed so much to the common Dano-Norwegian literature of that time that their Norwegian Society occupies a special place in Danish literary history. Especially active in drama, these writers in more ways than one were the forerunners of the National-Romantic school which was to become so prominent in the following century.

The 19th century marked a turning point in the life of the country. In 1814, Denmark and Sweden, having taken part in the Napoleonic wars on different sides, negotiated a peace treaty in Kiel. The treaty ended more than four centuries of Danish rule in Norway; by one stroke of the pen, Norwegians became subjects of the Swedish king—or so it was hoped. But the transfer, which had not been sanctioned by the Norwegian people, brought on a revolt. A Norwegian general assembly enacted a liberal, parliamentary constitution, and a king was elected. With an armed conflict imminent, however, a compromise with Sweden was reached whereby the Norwegians recognized the Swedish king as their sovereign in return for Swedish approval of Norwegian independence.

These great events had an enormous effect on the literary scene. In a remarkably short time Norwegian literature burst into bloom. Although National-Romanticism was the dominant school, two conflicting camps arose, both closely connected with the political struggle. One thought it necessary to maintain close cultural contact with Denmark (see Welhaven, p. 113), while the other wanted a clear break with the Danish tradition in order to shape an independent Norwegian culture (see Wergeland, p. 119). The conflict undoubtedly gave impetus to the bustling literary life, with nationalistic enthusiasm adding further color. Outstanding writers emerged; the old folk literature was systematically collected (see Asbjørnsen and Moe, p. 124); and above all, a new literary language was devised, based on those Norwegian dialects which had survived the Danish influence of the preceding centuries. Alternately called *Landsmål* and *Nynorsk,* it was immediately used by some 19th-century writers, and today its legal status is equal to that of the Dano-Norwegian *Riksmål,* or *Bokmål.*

As the 19th century grew older, Romanticism gave way to Naturalism and Realism, though not without individual differences. Thus, one detects in the works of some prominent writers ideas which are half-Romantic and half-Realist (see Bjørnson, p. 136), while others literally heeded the call of those who "debated problems" in their works (see Ibsen, p. 130). It was the most fruitful period in Norway's literary history. The literature was loaded with ideas which were expressed in a genuinely artistic fashion. Both the novel and the drama were serious and purposeful, and reached a high literary level.

In Norway, as in other countries, the unchallenged reign of Realism was a relatively short period. A Neo-Romantic reaction soon set in. Young writers, and even some of the older ones, grew tired of the orderly and factual literature of ideas. They called for more attention to personal emotions and stressed the validity of the inexplicable, even mystical sensations of human beings. Rejecting the emphasis on social problems, they wrote enthusiastically about nature (see Hamsun, p. 144). Above all, they insisted on artistry as a fundamental requirement of literature. It was to be expected that lyrical poetry would have a renaissance.

As in Denmark, by 1900 Norwegian Neo-Romanticism was replaced by two distinctive trends: regionalism and a new realism. Common to both, however, was a new national outlook created by the final separation of Norway and Sweden in 1905.

Although Norway escaped physical destruction in World War I, the effects of the emotional and intellectual chaos of postwar Europe were visible. Old foundations had crumbled, and Norwegian writers, like those of other countries, began to grope for new ideals. Some sought refuge in their faith in God (see Undset, p. 163), some in a belief in the fundamental strength of mankind (see Duun, p. 149), while others found an outlet for their idealistic energies in political radicalism (see Øverland, p. 175). With the thirties, many Norwegian writers raised their voices in warning against the growing menace of military totalitarianism. Unfortunately, their cries went unheeded.

ANONYMOUS

(c. 1300)

Norway cannot boast of many treasures of medieval literature. It was in Iceland that most of the works dealing with
this period in Norwegian history were written and preserved.
However, some ballads from the late Middle Ages survived
orally in various parts of Norway. One of these was called
"The Dream Poem." Discovered in the Telemark district of
southern Norway in the middle of the last century, it was
written down by the scholar M. B. Landstad.

As its name indicates, the piece is a dream vision, a genre
that achieved universal popularity in the literature of the
Middle Ages. Composed around 1300, "The Dream Poem"
is a highly sophisticated example of the type, distinguished
as it is by an original, strong, and impressive diction, and by
the multitude of fascinating scenes it describes. It is given
here in a slightly abridged form.

The Dream Poem

Come list to me, and I will tell
of a lad so brave and strong;
I'll tell you of Olav Asteson[1]
who slept a sleep so long.

He laid him down on Christmas Eve
and fell asleep full fast,
and he woke not till Epiphany,
when folk to church did pass.
For it was Olav Asteson
who slept a sleep so long.

---

[1] It is not quite clear who Olav Asteson is really meant to be, but some
scholars have identified him with King Olaf Haraldsson of Norway (1015–
30), later known as St. Olaf. His mother's name was Asta. However, recent
scholarship does not acknowledge the validity of such an identification.

He woke not till Epiphany,
when the sun shone far and wide,
and then he saddled his swift young steed,
to church he then would ride.
　　For it was &c.

Before the altar stands the priest
and long he reads the prayer.
Olav down in the porch he sits
and tells his dreams out there.
　　For it was &c.

Now give ye heed, as best ye may,
all men, both young and old,
till the brave swain Olav Asteson
his dream so strong has told.
　　For it was &c.

I laid me down on Christmas Eve
and fell asleep full fast,
and I woke not till Epiphany,
when folk to church did pass.
　　The moon it shines
　　and the roads do stretch so wide.

I have been up to the clouds above
and down to the dyke full dark.
Both have I seen the flames of hell
and of heaven likewise a part.
　　The moon &c.

I have fared over holy water
and over the valleys low.
I heard the waters but saw them not,
for under the earth they flow.
　　The moon &c.

Neither did my good horse neigh,
nor barked my dog aloud,
none of the early birds did sing,
and I did wonder why.
　　The moon &c.

I was in the other world
for many a weary night,
and God in heaven knows I saw
full many a sorry sight.
The moon &c.

First I went forth with my soul,
I went through briar and thorn,
and torn was then my scarlet cloak,
and the nails from my feet were torn.
The moon &c.

Came I then to Gjallar Bridge,[2]
so high up in the air.
With red gold it is decked above
and the pinnacles gold so fair.
The moon &c.

The serpent strikes, and the dog he bites,
and the bull stands on the path;
these three things are on Gjallar Bridge,
and all are fierce and wroth.
The moon &c.

Waded have I the miry marsh,
where never a foot finds hold.
Crossed have I also Gjallar Bridge,
my mouth filled with grave-mold.
The moon &c.

Then I came to those lonely lakes,
where the glittering ice burns blue;
but God put warning in my heart,
and thence my step I drew.
The moon &c.

[2] In Scandinavian mythology the bridge leading to the realm ruled by Hel, the fearful goddess of death. However, in the poem there seems to be some confusion as to the location of the bridge "so high up in the air," for the domain of Hel, according to tradition, was situated far down below the root of Yggdrasil, the tree of the universe. Possibly, the poet (or the oral tradition) had the Gjallar Bridge mixed up with Bifrost (identified with the rainbow), the bridge which the gods built between heaven and earth.

Then I turned to my right hand,
where the Milky Way does rise,
and over lovely lands I saw
the shining paradise.
    The moon &c.

There was again godmother mine,
command she gave full soon:
"Betake thee to the trial-porch,
where stands the seat of doom!"
    The moon &c.

Came I to the pilgrims' church
no one knew I there,
but only blest godmother mine
with gold on her fingers fair.
    In the trial-porch
    shall stand the seat of doom.

There came the host from out the north,
God save us from its course!
In front rode Grim the Graybeard[3]
upon a jet-black horse.
    In the trial-porch &c.

There came the host from out the south—
the best 'twas in my sight—
and first rode Michael, lord of souls,
upon his charger white.
    In the trial-porch &c.

It was St. Michael, lord of souls,
he blew his trumpet clear:
"And now must every living soul
to judgment forth appear!"
    In the trial-porch &c.

---

  [3] Norwegian: Grutte Gråskjegge. Most likely, this figure is Odin himself (see note 10, p. 190), one of whose many names was Hárbardr, i.e., "Gray-beard." The fact that Odin's horse was not black, but gray, need not refute the identification. In some versions of the poem the horse is not mentioned at all. Instead, Grim the Graybeard is said to wear a black hat. Two of Odin's names were Höttr ("Hat") and Síðhöttr ("Long Hat").

Then every sinful soul did shake
like aspens in the wind,
and every single soul there was
wept sore for every sin.
    In the trial-porch &c.

I saw a young man trudge along—
the first that I did see—
he bore a boy-child in his arms
and sank in earth to's knee.
    In the trial-porch &c.

The men I next came up with,
they carried burning clay:
God's mercy be with those poor souls
that carried bournes[4] away!
    In the trial-porch &c.

Children then I came to,
in fiery pit immersed:
God's mercy be with sinful souls
who father and mother cursed!
    In the trial-porch &c.

Next I came on serpents twain,
each other's tails they chewed:
cousins they who in this life
were joined in marriage lewd.
    In the trial-porch &c.

Then to the house of toil I came,
there witches were within:
they stood and churned the red, red blood,
so heavy was their sin.
    In the trial-porch &c.

Hot it is in the vaults of hell,
and foul is there the feast:
they swung a pot of pitch o'er fire,
flung in a back of priest.
    In the trial-porch &c.

[4] Boundaries, or boundary markers.

Blest is he who in his life
gave shoes to the needy poor:
he will not have to walk barefoot
on the sharp and thorny moor.
  Tongue shall speak and truth
  reply on Judgment Day.

Blest is he who in his life
did give the poor man bread:
he shall not stand in the other world
of fierce dogs' bark in dread.
  Tongue &c.

Blest is he who in his life
did give the poor man corn:
he need not fear on Gjallar Bridge
the bull with the pointed horn.
  Tongue &c.

Blest is he who in his life
gave clothes to the needy poor:
he need not fear in the other world
the glacier's ice-crest hoar.
  Tongue &c.

Now give ye heed, as best ye may,
all men, both young and old:
for it was Olav Asteson,
and this the dream he told.

Translated by Illit Grøndahl

PETTER DASS

(1647–1708)

In his large parish in northern Norway, it was no less important for the Reverend Petter Dass to be a good businessman than a good minister, for his income was largely made up of fish which he, like the fishermen, had to sell in Bergen. Apparently endowed with an astute pecuniary sense, he soon acquired some wealth and is said to have owned several fishing boats.

His reputation as a poet rests largely upon his *Trumpet of Nordland* (first published in 1739), parts of which are printed below. This long, detailed poem is a lyrical-topographical description of the Nordland district and the everyday life and toil of its people. Although Dass is sometimes moralistic in tone, as becomes his calling, the whole poem is warmed by a light humor and a sympathetic feeling for the land and the simple people who inhabit it.

From

"The Trumpet of Nordland"

Concerning the Trading Posts

The lands of the North have their seasonal fairs
Where parishes gather in festival airs,
   Their various products displaying.

Men come from the fiords and the outermost reefs
Their taxes to pay, to escape from the grief
   That comes from delinquency mainly.

The diligent trader will also be there
In time for his tents and his booths[1] to prepare,
   To show both his cloth and his muslin.

---

[1] Temporary sheds (see note 13, p. 200).

However, the beerkeg must centrally stand.
They draw with a measure made by their own hand
  Without much concern for their conscience.

If one in the crowd shall desire a good drink,
He gets from short measure the ale to the brink—
  Gives eight shillings precious in payment.

When commoner Gregus this ruse understands,
He warns and informs all his visiting friends;
  The trader is hurt in his business.

He shouts to Old Gregus, "Come here, have a drink!
I am not as stingy as some of you think;
  I give you a stein for the asking."

And Gregus is thirsty, one bowl cannot do;
He asks for another, a third after two;
  The woman draws ale from the barrel.

Then, meanwhile, a comrade comes near to the stand,
And Gregus shouts, "Brother, come give me a hand—
  I give you a drink, my good fellow!"

They drink until both of them badly are wet;
Their fish has been taken, they wonder and fret,
  But what can Old Gregus complain of?

Next morning he sleeps until sober he wakes.
He knows fully well that some money it takes
  To buy what he needs for the household.

He ordered his grindstone, some hemp and a scythe.
Bring fish to the merchant, the outlook is bright,
  But now all his wares have quite vanished.

Since nothing to barter he now can produce,
He buys at a price that he ought to refuse
  And sinks into poverty's quagmire.

For if you forever will moisten your throat,
You must be prepared to relinquish your coat
  And go with a patch on your trousers.

The trader puts all of his boats in a row;
His flag is at topmast, he makes quite a show
  Of merchandise, money and power.

Each closes his deal and loads all that he gained
On flag-flying ships; through both sunshine and rain,
  He sails to the trading post nearest.

Description of Vesteraalen

A parish is counted a farthing to stand
By those who make living and dwell in this land;
  It called is the farthing community.

Now farthing means quarter, a merchant must stay
Within his own farthing and there make his way,
  Must have there his boatstead and dwelling.

To trading post come they, by oar or by sail,
Are happy to come for their brandy and ale—
  Tobacco must not be forgotten.

They chew it like bread, poke it into the cheek;
They munch it and spit till their whole mouth must reek,
  As if some black gore they were eating.

The blackest tobacco is used in the cud;
Their breath, hence, is stinking like rottenest mud—
  A devil might throw up his stomach.

Some of it is ground for the women to snuff,
And thus can Hans Poverty do his worst stuff;
  Both parents and children must suffer.

Well, listen good woman, go on, be a hog!
If snuffhorn is small, you can make you a bag
  And ornately have it embroidered.

Then take from this bag as the heart may desire—
In time you may probably also aspire
  To grunting like hog in the pigsty.

Your nose will become as attractive and clean
As yeomen's old chimneys can ever have been—
Attractive as midsummer sows are.

Your husband invite at this supper to be!
I know that you him very happy will see—
Together heave to and be snoring!

You draw in the snuff, he tobacco may chew;
As beggars you dwell without further ado—
One cannot the other be blaming.

Take flour or take groceries on credit, at loan,
And as for the payment, do not it bemoan;
Let judgment day handle that problem!

There is in this country a habit right foul:
Men take goods on credit, they borrow, they growl,
And written in books their account is.

But when a full year has run out without pay,
They run from their homes and their houses away,
And thereby their debts have been canceled.

I ask you: Are not these a sinner's bad acts?
A sinner gets credit but leaps from the facts;
What is there to do with such people?

If one is to take them to city, to jail,
Expenses will double and everything will fail—
The last will get worse than the former.

But if one a tooth struck from mouth of a man
Who loves to deceive just as much as he can,
Some might think it over a little.

Translated by Theodore Jorgenson

JOHAN WELHAVEN

(1807–73)

As a young man Welhaven dreamt of becoming a painter. Instead, he became the second most prominent name in early 19th-century Norwegian literature. Because of a continuous feud, which covered the spheres of both literature and politics, his name is nearly always linked with that of Wergeland (see p. 119).

It was Welhaven's bad luck to be a conservative in a period alive with the liberal and National-Romantic ideas Wergeland promulgated. Welhaven was an ardent admirer of Danish culture and strove for the continuance of the tradition which centuries of Danish rule had created. His poetry is characterized by highly polished form and quiet moods. His admiration for Norwegian landscape and his ability to express his feelings in terms of it have prompted some critics to speak of the "landscape of his mind."

Of the following selections, the first three appeared in *Digte* ("Poems"), 1839, while "Bird-Notes" is taken from *En Digtsamling* ("A Collection of Poems"), 1860, and "Norway's Highlands" from *Halvhundrede Digte* ("Fifty Poems"), published in 1848.

Like an April Day

The buds of April dare not yet unfold
Their eager store of beauty to the sight,
While spring still battles with the winter's cold.

The broken sunbeams are but faintly bright,
The blossom swells within its narrow bower
In longing silence as it drinks the light.

Already it divines the Maytime hour
At whose brave touch the clouds will melt away
And cold no more constrain the heart-shaped flower.

Lover, your sweetheart's like an April day:
These chilly looks, the arrows of her glance—
You cannot tell as yet what they would say.

Her little heart, too, may be all adance,
As the unrest in it wells even higher,
Her lips would gladly smile, had they the chance.

Soon May will kiss the longing leaves with fire,
Soon through the air the wingèd loves will dart,
And if you then dare show your deep desire,
The flower will then reveal its blossom-heart.

Translated by Charles Wharton Stork

The Lotus

Out in the lake a lotus flower, full-blown,
Rising and dipping with the waves' unrest,
Her cheeks by zephyrs coolingly caressed,
Hears from the land a voice with mocking tone:
"Frail blossom, you were made for this alone,
That vanity in you might be expressed.
You must obey the storm-wind's rude behest,
And all your petals on the shore be strown."

The lotus then, untroubled and serene,
Replied, "My deep root reaches down unseen
And holds me steadfast, though the tempest roars.
No forest branches roof me from the light,
And in my cradle on the waters bright
My spirit holds communion with the stars."

Translated by Charles Wharton Stork

The Nixie

I laid my ear to the brooklet's brim
And harked to the nixie's chanting,
When all around me was wrapped in dream,
And day grew dim,
And long the shadows were slanting.

Folk tell that the nixie can dance all day
Down there where the pebbles glisten;
But the bird on the bough knows better than they
His mournful lay,
And hushes its notes to listen.

When twilight has settled the dales among
And earth in silence reposes,
'Tis then he intones his loveliest song;
For his night is long,
His eyelids he never closes.

I heard him sob, when behind the wood
The glow of even had faded,
And flowers and grasses were all bedewed
From the trees that stood
By the brink of the stream they shaded.

With muted string on his harp he played,
As he sang with tenderest feeling,
"Good night, sweet rose. To thy virgin bed
From forest and mead
The dream-elves will soon be stealing.

"So warm dost thou glow in thy leafy nest,
Unwitting of my anguish.
I deaden my grief with loud unrest;
But oh! my breast
For thee in the dark must languish."

Translated by Charles Wharton Stork

Bird-Notes

There flew a bird at the close of day,
With the lilt of its song it caught me;
It lured me off from the beaten way
And to shadowy bypaths brought me.
I came upon hidden spring and pool,
Where the thirsty elk were drinking;
But the song of the bird was far and cool,
Like a sigh of a zephyr sinking.
"Tirilil tiri!"
Deep, deep in the woods so eerie.

The walls of the birches rose left and right,
And the midsummer evening listened.
The dew in the valley was starry bright,
And the golden snow-peaks glistened.
The little leaves trembled close to me,
Like elves through the forest winging;
As rapt I heard how from cliff and tree
The magical notes came ringing.
"Tirilil tiri!"
Deep, deep in the woods so eerie.

A path leads on through the distant hills
To a nest high up mid the heather,
And thence it is that the bird-song trills,
Where the dark pines group together.
But though I never may win so far,
I thrill to the notes entrancing;
For oh, how ineffably sweet they are
When the dew on the sward is glancing!
"Tirilil tiri!"
Deep, deep in the woods so eerie.

Translated by Charles Wharton Stork

Norway's Highlands

High o'er the dales with their verdant pride,
Up mid the clouds, extending wide,
Is a desolate region of bleak plateau,
Lakes under jagged mountain walls,
Where a billowy mantle of virgin snow
Across the black knees of the cliffs is spread,
And over the teeming waterfalls
A turreted ice field lifts its head.

Oft from beneath the glacier's frown
The headlong avalanche thunders down.
But flowers peep out from the jagged rocks,
On the naked summits their petals gleam;
And there are nourished the reindeer flocks,
Over crag and marsh they go rushing past.
The mind of the hunter is lost in dream,
But wakes at the call of Adventure's blast.

So freshly resounds the clarion cry,
It summons up tales of the days gone by.
Like sable giants the cliffs uprear,
Till he who beholds must quake with fright.
On every form one encounters here
These demons have cast an evil spell,
But the race of the gods in their armor bright
Can trample to chaff the deceits of hell.

A freer life and a nobler ring
Wells up in the songs that the Norsemen sing;
For when they are passed from mouth to mouth,
The voice of the mountains echoes through,
Like a torrent that leaps to the valleys drouth;
And vigor is breathed by the storm-wind's roar,
When grove and hedge are budding anew
With April blossoms of legend lore.

The mystic spirits that walk the gale
Descend to the folk of the listening dale.
And faces look up from garth and croft,

And thought rushes on the saga's trace,
The soul spreads its wings and soars aloft
To share the wild joy of the mountain's mirth,
Where heaven has wrought of the clouds' thin lace
A veil for the mightiest forms of earth.

This home of the tales the Vikings told,
This realm in the clouds, is worth more than gold,
The torrent that seethes from its rugged brim
Is a fountain of life, and the swelling throat
Of the whirlwind chants an exultant hymn.
It sends us a surge of fierce delight
With a victory thrill in every note,
This mountain realm of the Norse gods' might.

Translated by Charles Wharton Stork

HENRIK WERGELAND
(1808–45)

Although he was above all a poet, it is not only because of his literary works that Wergeland occupies a very special place in the hearts of his countrymen. He lived during a period of great national awakening and his life has, in many ways, become identified with the rebirth of the Norwegian nation. A National-Romantic, liberal, and rationalist at once, Wergeland believed in mankind's perfectibility and in the power of Christianity and freedom to ennoble people's hearts. His faith was manifested in action, for he devoted his life to furthering those ideals. He swept over the country like a fire-brand, founding public libraries, distributing leaflets on education and writing political pamphlets, verses, and farces. He fought for the right of Jews to enter Norway, and two of his works, *The Jew* and *The Jewess*, became major weapons in that battle. In addition to all these activities, he still found time to write a voluminous amount of poetry. At twenty-two, he had already published *The Creation, Man, and Messiah,* a poem some seven hundred pages in length which he later revised and published as *The Creation.* Although faulty in many respects, it is still the most grandly conceived poem in Norwegian literature. However, it is really in his shorter works that his poetic genius sparkles. His powers increased as he aged, and he wrote some of his finest lyrics on his deathbed. Among them, "To My Wallflower" and "To Spring" are printed below. "Myself" (1841) was written as a reply to a newspaper article which had accused him of being "angry and in bad spirits."

Myself

I in bad spirits, did you say? I, who need only a glimpse of the sun
To break out into a loud laughter from a joy I cannot explain?

When I smell a green leaf, dazed I forget poverty, riches, friends and foes.

My cat rubbing against my cheek smoothens all heartsores.
Into my dog's eye I lower my sorrow as in a deep well.

My ivy has grown. Out of my window it has borne on its broad leaves
All the memories I do not care to keep.

The first spring rain will fall on the leaves and wipe out some faithless
names.
They will fall down with the drops and poison the burrows of the
earthworm.

I who read rapture in each petal of the hundred-leaved rose, that gift
of spring—
Me should a wretched rag cause to quench one second with vexation?

That would be like killing sky-blue and rose-colored butterflies.
Such crime, verily, my heart recoils from.

It would be like strewing ashes on my head which is not yet gray,
And throwing away the diamonds of sparkling seconds which Time yet
sows thereon.

Come on, journalists! Sharpen your fox's claws on the rock!
You only tear off flowers and a little moss for a soft grave.

Like the insect's sting in the mussel, insults breed pearls only in my
heart.
They shall one day adorn the diadem of my spirit.

I hate? When a bird flies over my head my hate is a thousand cubits
hence,
It melts away with the snow, it passes with the first waves from the
shore and far out to sea.

But why should not my veins be wroth?
Rob not the landscape of its rushing streams!
Right honorable osiers, permit the brook to foam when it runs among
boulders!

I love not blue sky everlasting, as I detest stupid staring eyes.
Have I no heaven because it is full of drifting clouds, fairylands of the
sun?

And if I had none—is not God's great and glorious enough?
Complain not under the stars of the lack of bright spots in your life!

Ha! Are they not twinkling as if they would speak to you?

How Venus sparkles tonight! Have the heavens also spring?
Now the stars have shone all through the winter; now they rest and
rejoice. Hallelujah!

What riches for a mortal.
My soul rejoices in heaven's joy of spring, and shall take part in that
of the earth.
It sparkles stronger than the eternal stars, and it will soon open with
the flowers.

Glorious Evening Star! I uncover my head.
A crystal bath upon it falls thy sheen.

There is kinship between the soul and the stars.
It steps in the starlight outside the curtain of the face, whose folds
have disappeared.

The rays cover my soul with calmness like that of alabaster.
Like a bust it stands within me. Gaze into its features!

Now they are as you would have them. The scornful ones are laid.
My soul has but the mild smile of a corpse. Are you still afraid?

The rascal! The bust has a laughing heart beneath its calm.
Alas for your feeble fingers: you cannot get hold of *that*.

Translated by Illit Grøndahl

To Spring

O Spring! Spring! Save me!
No one has loved thee more dearly than I.

Thy first grass to me is worth more than emeralds.
I call thy anemones the pride of the year,
Altho' I know that the roses are coming.

Often did they, fiery, stretch out after me.
It was like being loved by princesses,
But I fled: Anemone, Spring's daughter had my troth.

Oh witness, Anemone, before whom I have fervently knelt.
Witness, contemned Dandelion and Colt's-foot,
That I have valued you more than gold, because you are Spring's
children.

Witness, Swallow! that I made ready for thee
As for a long-lost child home again returned—
Thou wast the messenger of Spring!

Seek the Lord of these clouds and pray
That they may no longer throw darts into my breast
From out of their cold, blue openings.

Witness, Old Tree! whom I have worshiped like a god,
And whose buds I have counted every spring more eagerly than pearls.

Witness, thou whom I have so often embraced,
With the reverence of a great-grandson for his great-grandfather.
Yea, how often have I not wished to be a young maple of thy deathless
    root,
And to blend my crown with thine!

Be my witness, Ancient One! Thou wilt be believed;
For thou art venerable as a patriarch.

Pray for me, and I will pour wine on thy roots
And heal thy scars with kisses.

Now thou art robed in thy fairest light green;
Thy leaves are rustling already.

O Spring! The old one is crying out for me, altho' he is hoarse.
He stretches his arms towards Heaven,
And the anemones, thy blue-eyed children, kneel and pray
That thou wilt save me—me who love thee so dearly.

                                        Translated by Illit Grøndahl

To My Wallflower

Wallflower mine, ere thy bright hues fade,
I shall be that whereof all is made;
Ere thou hast shattered thy crown of gold,
        I shall be mold.

When "Open the window!" I cry from bed,
My last look lights on thy golden head;
My soul will kiss it, as over thee
    It flieth free.

Twice do I kiss thy lips so sweet,
Thine is the first, as it is meet;
The second, dearest, my will bestows
    On my fair rose.

In bloom no more I shall it see;
So give it my greeting, when that shall be,
And say I wished on my grave should all
    Its petals fall.

Yes, say I wish that upon my breast
The rose thou gavest my kiss shall rest;
And, Wallflower, be in Death's dark porch
    Its bridal torch!

                     Translated by Illit Grøndahl

P(ETER) CHR(ISTEN) ASBJØRNSEN
(1812–85)
and
JØRGEN MOE
(1813–82)

Few works of Norwegian literature have become as well known and as widely acclaimed outside Scandinavia as the folk and fairy tales collected and edited by Asbjørnsen and Moe. Because of this collaboration, their names have become so closely linked that they have, for most people, lost their individual identities. Asbjørnsen and Moe first met when they were both in their early twenties, and their friendship was strengthened by their common interest in folktales. But apart from this hobby—for hobby it was—their professional interests were almost diametrically opposed.

Asbjørnsen studied medicine and natural history, conducted zoological research of the marine fauna along the Norwegian coast and wrote a number of scientific essays. He became a state official responsible for the preservation of Norway's extensive forests and, later, supervised preparatory investigations for the state's peat industry.

Moe, on the other hand, studied theology, became a teacher for a number of years, then a chaplain, a minister of the church, and, finally, a bishop in the Kristiansand diocese. For a time, he had a stipend from the University to collect folk poetry, but he was also a lyric poet in his own right. His poetry is a mixture of childlike charm and mature manliness.

The two friends' collection was published as *Norske folkeeventyr* ("Norwegian Folk and Fairy Tales"), between 1841 and 1844.

The Squire's Bride

Once upon a time there was a rich squire who owned a large farm, and had plenty of silver at the bottom of his chest and money in the bank besides; but he felt there was something wanting, for he was a widower.

One day the daughter of a neighboring farmer was working for him in the hayfield. The squire saw her and liked her very much, and as she was the child of poor parents he thought, if he only hinted that he wanted her, she would be ready to marry him at once.

So he told her he had been thinking of getting married again.

"Ay! one may think of many things," said the girl, laughing slyly. In her opinion the old fellow ought to be thinking of something that behooved him better than getting married.

"Well, you see, I thought that you should be my wife!"

"No, thank you all the same," said she, "that's not at all likely."

The squire was not accustomed to be gainsaid, and the more she refused him the more determined he was to get her.

But as he made no progress in her favor, he sent for her father and told him that if he could arrange the matter with his daughter he would forgive him the money he had lent him, and he would also give him the piece of land which lay close to his meadow into the bargain.

"Yes, you may be sure I'll bring my daughter to her senses," said the father. "She is only a child, and she doesn't know what's best for her." But all his coaxing and talking did not help matters. She would not have the squire, she said, if he sat buried in gold up to his ears.

The squire waited day after day, but at last he became so angry and impatient that he told the father, if he expected him to stand by his promise, he would have to put his foot down and settle the matter now, for he could not wait any longer.

The man knew no other way out of it, but to let the squire get everything ready for the wedding; and when the parson and the wedding guests had arrived the squire should send for the girl as if she were wanted for some work on the farm. When she arrived she would have to be married right away, so that she would have no time to think it over.

The squire thought this was well and good and so he began brewing and baking and getting ready for the wedding in grand style. When the guests had arrived the squire called one of his farm lads and told him to run down to his neighbor and ask him to send him what he had promised.

"But if you are not back in a twinkling," he said, shaking his fist at him, "I'll——"

He did not say more, for the lad ran off as if he had been shot at.

"My master has sent me to ask for what you promised him," said the lad, when he got to the neighbor, "but there is no time to be lost, for he is terribly busy today."

"Yes, yes! Run down into the meadow and take her with you. There she goes!" answered the neighbor.

The lad ran off and when he came to the meadow he found the daughter raking the hay.

"I am to fetch what your father has promised my master," said the lad.

"Ah, ha!" thought she. "Is that what they are up to?"

"Ah, indeed!" she said. "I suppose it's that little bay mare of ours. You had better go and take her. She stands there tethered on the other side of the pease field," said the girl.

The boy jumped on the back of the bay mare and rode home at full gallop.

"Have you got her with you?" asked the squire.

"She is down at the door," said the lad.

"Take her up to the room my mother had," said the squire.

"But, master, how can that be managed?" said the lad.

"You must do as I tell you," said the squire. "If you cannot manage her alone you must get the men to help you," for he thought the girl might turn obstreperous.

When the lad saw his master's face he knew it would be no use to gainsay him. So he went and got all the farm tenants who were there to help him. Some pulled at the head and the four legs of the mare and others pushed from behind, and at last they got her up the stairs and into the room. There lay all the wedding finery ready.

"Now, that's done, master!" said the lad; "but it was a terrible job. It was the worst I have ever had here on the farm."

"Never mind, you shall not have done it for nothing," said his master. "Now send the women up to dress her."

"But I say, master——!" said the lad.

"None of your talk!" said the squire. "Tell them they must dress her and mind and not forget either wreath or crown."

The lad ran into the kitchen.

"Look here, lasses," he said; "you must go upstairs and dress up the bay mare as bride. I expect the master wants to give the guests a laugh."

The women dressed the bay mare in everything that was there, and then the lad went and told his master that now she was ready dressed, with wreath and crown and all.

"Very well, bring her down!" said the squire. "I will receive her myself at the door," said he.

There was a terrible clatter on the stairs; for that bride, you know, had no silken shoes on.

When the door was opened and the squire's bride entered the parlor you can imagine there was a good deal of tittering and grinning.

As for the squire you may be sure he had had enough of that bride, and they say he never went courting again.

Translated by H. L. Brækstad

The Contrary Woman

There was once upon a time a man who had a wife, and she was so contrary and cross-grained that it was not an easy thing at all to get on with her. The husband fared worst of all; whatever he was for, she was always against.

So it happened one Sunday in summer that the man and the woman went out to see how the crops looked.

When they came to the cornfield on the other side of the river the man said:

"It's ready for reaping; tomorrow we must begin."

"Yes, tomorrow we can begin and clip it," said the woman.

"What is it you say? Are we going to clip it? Are we supposed not to reap corn any longer?" said the man.

"No, it must be clipped," said the woman.

"There is nothing so dangerous as a little knowledge," said the man; "one would think you had lost what little sense you had! Have you ever seen anybody clipping corn?" said he.

"Little I know, and less I want to know," said the woman; "but this I do know, that the corn shall be clipped and not reaped." There was no use talking any more about that; clipped it should be.

So they walked on wrangling and quarreling, till they came to the bridge across the river, close to a deep pool.

"There's an old saying," said the man, "that good tools make good work; I fancy that'll be a queer harvest which is cut with a pair of shears," said he. "Shall we not settle to reap the corn, after all?"

"No, no! it must be clipped, clipped, clipped!" shouted the woman, jumping up and clipping her fingers under the man's nose.

In her passion she forgot to look where she was going, and all at once she stumbled over one of the beams on the bridge and fell into the river.

"Old habits are hard to change," thought the man, "but it would be a wonder if I, for once, got my way."

He waded out into the pool and got hold of her by the hair, till her head was just out of the water.

"Shall we reap the corn then?" he said.

"Clip, clip, clip!" screamed the woman.

"I'll teach you to clip," thought the man, and ducked her under the water. But that wasn't of much use; "they must clip it," she said, as he brought her to the surface again.

"I do believe the woman is crazy," said the man to himself; "many are mad and don't know it, and many have sense and don't use it; but I must try once more, anyhow," said he. But no sooner had he ducked her under again than she held her hand above the water and began to clip with her fingers, like a pair of shears. Then the man got furious and kept her under so long that her hand all of a sudden fell under the water, and the woman became so heavy that he had to let go his hold.

"If you want to drag me down into the pool with you, you may lie there, you wretch!" said the man. And so the woman was drowned.

But after a while he thought it wasn't right that she should lie there and not be buried in Christian soil, so he went along the river and searched and dragged for her; but for all his searching and all his dragging he could not find her. He took the people on the farm and others in the neighborhood with him, and they began dragging the river all the way down; but for all the searching they could not find the woman.

"Well," said the man, "this is not much use! This woman was a sort by herself; while she was alive she was altogether a contrary one, and it is not likely she'll be different now," he said, "we must search up the river for her, and try above the fall; perhaps she has floated upward."

So they went up the river and searched and dragged for her above the fall, and there, sure enough, she lay. That shows what a contrary woman she was!

Translated by H. L. Brækstad

HENRIK IBSEN

(1828–1906)

So much has been written about Henrik Ibsen and his plays, and so great has been his influence even in the English-speaking world, that it would seem like carrying coals to Newcastle to dwell on that subject.

There is, however, one area of Ibsen's work with which people in general are unfamiliar, and that is his poetry. While he wrote some of his most famous plays, such as *Brand* and *Peer Gynt*, in verse, people continue to think of him solely as a dramatist, forgetting that he was also an accomplished lyric poet.

Of the poems that appear below, some present the poet, like the dramatist, as an assailant of hypocrisy; some are marked by a touching lyricism; still others reveal his sense of humor. Together they make it clear that Ibsen merits serious consideration as a poet, and not alone as a social critic and dramatist.

The selections below date from an eighteen-year period. "Wildflowers and Hothouse-Plants" (1853) is the oldest, "Burnt Ships" (1871), the youngest. In between were "Light-Shy" (1859), "With a Water Lily" (1863), "Gone" (1864), and "To My Friend the Revolutionary Orator" (1869). "Agnes" is taken from the first act of *Brand* (1866). All were included in Ibsen's *Digte* ("Poems"), 1871.

Burnt Ships

He turned his prow to
The southern seas,
He made his vow to
The gods of ease.

Quenched in the wave was
The snow-clad peak;

The sun-land brave was
Now his to seek.

He burned his ships there—
The smoke welled forth
To build with blue strips there
A bridge to the north.

Over the span-road
Faintly bright
Northward a man rode
Every night.

Translated by Charles Wharton Stork

With a Water Lily

Look, my lady, what I've brought here,
With white pinions overwrought here!
On the tranquil streamlet floating,
Deep in reverie 'twas gloating.

Home 'twould be to such a blossom,
If you set it on your bosom,
For beneath it, softly gliding,
Deep the current would be hiding.

Linger not beside the stream there!
Peril-fraught it were to dream there.
Lo, a sprite of cunning power
Sleepless lurks to threat the flower!

'Tis your breast, the quiet stream there.
Peril-fraught it were to dream there.
Sleepless underneath the flower
Lurks a sprite of cunning power.

Translated by Charles Wharton Stork

Light-Shy

I used to be stout-hearted,
Untroubled my boyish breast
Till the time when the sun departed
Behind the mountain's crest.

But ever the dark would daunt me
As it settled on moor and vale,
And specters would come to haunt me
From legend and fairy tale.

No sooner sleep overtook me
Than dreams would throng to my bed;
With that my courage forsook me—
God only knows where it fled.

But things are quite reversed now
Compared with long ago;
My courage is dispersed now
By morning's radiant glow.

'Tis day-trolls now attack me,
'Tis din of noonday clear
Distils the drop to wrack me
With clammy throes of fear.

I hide beneath the cover
Of night's dread blanket then,
And all my fears are over,
I'm eagle-bold again.

Defying my garish terror,
On high like hawk I sail,
Forgetting my doubt and error—
Till next the dawn grows pale.

But, stripped of the night's protection,
Completely I miss the mark.
What I may bring to perfection
Must be a deed of the dark.

Translated by Charles Wharton Stork

Wildflowers and Hothouse-Plants

"Good Heavens, man, what a freak of taste!
What blindness to form and feature!
The girl's no beauty, and might be placed
As a hoydenish kind of creature."

No doubt it were more in the current tone
And the tide today we move in,
If I could but choose me to make my own
A type of our average woman.

Like winter blossoms they all unfold
Their primly maturing glory;
Like pot-grown plants in the tepid mold
Of a window conservatory.

They sleep by rule and by rule they wake,
Each tendril is taught its duties;
Were I worldly-wise, yes, my choice I'd make
From our stock of average beauties.

For worldly wisdom what do I care?
I am sick of its prating mummers;
She breathes of the field and the open air
And the fragrance of sixteen summers.

Translated by Fydell Edmund Garret

Gone

The last, late guest
To the gate we followed;
Good-bye—and the rest
The nightwind swallowed.

House, garden, street,
Lay tenfold gloomy,

Where accents sweet
Had made music to me.

It was but a feast
With the dark coming on;
She was but a guest—
And now she is gone.

Translated by Fydell Edmund Garret

To My Friend the Revolutionary Orator

They say I've become a conservative.
I am what I was and thus I'll live.

I don't play your chess; it can only wrack you.
Knock over the board and then I'll back you.

I recall only one revolution
that wasn't made in lukewarm confusion.

It retains over all the later the glory.
What I mean, of course, is the Deluge story.

Yet, even then was Lucifer cheated
and Noah's dictatorship later completed.

Let's do it again in an all-out battle,
but that will need men who do more than prattle.

You see to the flood; as a final measure
I shall torpedo the Ark with pleasure.

Translated by Hallberg Hallmundsson

Agnes

Agnes, my beautiful butterfly,
Playfully shalt thou be caught!
I am weaving a net, and its meshes fine
Are all of my music wrought!

And am I a butterfly, dainty and slight,
Let me sip of the heather-bell blue,
And art thou a boy, let me be thy sport,
But oh! not thy captive too!

Agnes, my beautiful butterfly,
I have woven my meshes so thin,
And never availeth thy fluttering flight,
Soon art thou my captive within.

And am I a butterfly, young and bright,
Full joyously I can play,
But if in thy net I a captive lie
Oh, touch not my wings, I pray!

Nay, I will lift thee with tender hand,
And lock thee up in my breast,
And there thou shalt play thy whole life long
At the game thy heart loves best.

Translated by C. H. Herford

BJØRNSTJERNE BJØRNSON
(1832–1910)

When, in 1903, Bjørnstjerne Bjørnson became the first Scandinavian to receive the Nobel Prize for literature, he was no longer young. For nearly fifty years he had been the moving force of his people, always present with his spirited, overwhelming vitality to incite them to bolder action, to castigate their vices, to rejoice in their good fortune, or to weep their tears. Nothing human had been alien to him. It was with good reason that Norway felt—and still feels—a fonder affection for him than for most of her other sons.

Bjørnson was a prolific writer. Influenced by Oehlenschläger's tragedies (see p. 46) on the one hand, and Snorri Sturluson's *Heimskringla* on the other, he wrote a series of historical plays. His aim was to show the continuity between the heroes of yore and the peasants of his own time, whom, for the first time, he introduced into Norwegian literature. In addition to plays and pastoral novels, Bjørnson wrote a substantial amount of poetry, of which the best-known single work is probably "Ja, vi elsker dette landet" ("Yes, We Love This Land of Ours"), the Norwegian national anthem.

"Synnöve's Song" is taken from Bjørnson's delightful, little peasant romance, *Synnøve Solbakken* (1857), first published serialized in *Illustreret Folkeblad* ("Illustrated People's Paper"), where "A Dangerous Wooing" had also been printed the year before. "The Princess" dates from 1860 and "I Love You, Ha! You Brown-Skin Devil" from 1875.

A Dangerous Wooing

When Aslaug had become a grown-up girl, there was not much peace to be had at Huseby; for there the finest boys in the parish quarreled and fought night after night. It was worst of all on

Saturday nights; but then old Knud Huseby never went to bed without keeping his leather breeches on, nor without having a birch stick by his bedside.

"If I have a daughter, I shall look after her, too," said old Huseby.

Thore Næset was only a houseman's son; nevertheless there were those who said that he was the one who came oftenest to see the gardman's[1] daughter at Huseby. Old Knud did not like this, and declared also that it was not true, for he had never seen him there. But people smiled slyly among themselves, and thought that had he searched in the corners of the room instead of fighting with all those who were making noise and uproar in the middle of the floor, he would have found Thore.

Spring came and Aslaug went to the sæter[2] with the cattle. Then, when the day was warm down in the valley, and the mountain rose cool above the haze, and when the bells tinkled, the shepherd dog barked, and Aslaug sang and blew the lur[3] on the mountainside, then the hearts of the young fellows who were at work down on the meadow would ache, and the first Saturday night they all started up to the mountain sæter, one faster than the other. But still more rapidly did they come down again, for behind the door at the sæter there stood one who received each of them as he came, and gave him so sound a whipping that he forever afterward remembered the threat that followed it—

"Come again another time and you shall have some more."

According to what these young fellows knew, there was only one in the parish who could use his fists in this way, and that was Thore Næset. And these rich gardmen's sons thought it was a shame that this houseman's son should cut them all out at the Huseby sæter.

So thought, also, old Knud, when the matter reached his ears, and said, moreover, that if there was nobody else who could tackle Thore, then he and his sons would try it. Knud, it is true,

---

[1] Norwegian: gårdmann or gaardmann, a "freeholder" (see note 1, p. 151).

[2] A second farm up in the mountains, used only during the summer.

[3] Trumpet or signal horn.

was growing old, but although he was nearly sixty, he would at times have a wrestle or two with his eldest son, when it was too dull for him at one party or other.

Up to the Huseby sæter there was but one road, and that led straight through the gard. The next Saturday evening, as Thore was going to the sæter, and was stealing on his tiptoes across the yard, a man rushed right at his breast as he came near the barn.

"What do you want of me?" said Thore, and knocked his assailant flat on the ground.

"That you shall soon find out," said another fellow from behind, giving Thore a blow on the back of the head. This was the brother of the former assailant.

"Here comes the third," said old Knud, rushing forward to join the fray.

The danger made Thore stronger. He was as limber as a willow and his blows left their marks. He dodged from one side to the other. Where the blows fell he was not, and where his opponents least expected blows from him, they got them. He was, however, at last completely beaten; but old Knud frequently said afterward that a stouter fellow he had scarcely ever tackled. The fight was continued until blood flowed, but then Huseby cried—

"Stop!" and added: "If you can manage to get by the Huseby wolf and his cubs next Saturday night, the girl shall be yours."

Thore dragged himself homeward as best he could; and as soon as he got home he went to bed.

At Huseby there was much talk about the fight; but everybody said—

"What did he want there?"

There was one, however, who did not say so, and that was Aslaug. She had expected Thore that Saturday night, and when she heard what had taken place between him and her father, she sat down and had a good cry, saying to herself—

"If I cannot have Thore, there will never be another happy day for me in this world."

Thore had to keep his bed all day Sunday; and Monday, too, he felt that he must do the same. Tuesday came, and it was such a beautiful day. It had rained during the night. The mountain was wet and green. The fragrance of the leaves was wafted in through the open window; down the mountainsides came the sound of the cowbells, and someone was heard singing up in the glen. Had it not been for his mother, who was sitting in the room, Thore would have wept from impatient vexation.

Wednesday came and still Thore was in bed; but on Thursday he began to wonder whether he could not get well by Saturday; and on Friday he rose. He remembered well the words Aslaug's father had spoken: "If you can manage to get by the Huseby wolf and his cubs next Saturday, the girl shall be yours." He looked over toward the Huseby sæter again and again. "I cannot get more than another thrashing," thought Thore.

Up to the Huseby sæter there was but one road, as before stated; but a clever fellow might manage to get there, even if he did not take the beaten track. If he rowed out on the fiord below, and past the little tongue of land yonder, and thus reached the other side of the mountain, he might contrive to climb it, though it was so steep that a goat could scarcely venture there—and a goat is not very apt to be timid in climbing the mountains, you know.

Saturday came, and Thore stayed withoutdoors all day long. The sunlight played upon the foliage, and every now and then an alluring song was heard from the mountains. As evening drew near, and the mist was stealing up the slope, he was still sitting outside of the door. He looked up at the mountain, and all was still. He looked over toward the Huseby gard. Then he pushed out his boat and rowed round the point of land.

Up at the sæter sat Aslaug, through with her day's work. She was thinking that Thore would not come this evening, but that there would come all the more in his stead. Presently she let loose the dog, but told no one whither she was going. She seated herself where she could look down into the valley; but a dense fog was rising, and, moreover, she felt little disposed to look down that way, for everything reminded her of what had occurred. So she moved, and without thinking what she was doing, she happened to go over to the other side of the mountain, and there she sat down and gazed out over the sea. There was so much peace in this far-reaching sea-view!

Then she felt like singing. She chose a song with long notes,

and the music sounded far into the still night. She felt gladdened
by it, and so she sang another verse. But then it seemed to her
as if someone answered her from the glen far below. "Dear me,
what can that be?" thought Aslaug. She went forward to the
brink of the precipice, and threw her arms around a slender
birch, which hung trembling over the steep. She looked down
but saw nothing. The fiord lay silent and calm. Not even a bird
ruffled its smooth surface. Aslaug sat down and began singing
again. Then she was sure that someone responded with the same
tune and nearer than the first time. "It must be somebody, after
all." Aslaug sprang up and bent out over the brink of the steep;
and there, down at the foot of a rocky wall, she saw a boat
moored, and it was so far down that it appeared like a tiny shell.
She looked a little farther up, and her eyes fell on a red cap, and
under the cap she saw a young man, who was working his way
up the almost perpendicular side of the mountain. "Dear me,
who can that be?" asked Aslaug, as she let go of the birch and
sprang far back.

She dared not answer her own question, for she knew very well
who it was. She threw herself down on the greensward and took
hold of the grass with both hands, as though it were *she* who
must not let go her hold. But the grass came up by the roots.

She cried aloud and prayed God to help Thore. But then it
struck her that this conduct of Thore's was really tempting God,
and therefore no help could be expected.

"Just this once!" she implored.

And she threw her arms around the dog, as if it were Thore
she was keeping from loosing his hold. She rolled over the grass
with him, and the moments seemed years. But then the dog tore
himself away. "Bow-wow," he barked over the brink of the steep
and wagged his tail. "Bow-wow," he barked at Aslaug, and threw
his forepaws up on her. "Bow-wow," over the precipice again;
and a red cap appeared over the brow of the mountain and
Thore lay in her arms.

Now when old Knud Huseby heard of this, he made a very
sensible remark, for he said—

"That boy is worth having; the girl shall be his."

Translated by Rasmus B. Anderson

The Princess

The princess sat high in her bower forlorn,
The boy down below played his shepherd's horn.
"You play and you play. Can you never let be?
It hinders my thoughts, boy, that long to go free,
When the sun goes down."

The princess sat high in her bower forlorn,
The boy ceased his tune on the shepherd's horn.
"Why stop with your playing? Go on, boy, for me.
It lifts up my thoughts, as they long to go free,
When the sun goes down."

The princess sat high in her bower forlorn,
The boy played again on his shepherd's horn.
She wept in the twilight, she sobbed with the smart:
"Dear God, oh, what is it, this lack in my heart—
Now the sun goes down?"

Translated by Charles Wharton Stork

Synnöve's Song

Oh, thanks for all since the days long past
When we played about the purple heather!
I thought that the merry times would last
Till we should grow old together.

I thought we should run on hand in hand
From the birches—and how we used to love them!—
To where the Solbakke houses stand,
And on to the church above them.

I waited many an eventide
And looked far off through the pines around me,
But shadows fell from the mountainside,
And you, oh you never found me.

I sat and waited, and often thought:
He'll surely dare it when dusk is falling.
But the twilight faded and then burnt out,
And the day was gone past recalling.

Poor eye, its wont it never forsook,
It never could get the trick o' turning;
It never knew anywhere else to look,
'Twas fixed in a deep-set yearning.

They tell of a place where peace may be:
It's in the kirk, as is rightly fitting.
But do not ask me to go and see—
He'd be right across from me sitting.

But still I know—and 'tis well and good—
Who let our farms be so near together,
And cut the opening in the wood
To look out on the bright spring weather.

But still I know—and 'tis right and fair—
Who built the kirk and its pointing spire,
And made the pews go pair and pair
Along the aisle to the choir.

Translated by Charles Wharton Stork

I Love You, Ha! You Brown-Skin Devil

I love you, ha! you brown-skin devil,
Your wine-hot blood, your smile of fire;
'Twas surely from the flame of Evil,
That sparkle, flickering with desire.

Your mad, unending play of passion
In eye, in gesture, mood and limb
Is all of Satan's restless fashion;
Your luring laughter is from him.

E'en so, yet this would rather make me
Love on and die with you, my dear,
Than slumber on a breast would take me
Cool to the grave for fifty year.

Better the queen of life to cherish,
Her tempting mystery to explore,
Though in the quest I vainly perish—
Than keep but what I've known before.

Translated by Charles Wharton Stork

KNUT HAMSUN

(1859–1952)

The figure of the wanderer in Norwegian literature was the creation of Knut Hamsun. It is, therefore, not surprising to learn that Hamsun himself led a wanderer's life in his youth. He was a shoemaker's apprentice, a longshoreman and a schoolmaster in Norway. Then, upon arriving in America, he worked as a farmhand on the prairie, a worker in a stone quarry and a streetcar conductor in Chicago. Not very happy in the new world, he returned to his native land and in 1888 published the short novel *Hunger*. The beauty of his style and the freshness of his literary approach immediately won him wide acclaim. His fame grew with every new book he wrote, and in 1920 he was awarded the Nobel Prize for literature.

In many of Hamsun's books we meet the wanderer, whose unrestricted liberty to taste the joys of life the writer exalts. Paradoxically, in *The Growth of the Soil* he hails the productive life of the farmer who, forfeiting his own freedom, remains to till his land, knowing that joy only which comes from contact with nature.

The last years of Hamsun's life were a series of sad events. During the occupation of Norway, he cooperated with the Nazis and, as a consequence, was ostracized by the Norwegian people. After the war he was formally sentenced to internment in an old people's home. However, bitterness toward him has subsided considerably in recent years.

The following selection is taken from his collection of short stories, *Siesta*, published in 1921.

Just an Ordinary Fly of Average Size

Our acquaintanceship began one day as I was writing. She came flying in through my open window and started to dance around my head, obviously attracted by the alcohol in my hair. I struck at her time and again, but she took no notice. It was then that I took up the paper scissors.

This is a big and wonderful pair of scissors which I use both as a pipe-scraper and a fire tong; I also drive nails into the walls with them. In my trained hand they are a terrible weapon. I swung them around several times and the fly flew away.

But a little later she came back and began dancing again. I stood up and moved my table to the door, but the fly followed. "I'll fix you," I thought. And quietly I went and washed the alcohol out of my hair. That helped. Shamefacedly the fly sat down on the shade of my lamp and didn't move.

It went on this way for quite a while. I continued my work and got much done. But in the end it became a little monotonous to see this fly every time I happened to look up. I observed her; she was just an ordinary fly of average size, well formed with gray wings. "Move a little," I said. She didn't. "Go away," I said and waved at her. Then she flew up, swung around the room, and returned to the lampshade.

Our real acquaintanceship stems from that moment. I began to respect her steadfastness; what she wanted she wanted. I was also touched by her expression; she turned her head to one side and looked at me sadly. Our feelings became mutual; she understood that I had taken to her and behaved accordingly. She became more and more impudent in her conduct, and by the afternoon when I started to go out she flew to the door ahead of me and tried to prevent my departure.

Next day I rose rather early. Just as I was leaving the breakfast table to begin my work, I met the fly in the doorway. I nodded to her. She buzzed around the room several times and then landed on my chair. I hadn't asked her to be seated, and I needed the chair. "Go away," I said. She rose a few inches into the air and landed on the chair again. Then I warned her I was going to sit down, and I did. The fly flew up and planted herself on my paper. "Go away," I said. No answer. I blew at her; she crouched down and wouldn't go. "No! Without mutual respect for each other this can't go on," I said. She listened to me and thought about it, but decided to sit all the same. Then I swung the paper scissors again. The window was open, a fact of which I was not aware, and the fly flew out.

She was gone for two hours. All that time I was regretting that I had let her go out all by herself. Where was she now? Who knew what might happen to her? At last I sat down to work again, but my mind was full of dark forebodings.

Then the fly returned. One of her hind legs was covered with dirt. "You've been out in the mud, you slob," I said. "Shame on you!" Yet, I was glad that she had come back and I closed the window carefully. "How could you do a thing like that?" I said. Then she looked at me triumphantly as if saying she had done a thing like that, and what was I going to do about it. I had never seen a fly triumphant like that before. It was amusing and I laughed heartily. "Ha ha, what an imp of a fly you are!" I said. "Come here, and I'll tickle you under the chin, you devil!"

In the evening she was up to her old tricks and attempted to block the door again. I pulled myself up and spoke to her with authority. It was all very well that she was fond of me, but keep me at home every evening, that she couldn't. And I forced my way out past her. I could hear that she was in a rage inside and I shouted in to her: "Well, you can see for yourself how nice it is to be alone. Now you can just sit there. Good-bye."

In the days following this little fly tried my patience in many ways. If I had visitors she became jealous and drove them away by being disagreeable. Afterward, when I reproached her for her conduct and wanted to teach her a little lesson, she took a neck-breaking swing from the floor right up to the ceiling where she remained and made me dizzy. "You'll fall down!" I shrieked. But my warnings were of no avail. "All right then, suit yourself and sit up there," I said and turned my back on her. Then she came down again. It never failed: if I didn't take any notice of her, she would come whisking past my nose and flop down on my manuscript with a thud. There she would start promenading back and forth, just as though I had no paper scissors in the house. "Try the sweet way with her in the future," I thought. And in a conciliatory voice I said: "Don't go there and smudge yourself with ink; I'm only thinking of your own good." She was deaf to my words. "Haven't I told you not to walk on this paper?" I repeated. "It's rough and you'll get splinters in your feet." Oh no, she was not afraid of that. "Did you ever see such stubbornness?" I yelled infuriated. "So the paper doesn't have any splinters?"

No, no, to her there seemed to be no splinters at all. "Then go to hell on it," I replied. "I'll take another sheet." But when I took another sheet, she went away.

Days and weeks passed. We got used to each other, worked together on many sheets of paper, and were partners in joy and grief. Her whims were innumerable, but I tolerated them. She had quite clearly indicated her distaste for drafts, and I kept the windows and doors closed for her sake. Nevertheless, she would often get the idea of jumping from the ceiling right against the window pane in order to break through it. "If you have any business outside, then come this way," I said. And I opened the door for her. No, she seemed not to want to go out. "Do you or don't you?" I asked. "One, two, three!" No answer. Then, in a rage, I slammed the door shut.

I was soon to regret my hot temper.

One day the fly disappeared. She had watched the door in the morning when the maid came in and then darted out. I understood that this was her revenge and I pondered long over what I should do. Then I went out to the garden and shouted that she could stay away if she pleased, I didn't miss her. But it was no use. I couldn't lure the fly back, and I did miss her. I opened everything that could be opened in my house, and I placed my manuscript in the window, exposed to weather and wind. She should see that nothing was too good for her to walk on. I asked my landlady for the fly; I soused my hair with alcohol again and I entreated her and called her my dearest friend and my queen of flies to exalt her—all in vain.

At last, the following morning, she returned. But she didn't come alone; she dragged in with her a lover from the street. In my joy over seeing her again, I forgave her everything and for quite a while even tolerated her sweetheart. But enough is enough; there are certain limits. They started sending each other glances and rubbing their legs. Then, all of a sudden, the lover threw himself over her in a way that made me blush. "What on earth are you doing right under people's noses?" I reprimanded harshly. "Don't you think you're a little too young for that?" This offended her and she threw up her head and let me clearly understand that I must be jealous. "I jealous?" I hissed. "Jealous of him there? Listen to that!" But she turned up her face still more and reiterated her point of view. Then I rose to my feet and declared the following: "With you I will not fight; it is contrary to the tenets of chivalry. But send your miserable lover against me; him I shall meet." And I snatched up the paper scissors.

Now they began to mock me. They sat on the corner of the table, shaking with laughter, and their looks seemed to say: "Ha ha, don't you have a pair of bigger scissors, just a little bigger scissors?" "I'll show you that it is not the weapons that matter," I answered. "I'll meet the chap with only a ruler in my hand." And I swung my weapon. They laughed still more and proved their contempt for me in the most obvious way. "Just what are you two starting again?" I said threateningly. But they didn't take any notice of me; the moment didn't seem fateful to them. They approached each other with shameless gestures and were just about to embrace again! "You won't do it!" I shouted to them. But they did. Then my patience was at an end. I raised the ruler and let it fall like a shaft of lightning. Something was crushed, something flowed. My well-aimed stroke had brought them both crashing to the ground.

That's how our acquaintanceship ended. . . .

She was just an ordinary little fly with gray wings. And there was nothing special about her. But she provided me with many pleasant moments while she lived.

Translated by Hallberg Hallmundsson

OLAV DUUN

(1876–1939)

The latest Norwegian to be awarded the Nobel Prize for literature was Sidgrid Undset, in 1928. Thereafter, while he lived, Olav Duun was popularly considered the strongest Norwegian contender for that honor. He had been constantly gaining stature as a writer; the year before his death saw the publication of one of his major works, *Menneske og Maktene* (published in English as "Floodtide of Fate"). Many felt that the great prize would surely fall to him; it was only a question of time. Apparently, it was also a question of fate.

Most of Duun's stories take place in the same district: Namdalen, in eastern Norway. This was an area which he knew and understood better than most others, and he succeeded in giving universal meaning to his descriptions of this special and narrow milieu. He wrote almost exclusively in *Nynorsk* (see Introduction, p. 101).

The following selection is from *Blind-Anders. Fortelingar* ("Blind Anders. Stories"), 1924.

At Christmas

There are other people at Moholmen now. When I was a boy, the man who had the place was named Gabriel. Moholmen had been in the family, had come down from father to son, from times immemorial. It was reputed a sizable gaard, and a good gaard, and Gabriel was very well off. One could see that he was aware of it, but otherwise he was as square and upright a fellow as you'd find for miles around. And he was well married, with three daughters, but no son. Massi was the eldest daughter—it is of her I am going to tell you. She was both pretty and good. I was only a lad at the time, but I remember her well. She was tall and straight, so fair of hue and kindly of eye that one was tempted to linger and look after her whenever she went by—and there were many who did so. When the young folks were together, and had no fiddler, they often got her to tra-la-la the dance, for she had a fine voice and was always merry and lighthearted. When she came, she always put life in the party, even if she said little or nothing.

At Nesstrand, right across from Moholmen, you can still see the site of old houses. A crofter lived there at the time, Andreas by name. He was of a freeholder family, from Ness, and he always managed pretty well; but, as I say, other than crofter he was not, and at that time the herring had not yet come to make the crofter equal with the freeholder. He had a son called Tarald; it was an old name in the family, and, as it happened, all who had borne it were fellows who had made something of themselves. He was of an age with Massi. What she saw in him I don't know, nor did anyone else; he was only one among many. But it was him she wanted. Others who offered themselves she merely laughed at. Massi and Tarald betrothed themselves, people said, but every time he suggested going to her father and asking for her, she lost courage.

"It's no use, I'm afraid," she said. "We'll have to wait."

"I have waited long enough and then some, it seems to me," Tarald pleaded.

"And does he wait too long who waits for something good?" she laughed. Massi always laughed most when matters were worst.

"But I'm not made to wait," he protested.

"Nor I either," she answered, and added, "but for you I could wait twenty years."

She told her mother she wanted to marry Tarald of Nesstrand. The mother was angry and upbraided her; she had better not try any such nonsense in that house! The girl went to her father, but he merely laughed at her, as one laughs at a child who wants to trade his silver shilling for a copper. Massi said no more, not even to Tarald, but he must have understood it, nevertheless, although he said nothing. One evening he rowed over the inlet, went straight up to Moholmen, and asked for Gabriel. He found him in the house. Almost all the help were present, but Tarald did not bite his lip on their account; he went straight to business and asked Massi's hand in marriage as if he were a real bigwig. It was deathly still in the room. Those who were present wished themselves elsewhere.

"Well, you haven't anything against it, have you?" asked Tarald.

Gabriel laid aside the boot he was patching. The sweat stood out on his brow.

"You don't really think you'll get my daughter, do you?" he asked.

"I shouldn't be here if I didn't," Tarald replied. "Maybe I'm not good enough—eh?"

"You don't know then that she is to have the gaard[1]?" said Gabriel.

"Oh yes, I do, and I have nothing against the gaard either," Tarald replied.

At that point Massi broke in.

"We'll be glad to give up the gaard—if it's that that stands in the way. Anne and Marja can have it, can't they, Tarald?" Anne and Marja were her two sisters.

"That we might," he answered, "and yet again I don't know whether we should."

"You keep still and leave us!" Gabriel shot at Massi.

She went to the door slowly.

Then he got up and faced Tarald squarely.

"You worthless crofter, you! Come back and plunk down real money for the gaard—then maybe there'll be another story. Then we'll talk business!"

The wife over on the bench coughed. She had great plans for Massi. But Gabriel repeated what he had said.

"And if you're any kind of man you'll do it!" he added.

"Very well," Tarald said. "I'll take you at your word. Massi has vowed she will wait twenty years for me. I'll go away, and I'll come back too—by God, I will. Now we have sworn it—Massi and I."

With that he left the room. Massi wept, but the others stood firm. And Tarald went away.

---

[1] Gaard in this connection means a freeholder farm, carrying with it allodial rights. The gaard is indivisible and the one who takes it often has to buy out the other heirs. Between the crofter (tenant farmer) and the freeholder there is a deep gulf.—*Transl.*

He had hinted to Massi he might go to sea—that seemed to him the quickest way to get the money. One year after another went by, and never a word they heard from him. Her parents and people generally argued with her that she had better put him out of her mind. She merely laughed at them; it was a long time yet till the twenty years were up. The wooers grew weary at last and did not come back. She still went about with the young folks, and kept her courage up, but she was not so full of song as before.

Then one summer, at Nærøy Fair, she met a young man who hailed from Sandöy, a lighthearted fellow, a pleasant chap to look at, and the best dancer at the fair. His name was Thor. How the two came to know each other is not told, but he said that he never would dance again for the rest of his life if he could not dance with her. And dance with her he did—all he wanted to. Gabriel and his wife were also present. They were delighted with her; she danced with all her old vim, and was just like herself again. They were pleased with the stranger too. Gabriel even made inquiries. Thor had not a little cash already, and a gaard in expectancy. People out his way had the reputation in those days of being wild and raw and a bit unmannered, but it was evident that Thor was not of their kind. It seemed almost certain there would be a betrothal, and a wedding, too, before very long, for Massi and he kept company. "In God's name, so be it," said the parents.

There would be no kicking over the traces there, people said. Yet when spring came Massi gave birth to a child.

It came so suddenly upon the Moholmens that they hardly knew which way to turn. It was rare in those days that a girl had a child; it was a tragedy. Gabriel journeyed over the Folla; he wanted to talk with Thor. But Thor was far up north fishing, and he was not likely to come home very soon—he was a wide-traveling fellow. His parents talked kindly with Gabriel, and promised that there would be a wedding as soon as Thor came home, if it stood in their power.

"Well, that's the least you could do," said Gabriel.

But he had to cross the Folla a second time, and this time he saw Thor. No—Thor did not want to marry. Marriage he considered too serious a matter, and he had furthermore learned that the girl was engaged. For all that Gabriel pressed him, he got nowhere—they said he both begged and threatened. Thor was the stronger. He planked money down on the table, and compelled Gabriel to take it—it was for the child, he said.

Gabriel was worn to a shred when he returned home. It is said he took to his bed the better part of two days. He summoned Massi and asked her if she had brought this disgrace on him for spite. She assured him she had not. She had trusted Thor implicitly; she had been only too fond of him. With that she sat down and wept.

Then came the particular Christmas and the Christmas party that I want to tell you about. I was there myself. I was only sixteen or seventeen at the time, but I wasn't so little for all that. It was the week between Christmas and New Year, a Saturday evening. We were at Ness, three score or so of young folks, and were just talking of taking a trip over the inlet to see how the Moholmen girls were celebrating Christmas. One hinted that now it might soon pay to make Massi an offer of marriage. A second intimated he'd like to go up and take a good look at this youngster of hers—he had not seen him yet. So we sat and gabbed. Her child at the time might have been three years or so, and for three years they had seen little of Massi, although she bore her shame with a high head.

Then we noticed a boat row up the inlet and put in at the Moholmen boathouse. There were four strangers in it. They pulled the boat up carefully, and went on to the house. Some Christmas drams they must have had, from what we could see, and one carried an accordion. They were from the other side of Folla, we concluded. And then we, too, started.

The four proved to be from Sandöy—Thor and his brother and two other madcap fellows. They had been at a Christmas party, a dance somewhere, and now they came here. They wanted to drop in on old friends. It was Christmas, wasn't it? Gabriel was alone except for the hired man, who was not much of a fellow, and it was little use showing them the door. Nor was Thor the kind one could turn away. There was something likable about him, so people said. Now he wanted to see his son. When we arrived, the Christmas ale had already been brought in, and the visitors were passing it round. They offered some to us too— a good holiday dram to each one, and a merry word to boot.

"You're not angry with me any longer?" asked Thor of Gabriel and his wife.

Neither answered. Thor looked at them perplexed. Then he turned to Massi.

"How about you—are you angry with me?"

Massi laughed; it was the first time in three years.

"Well, I can't say that I am especially pleased with you."

"Well, but it's Christmas, isn't it!" he said. "And where is he? Our boy, I mean. You'll let me have a look at him surely?"

She turned red as a rose haw as she went to fetch him. The youngster was exhibited before the whole room; he stood it well, although toward the last he was near crying.

"Oh, Massi, Massi, who'd ever think it of you!" laughed Thor and drank her health.

There was another round of drinks, and afterward still more. "More! More!" we laughed. It was Christmas in full swing, and Gabriel Moholmen was as if come to life again. One thing helped another, of course, but it was Massi especially that livened it up. For she had not been herself lately—hers had been a hard lot; but now she glowed like the morning sun on the mountaintop.

"What sort of box is this?" she laughed, as she dragged out the accordion.

Such an accordion there were few of us had seen. She worked it out and in, as if she hardly knew it was made to play on, and all at once it began to sound. She had touched the keys with her fingers. The girls crowded around her. They tried it and laughed, they laughed and tried it again, and she who laughed most heartily was Massi.

The owner had to take it and show his art, and before we knew it we were dancing, every last one of us. For it was Christmas, and it was a long time between Christmas and Christmas in those days too. Other young folk came, and, as always happened, when the music sounded, we turned everything upside down at old Moholmen. And the one who was lightest of foot and whose laugh rang most gaily was Massi. Even old Gabriel himself had to take the floor with his wife. One madcap fetched the ale keg from the cellar; we placed it on the table, and tapped as we found time and were thirsty. Once or twice we stopped to get something to eat—we had never had such a Christmas! Now and again we noticed that it was Thor who danced with Massi, or that she sat on his lap when they rested; but we forgot it the next instant.

"Now things are going as they should," said Gabriel.

The sweat and the joy almost overcame him. Happy also were her two sisters; they were wonderfully light on their feet in the dance.

When we stopped at last, it was broad daylight outside. A glorious Sunday morning.

"It's getting light, Gabriel Moholmen," Thor called to Gabriel across the room.

"That may be," said Gabriel.

"It's dawn for us too!" called Thor, who sat with Massi on his knee.

"I was thinking about that myself," laughed Gabriel.

Thor asked whether it was far to the minister. He meant to have the banns published that very Sunday.

"For Massi has grown prettier and prettier, and I believe I must take her home with me."

It was only a short stretch, Gabriel said, "We can reach the minister just in time."

"Is this one of the Sundays he preaches?" asked someone.

"It certainly is," answered Gabriel. "This, let me tell you, has all been foreordained. Get me something to eat, wife, and fetch me my Sunday clothes, and we'll be off. And get some breakfast for the whole company. It was written in the stars, this was. He who rules on high is mighty. Have you your papers with you, Thor?" he asked.

No, Thor did not have them—he had not thought so far ahead. One or two of the guests looked up.

"Oh, I'll fix it somehow," Gabriel reassured him—he was no small man. "It'll go through as if greased," he said. "I know the minister."

Four men rowed them over the bay and requested the publication of the banns. The minister interposed no obstacles. While they were gone, the rest of us danced with the bride, each in his turn.

Now there was a fellow there named Karl Kvingstad. He was an exceptionally comely fellow, of a freeholder family, though without any expectancy, and had frequently tried his luck with Massi. Gabriel's next oldest daughter was Anne. She was a thoroughly genuine person, and kindhearted, people said, but, compared to Massi, not particularly pretty. She had scarcely had a single wooer, for it was Massi they all wanted. Karl Kvingstad thought quickly. No sooner had it become clear to him that it was Anne who would now get the gaard, than he drew her out in the hall and made her an offer. She accepted him on the spot, but they said nothing about it for the time being.

The festive table was decked again—sausages and collared beef and smoked mutton, the finest Christmas bread, butter and cheese and lefse,[2] and aquavit and ale aplenty. Then we danced again. Massi was too happy to dance. She sat and talked with some of the girls as they sipped their glasses, and every now and then she looked out after those who had gone to the parson, for Thor was among them. Finally they came, their work accomplished. One of the girls said to her—she could be heard throughout the room—"To think that you should become so happy. You little dreamed it yesterday."

Massi laughed.

"No, I little dreamed it," she answered. "I only wished I would not live the year out. Now I wish I could wipe out that wish."

"But are you happy—deep in your heart?" asked the others.

"Yes, that I am. Except for one little thing."

"And what is that?" they demanded.

"It's this," she said, "I only wish *he* might see what's happening now. He who left me and never returned. I haven't heard a word from him!" She was so angry she trembled.

It was not certain that he was still alive, some suggested.

"I rather wish he were not," Massi answered. "Then I should not have to hate him. But I shouldn't object to his being here and seeing how happy I am. That joy I should not begrudge him," she added.

[2] A certain Norwegian type of fine-grade flatbread.

They did not wonder at that. Then we were all silent.

But not for long. A stranger entered, and there was soon something else to think about. He was a tall bearded fellow in a blue suit, and a stranger in his whole manner. He greeted them, wished them a merry Christmas, and then simply stood and looked about the room. They invited him to come forward and be seated, but he seemed not to hear them. All at once Massi gave a little cry, and grew deathly pale. *She* had recognized him. It was Tarald. Then one after the other recognized him.

Thor went over to her quickly and supported her; she had all but fainted outright. He did not know what the trouble was.

Tarald went up and shook hands first with Gabriel and his wife, and then he approached Massi, but she sat rigid, her eyes glued fast to him.

"Who are you?" Thor asked.

"Well, who are you?" Tarald answered.

"I am Massi's husband-to-be," he answered. "If you must know," he added.

"No, you're wrong there," said Tarald. "It is I am her husband-to-be. Come, Massi, your hand!"

Massi put her hand behind her. At length Gabriel had recovered his speech. He went up and put his hand on Tarald's shoulder and explained how matters stood.

"You stayed too long," he said. "There was none of us thought you were still alive."

Tarald looked at him and then at Massi.

"Yes, I stayed a long time. But I couldn't get ready sooner. You it was who set me the task, and Massi had promised to wait twenty years. I traveled fast homeward."

Gabriel answered it were best he said farewell and departed again whence he had come; it were best both for himself and these two.

"You have come too late, and there is nothing to be done about it," he said. "It isn't my fault."

Tarald stood silent for a moment. The others crowded around him and begged him to leave like a sensible fellow. Some of the men pressed him pretty hard—they had had a good many drinks.

"Easy, folks, easy," he said, his eyes darkening. "You can't scare me, and you may as well know it."

There was among them a fellow who was very strong. He didn't think twice, but seized the stranger and heaved him out. But a moment later Tarald again stood in the doorway. He was still as calm as ever.

"I have been shown the door here once before," he said. "As yet only half the twenty years have gone, Massi, and here, Gabriel, here is the money for the gaard. Now speak up and say your say."

He drew forth a large purse with money—it was almost all in gold. Then he called out over the heads of those who stood in front of him. "One thing I ask of you, Massi: that you have the banns annulled and take a fortnight to think things over."

They all shouted "No!" to a man. They said his money was stolen money, and much that was worse. They were about ready to lay hold of him as a vagabond. But then they heard Massi behind them.

"I'll do as you say, Tarald," she said, "if that will give you any joy. I have waited so long already. But here's my child, that Thor is father to," she laughed.

"Yes, I see him," Tarald answered. "I'll be a good father to him —you needn't worry about that. Even though it may not be so easy for me at first. Not one word of reproach from me shall you hear for what has happened. And this money is an honest man's money—I believe you know that. I have both ventured and won."

Thor of Sandöy was a good-natured fellow, and he was sure of Massi. He came forward and offered Tarald his hand.

"Well, all right then! And welcome home! After all we're grown men, aren't we? Shall we drink to his homecoming? And this other matter will surely straighten itself out."

To this they all loudly assented. Many of them were so relieved, they thought the roof of the house had been lifted. They drank to the stranger's homecoming and asked him to tell about his travels. That he would do some other time, he promised. He gave them only a few hints. He had scars both on his hands and on his face, and he admitted he had been up against all sorts of people. He had some fine things, both of silver and gold, and had traveled wide and far. "And now I am here," he concluded.

Gabriel had to go to the minister again—he had scarce time to reach him before church. Whether he relished going or not no one knew, but his wife laughed.

"First we sigh for want of *one* man for Massi, and now we sigh because there are two. *Now* surely she is bound to be married."

She was fond of money, though a fine woman in other respects.

It was as good as a wedding that day at Moholmen. One continuous round of eating and drinking and dancing. Massi for the most part looked on, but when we cleared the room in the evening, she, too, joined in the dance. She danced with both suitors and with all of us, and she was gayer than ever before. And so pretty was she that it almost hurt one to look at her. Her mother begged her to go more slowly, but Massi laughed and called out that she wouldn't mind dancing now till she died! We heard it, all of us. She was perhaps not so happy as she let on. We understood her pretty well; it was not easy for her to choose between the two.

Karl Kvingstad had become dubious.

"Do you think that Tarald will take the gaard?" he said to Anne in a corner. That she did not know. But she eyed him.

And the night went by; we hardly knew what became of it. There had gathered at Moholmen a great crowd of young people, and there was drinking all the way round, and loud reveling, and no sleep. It had all come about so strangely.

"This, boys, this *is* a wedding!" someone shouted.

But almost in the same moment another shouted something else.

"They're fighting outside!"

We rushed out, and there stood Tarald and Thor facing each other. It was a glittering moonlight night, crackling cold and clear, and there they were with knives drawn. We stood stock still and looked on. Our wits and our strength failed us. A weird light enveloped us as well as the fighters. Back and forth they moved, back and forth, without a sound; it meant life or death.

All at once Massi appeared among us, paused a moment, and called to them, her voice breaking with tears.

"Thor and Tarald! Tarald and Thor!"

She rushed forward and tried to get to them. They did not heed her. People seized her and held her back and forced her inside again, for here she merely made matters worse. All the menfolk closed in and separated the fighters and took from them their knives. Then we let them go to it and settle their differences as best they might. It was a bully fight. Blood flowed. Thor was as strong as an ox, and he had the upper hand, but Tarald was wild and rushed blindly in on him. And presently he whipped forth a new weapon, a large pistol, and aimed at Thor. There was a loud outcry all over the gaard, and then a deadly silence. And deadly still and pale the two rivals faced each other.

Tarald then threw his weapon aside; it struck the cowshed with a thud.

"Now!" he shouted. "Come on, if you dare!"

Thor came, and they closed anew; and none of the others wanted to interfere, for it was a serious business they had to settle between themselves. It was Gabriel who finally put a stop to the madness. He appeared at the door, completely beside himself, as a full-grown man rarely is, so hoarse of speech we could not understand what he said. Within we heard womenfolk crying. Finally he recovered his speech.

"Come in!" he shouted. "Both of you—right away. It's Massi!"

When they came in, it was all over with her. She breathed no longer. She had collapsed as they carried her in, had called the names of the two suitors, the last words she spoke, and had then become rigid almost at once. She lay a corpse on the bed.

There was no one then but was sober.

Thor and Tarald stood near each other, a short distance from the bed, the rest in a half-circle about them. The mother bent down over her time and again, begged her to answer, for she could not yet believe that it was all over. None of us could believe it. Thor stalked across the floor and went out, Tarald after him, and finally the rest of us. We could not bear to stay within.

"Well, you didn't get her anyway." It was Tarald who spoke.

The other whirled about and stared at him. It seemed as if he woke up.

"That was an ugly thing to say," he answered, "but I say, would to God you had got her rather!"

Before the guests had all taken their departure, Tarald went up to Thor.

"I'm leaving the country again and this time for good. I don't suppose you can ever forgive me for coming here as I did?"

Thor turned white as he faced him. It was a hard struggle

for him. Many of those who stood around urged that he ought
to forgive Tarald, and talked seriously with him. And Thor offered him his hand.

"There's little now to quarrel about. And what has happened
was perhaps for the best; we can't think otherwise. Nor shall
you leave the country before we have followed Massi on her
last journey."

Tarald was unable to say anything, but to judge from his
silence, he agreed.

It turned out to be a large funeral—larger than any the dale
people could remember. All who had known her had thought
a great deal of Massi. She had been of different stuff from most
people, and now she loomed large in their thoughts, and they
sorrowed greatly. Half the neighborhood turned out and accompanied her to the grave. It was a memorable funeral procession.

Thor had remained at Moholmen up to the time of the funeral.
After the funeral he came forth and said he was not minded to
leave Moholmen alone this time. He and Marja stood side by
side, and they could see he held her hand. Marja was the
youngest daughter in the family, a beautiful girl, and of mar-
riageable age. She dared not look up, as she stood there, so
young and modest, but they could see that she was supremely
happy. The parents brightened up when they heard what Thor
said, and the whole company wished both them and the children joy.

Karl Kvingstad then wanted to be no less a man. He crossed
the floor to Anne.

"You know what we have agreed on," he said. "Now we can
make it public, we too."

"We have agreed on nothing," she answered.

"You surely don't mean to go back on me?" he asked.

But she looked him straight in the eyes.

"Remember what you asked when Tarald came. It was you
then that went back on me."

"What's become of you, Tarald?" Thor then asked, looking
about him.

Tarald went up to Anne, took her by the hand, and led her
out on the floor.

"What do you say to that, Gabriel?" he asked.

Gabriel said "Amen!" and blessed them, and so did his wife. Thor then spoke up again—he was so light of heart, and the words came easily to him.

"We're robbing your home," he said. "But we have talked the matter over, Tarald and I, and we couldn't do otherwise. It's pretty soon, to be sure, but better too early than too late," he added.

It came out later that both of them had wanted Marja, for she was the prettier of the two sisters, but when one of them heard of it he refused to get in the other's way—they had had enough of that already. There was quite a struggle over it. But the upshot was, as we have seen, that Tarald was to have Anne and the gaard, and Thor to have Marja. That was what the girls wanted, too, it was said.

They lived happily each with his own. They were such good friends that they had to visit each other often.

—And that's the way it went. And the moral—I had it in mind all the time I was telling the story, but now it's clean gone. Well, it's all the same.

Translated by Anders Orbeck

SIGRID UNDSET

(1882–1949)

The daughter of an archeologist, Sigrid Undset was early an eager student of the Middle Ages. Even as she was writing her first novels on contemporary life, she was constantly at work increasing her knowledge of medieval Norway. Her studies, which led to a profound understanding of the role played by the Catholic Church in the Middle Ages, enabled her to describe the period with especial perceptiveness. These extensive studies are evident in the two major works upon which her fame mainly rests: *Kristin Lavransdatter* (1920–23) and *The Master of Hestviken* (1925–27).

The qualities which make *Kristin Lavransdatter* among the finest examples of historical fiction are its truthful depiction of the past, its complex and colorful characterizations, and, finally, its unique grasp of the medieval mind. It was primarily for these historical novels on the Middle Ages that she received the Nobel Prize in 1928.

The following pages contain excerpts from chapters 6 and 7 of "Jødunrgaard," the first part of *Kristin Lavransdatter*.

The Death of Arne

It was all but dark when Kristin and Arne had said their last farewell. She stood and looked after him when at length he rode away. A streak of yellow light shone through a rift in the clouds, and was reflected in the footprints, where they had walked and stood in the slush on the road—it all looked so cold and sorrowful, she thought. She drew up her linen neckerchief and dried her tear-stained face, then turned and went homeward.

She was wet and cold, and walked quickly. After a time she heard someone coming along the road behind her. She was a little frightened; even on such a night as this there might be strange folk journeying on the highway, and she had a lonely stretch before her. A great black scree rose right up on one side, and on the other the ground fell steeply and there was fir-forest all the way down to the leaden-hued river in the bottom of the Dale. So she was glad when the man behind her called to her by name; and she stood still and waited.

The newcomer was a tall, thin man in a dark surcoat with lighter sleeves; as he came nearer she saw he was dressed as a priest and carried an empty wallet on his back. And now she knew him to be Bentein Priestson, as they called him—Sira Eirik's daughter's son. She saw at once that he was far gone in drink.

"Ay, one goes and another comes," said he, laughing, when they had greeted one another. "I met Arne of Brekken even now—I see you are weeping. You might as well smile a little now I am come home—we have been friends, too, ever since we were children, have we not?"

"'Tis an ill exchange, methinks, getting you into the parish in his stead," said Kristin bluntly. She had never liked Bentein. "And so, I fear, will many think. Your grandfather here has been so glad you were in Oslo making such a fair beginning."

"Oh, ay," said Bentein, with a nickering laugh. "So 'twas a fair beginning I was making, you think? I was even like a pig in a wheatfield, Kristin—and the end was the same, I was hunted out with cudgels and the hue and cry. Ay, ay! ay, ay! 'Tis no great thing, the gladness my grandfather gets from his offspring. But what a mighty hurry you are in!"

"I am cold," said Kristin curtly.

"Not colder than I," said the priest. "I have no more clothes on me than you see here—my cloak I had to sell for food and beer in Little Hamar. Now, you should still have some heat in your body from making your farewells with Arne—methinks you should let me get under your fur with you——" and he caught her cloak, pulled it over his shoulders and gripped her round the waist with his wet arm.

Kristin was so amazed with his boldness it was a moment before she could gather her wits—then she strove to tear herself away, but he had a hold of her cloak, and it was fastened together by a strong silver clasp, Bentein got his arms about her again, and made to kiss her, his mouth nearly touching her chin. She tried to strike, but he held her fast by the upper arm.

"I trow you have lost your wits," she hissed, as she struggled, "dare you lay hands on me as if I were a . . . dearly shall you rue this tomorrow, dastard that you are——"

"Nay, tomorrow you will not be so foolish," says Bentein, putting his leg in front of her so that she half fell into the mud, and pressing one hand over her mouth.

Yet she had no thought of crying out. Now for the first time it flashed on her mind what he dared to want with her, but rage came upon her so wild and furious she had scarce a thought of fear: she snarled like an animal at grips with another, and fought furiously with the man as he tried to hold her down, while the ice-cold snow-water soaked through her clothes on to her burning skin.

"Tomorrow you will have wit enough to hold your tongue," said Bentein, ". . . and if it cannot be hidden, you can put the blame on Arne—'twill be believed the sooner——"

Just then one of his fingers got into her mouth, and at once she bit it with all her might, so that Bentein shrieked and let go his hold. Quick as lightning Kristin got one hand free, seized his face with it, and pressed her thumb with all her might against the ball of one of his eyes: he roared out and rose to his knees; like a cat she slipped from his grasp, threw herself upon him so that he fell upon his back, and, turning, rushed along the road with the mud splashing over her at every bound.

She ran and ran without looking back. She heard Bentein coming after, and she ran till her heart thumped in her throat, while she moaned softly and strained her eyes forward—should she never reach Laugarbru? At last she was out on the road where it passed through the fields; she saw the group of houses down on the hillslope, and at the same moment she bethought her that she durst not run in there, where her mother was—in the state she was now in, plastered with clay and withered leaves from head to foot, and with her clothing torn to rags.

She marked that Bentein was gaining upon her; and on that she bent down and took up two great stones. She threw them when he came near enough; one struck him with such force it felled him to the ground. Then she ran on again and stayed not before she stood upon the bridge.

All trembling, she stood and clutched the railing of the bridge;

a darkness came before her eyes, and she feared she would drop down in a swoon—but then she thought of Bentein; what if he should come and find her. Shaken with rage and shame she went onward, though her legs would scarce bear her, and now she felt her face smart where fingernails had scarred it, and felt too she had hurts upon both back and arms. Her tears came hot as fire.

She wished Bentein might have been killed by the stone she had thrown; she wished she had gone back and made an end of him; she felt for her knife, but found that she must have lost it.

Then again came the thought, she must not be seen at home as she was; and so it came into her mind that she would go to Romundgaard. She would complain to Sira Eirik. . . .

Bentein went southward not more than a week later; he carried letters from Sira Eirik to the Bishop of Hamar, begging the Bishop to find work for him or otherwise to help him.

One day at Yuletide Simon Andressön came riding to Jörundgaard, a quite unlooked-for guest. He craved pardon for coming thus, unbidden and alone, without his kinsfolk. But Sir Andres was in Sweden on the King's business; he himself had been home at Dyfrin for a time, but only his young sisters and his mother, who lay ill abed, were there; so time had hung on his hands, and a great longing had taken him to look in upon them up here.

Ragnfrid and Lavrans thanked him much for having made this long journey in the depth of winter. The more they saw of Simon the more they liked him. He knew of all that had passed between Andres and Lavrans, and it was now fixed that his and Kristin's betrothal ale should be drunk before the beginning of Lent if Sir Andres could be home by that time, but, if not, then as soon as Easter was past.

Kristin was quiet and downcast when with her betrothed; she found not much to talk of with him. One evening when they had all been sitting drinking, he asked her to go out with him a little into the cool. Then, as they stood on the balcony in front of the upper hall, he put his arm round her waist and kissed her. After that he did the same often when they were alone. It gave her no gladness, but she suffered him to do it, since she knew the betrothal was a thing that must come. She thought of her wedding now only as something which she must go through with, not as something she wished for. Nonetheless she liked Simon well enough—most, though, when he talked with others and did not touch or talk to her.

She had been so unhappy through this whole autumn. It was of no use, however often she told herself Bentein had been able to do her no harm; nonetheless she felt herself soiled and shamed.

Nothing could be the same as it had been before, since a man had dared try to wreak such a will on her. She lay awake of nights and burned with shame and could not stop thinking of it. She felt Bentein's body close against hers as when they fought, his hot, beery breath—she could not help thinking of what might have happened—and she thought, with a shudder through all her body, of what he had said: how Arne would get the blame if it could not be hidden. There rushed through her mind all that would have followed if such a calamity had befallen and then folk had heard of her meeting with Arne—what if her father and mother had believed such a thing of Arne—and Arne himself. . . . She saw him as she had seen him that last evening, and she felt as though she sank crushed before him at the very thought that she *might* have dragged him down with her into sorrow and disgrace. And then she had such ugly dreams. She had heard tell in church and in holy stories of fleshly lusts and the temptations of the body, but they had meant naught to her. Now it was become real to her that she herself and all mankind had a sinful, carnal body which enmeshed the soul and ate into it with hard bonds.

Then she would think out for herself how she might have killed or blinded Bentein. It was the only solace she could find— to sate herself with dreams of revenge upon the dark, hateful man who stood always in the way of her thoughts. But this did not help for long; she lay by Ulvhild's side of nights and wept bitter tears at the thought of all this that had been brought upon her by brute force. Bentein had not failed altogether—he had wrought scathe to the maidenhood of her spirit.

The first workday after Christmas all the women on Jörund-gaard were busy in the kitchen-house; Ragnfrid and Kristin had been there, too, for most of the day. Late in the evening, while some of the women were clearing up after the baking, and others making ready the supper, the dairymaid came rushing in, shrieking and wringing her hands:

"Jesus, Jesus—did ever any hear such a dreadful thing—they are bringing Arne Gyrdsön home dead on a sleigh—God help Gyrd and Inga in this misery——"

A man who dwelt in a cottage a little way down the road came in with Halvdan. It was these two who had met the bier.

The women crowded round them. Outside the circle stood Kristin, white and shaking. Halvdan, Lavrans' own body-servant, who had known Arne from his boyhood, wept aloud as he told the story:

It was Bentein Priestson who had killed Arne. On New Year's Eve the men of the Bishop's household were sitting and drinking in the men's hall, and Bentein had come in—he had been given a clerkship now with the Corpus Christi prebendary. The men did not want him amongst them at first, but he had put Arne in mind that they were both from the same parish, and Arne had let him sit by him, and they had drunk together. But presently they had quarreled and fought, and Arne had fallen on so fiercely that Bentein had snatched a knife from the table and stabbed him in the throat and then more than once in the breast. Arne had died almost at once.

The Bishop had taken this mischance much to heart; he himself had cared for the laying-out of the corpse, and had it brought all the long way home by his own folk. Bentein he had thrown into irons, cast him out from the church, and if he were not already hanged, he was going to be.

Halvdan had to tell all this over again many times as fresh people streamed in. Lavrans and Simon came over to the kitchen too, when they marked all the stir and commotion about the place. Lavrans was much moved; he bade them saddle his horse, he would ride over to Brekken at once. As he was about to go, his eyes fell on Kristin's white face.

"Maybe *you* would like to go with me?" he asked. Kristin faltered a little; she shuddered—but then she nodded, for she could not utter one word.

"Is't not too cold for her?" said Ragnfrid. "Doubtless they will have the wake tomorrow, and then 'tis like we shall all go together——"

Lavrans looked at his wife; he marked Simon's face too; and then he went and laid his arm round Kristin's shoulders.

"She is his foster sister, you must bear in mind," said he. "Maybe she would like to help Inga with the laying-out of the body."

And though Kristin's heart was benumbed with despair and fear, she felt a glow of thankfulness to her father for his words. . . .

The sound of singing and the glitter of many lighted candles met them in the doorway. In the middle of the room stood the coffin Arne had been brought home in, covered with a sheet; boards had been laid on trestles and the coffin placed upon them. At the head of the bier a young priest stood with a book in his hands, chanting; round about knelt the mourners with their faces hidden in their heavy cloaks.

Lavrans lit his candle at one of those already burning, set it firmly upon one of the boards of the bier and knelt down. Kristin tried to do the like, but could not get her candle to stand; so Simon took it and helped her. As long as the priest went on chanting, all stayed upon their knees and repeated his words in whispers, their breath hanging like steam about their mouths in the bitter cold of the room.

When the priest shut his book and the folks rose—there were many gathered in the death-chamber already—Lavrans went forward to Inga. She stared at Kristin, and seemed scarce to hear what Lavrans said; she stood holding the gifts he had handed to her, as though she knew not she had aught in her hand.

"Are *you* come, too, Kristin," she said in a strange, choking voice. "Maybe you would like to see my son, so as he is come back to me?"

She pushed some of the candles aside, seized Kristin's arm with a shaking hand, and with the other swept the napkin from the face of the dead.

It was grayish-yellow like clay, and the lips had the hue of lead; they had parted a little, so that the small, even, bone-white

teeth showed through as in a mocking smile. Under the long
eyelashes there was a gleam of the glassy eyes, and there were
some livid stains below the temples, either marks of blows or the
death-spots.

"Maybe you would kiss him?" asked Inga, as before; and
Kristin bent forward at her bidding and pressed her lips upon
the dead man's cheek. It was clammy as with dew, and she
thought she could feel the least breath of decay; the body had
begun to thaw perhaps with the heat from all the tapers round.

Kristin stayed still, lying with her hands on the bier, for she
could not rise. Inga drew the shroud farther aside, so that the
great gash above the collarbone came to sight. Then she turned
toward the people and said with a shaking voice:

"They lie, I see, who say a dead man's wounds will bleed when
he is touched by him who wrought his death. He is colder now,
my boy, and less comely, than when you met him last down
there upon the road. You care not much to kiss him now, I see—
but I have heard you scorned not his lips then."

"Inga," said Lavrans, coming forward, "have you lost your
wits—are you raving——"

"Oh, ay, you are all so fine, down at Jörundgaard—you were
far too rich a man, you Lavrans Björgulfsön, for my son to dare
think of courting your daughter with honor—and Kristin, too, she
thought herself too good. But she was not too good to run after
him on the highway at night and play with him in the thickets
the night he left—ask her yourself and we will see if she dare
deny it here, with Arne lying dead—and all through her light-
ness——"

Lavrans did not ask; he turned to Gyrd:

"Curb your wife, man—you see she has clean lost her wits——"

But Kristin lifted her white face and looked desperately about
her:

"I went and met Arne the last evening because he begged me
to. But naught of wrong passed between us." And then, as she
seemed to come to herself and to understand all, she cried out:
"I know not what you mean, Inga—would you slander Arne and
he lying here—never did he tempt me nor lure me astray——"

But Inga laughed aloud:

"Nay, not Arne! but Bentein Priest—*he* did not let you play with him so—ask Gunhild, Lavrans, that washed the dirt off your daughter's back; and ask each man who was in the Bishop's henchmen's hall on New Year's Eve, when Bentein flouted Arne for that he had let her go, and leave him standing like a fool. She let Bentein walk homeward with her under her cloak, and would have played the same game with him——"

Lavrans took her by the shoulder and laid his hand over her mouth:

"Take her away, Gyrd. Shameful it is that you should speak such words by this good youth's body—but if all your children lay here dead, I would not stand and hear you lie about mine— you, Gyrd, must answer for what this madwoman says——"

Gyrd took hold of his wife and tried to lead her away, but he said to Lavrans:

"'Tis true, though, 'twas of Kristin they talked, Arne and Bentein, when my son lost his life. Like enough you have not heard it, but there hath been talk in the parish here, too, this autumn——"

Simon struck a blow with his sword upon the clothes chest beside him:

"Nay, good folk, now you must find somewhat else to talk of in this death-chamber than my betrothed. . . . Priest, can you not rule these folk and keep seemly order here?"

The priest—Kristin saw now he was the youngest son from Ulvsvolden, who had been home for Yule—opened his book and stood up beside the bier. But Lavrans shouted that those who had talked about his daughter, let them be who they might, should be made to swallow their words; and Inga shrieked:

"Ay, take my life then, Lavrans, since she has taken all my comfort and joy—and make her wedding with this knight's son; but yet do all folk know that she was wed with Bentein upon the highway. . . . Here . . ." and she cast the sheet Lavrans had given her right across the bier to Kristin, "I need not Ragnfrid's linen to lay my Arne in the grave—make headcloths of it, you, or keep it to swaddle your roadside brat—and go down and help Gunhild to moan for the man that's hanged——"

Lavrans, Gyrd and the priest took hold of Inga. Simon tried

to lift Kristin, who was lying over the bier. But she thrust his arm fiercely aside, drew herself up straight upon her knees, and cried aloud:

"So God my Savior help me, it is false!" and, stretching out one hand, she held it over the nearest candle on the bier.

It seemed as if the flame bent and waved aside—Kristin felt all eyes fixed upon her—what seemed to her a long time went by. And then all at once she grew aware of a burning pain in her palm, and with a piercing cry she fell back upon the floor.

She thought herself she had swooned—but she was aware that Simon and the priest raised her. Inga shrieked out something; she saw her father's horror-stricken face, and heard the priest shout that no one must take account of this ordeal—not thus might one call God to witness—and then Simon bore her from the room and down the stairs. Simon's man ran to the stable, and soon after Kristin was sitting, still half-senseless, in front of Simon on his saddle, wrapped in his cloak, and he was riding toward Jörundgaard as fast as his horse could gallop.

They were nigh to Jörundgaard when Lavrans came up with them. The rest of their company came thundering along the road far behind.

"Say naught to your mother," said Simon, as he set her down at the door of the house. "We have heard all too much wild talk tonight; 'tis no wonder you lost your wits yourself at the last."

It was Simon who told Ragnfrid of what had happened in the corpse-chamber at Brekken the night before. He did not make more of it than he needs must. But Kristin was so mazed with sorrow and night-waking that she felt a senseless anger against him because he talked as if it were not so dreadful a thing after all. Besides it vexed her sorely that her father and mother let Simon behave as though he were the master in the house.

"And you, Simon—surely you believe not aught of this?" asked Ragnfrid fearfully.

"No," replied Simon. "Nor do I deem there is anyone who believes it—they know you and her and this Bentein; but so little befalls for folk to talk of in these outparishes, 'tis but reason they should fall to on such a fat titbit. 'Tis for us to teach them Kristin's good name is too fine fare for such clowns as they. But pity it was she let herself be so frighted by his grossness that she went not forthwith to you or to Sira Eirik with the tale—methinks this bordel-priest would but too gladly have avowed he meant naught worse than harmless jesting, had you, Lavrans, got a word with him."

Both Kristin's parents said that Simon was right in this. But she cried out, stamping her foot:

"But he threw me down on the ground, I say—I scarce know myself what he did or did not do—I was beside myself; I can remember naught—for all I know it may be as Inga says—I have not been well nor happy a single day since——"

Ragnfrid shrieked and clasped her hands together; Lavrans started up—even Simon's face fell. He looked at her sharply, then went up to her and took her by the chin. Then he laughed:

"God bless you, Kristin—you had remembered but too well if he had done you any harm. No marvel if she has been sad and ill since that unhappy evening she had such an ugly fright—she who had never known aught but kindness and goodwill before," said he to the others. "Any but the evil-minded, who would fain think ill rather than good, can see by her eyes that she is a maid and no woman."

Kristin looked up into her betrothed's small, steady eyes. She half lifted her hands—as if to throw them round his neck—when he went on:

"You must not think, Kristin, that you will not forget this. 'Tis not in my mind that we should settle down at Formo as soon as we are wed, so that you would never leave the Dale. No one has the same hue of hair or mind in both rain and sunshine, said old King Sverre, when they blamed his Birch-legs[1] for being overbearing in good fortune——"

Lavrans and Ragnfrid smiled—it was pleasant enough to hear the young man discourse with the air of a wise old bishop. Simon went on:

" 'Twould ill beseem me to seek to teach you, who are to be my father-in-law; but so much, maybe, I may make bold to say, that we, my brothers and sisters and I, were brought up more

---

[1] The political faction, with whose help Sverre made himself the king of Norway. King Sverre ruled from 1184 to 1202.

strictly; we were not let run about so freely with the house folk as I have seen that Kristin is used to. My mother often said that if one played with the cottar-carls' brats, 'twas like one would get a louse or two in one's hair in the end—and there's somewhat in that saying."

Lavrans and Ragnfrid held their peace; but Kristin turned away, and the wish she had felt but a moment before, to clasp Simon round the neck, had quite left her.

Translated by Charles Archer
AND *J. S. Scott*

ARNULF ØVERLAND
(1889–   )

In his first volume of poetry *Den ensomme Fest* ("The Lonely
Feast"), in 1911, Arnulf Øverland showed the sure touch of
a major poet. His unabashed radicalism made him the natural
spokesman of the working classes, and during the period
between the wars he joined with them in their attack upon
bourgeois tepidity and pettiness. At the same time, he con-
demned religious narrow-mindedness and superstition, while
hailing the universal virtue of neighborly love.

Øverland was early aware of the Nazi menace and already
in 1936 gave warning in the magnificent poem *Du må ikke
sove* (translated as "Europe on Fire"). During the Nazi occupation of Norway, he survived four years of German prisons
and concentration camps. An avid opponent of any kind of
totalitarianism he has, since the end of the war, clamored
against the danger of Soviet Communism.

Besides his poetry, Øverland has written many volumes of
essays and short stories, many of which contain a curious
and strangely haunting mixture of Freudian and mystical
ideas. The theme of "Thirty Dollars," from his collection *Gud
plantet en have* ("God Planted a Garden"), 1931, is borrowed from the poem "Der Haideknabe" by Friedrich
Hebbel.

Thirty Dollars

There was a mill here down the hill, just below Lake Horn. The
man who owned it moved away and nobody took over the place,
so the mill stood empty for a long time. At last it collapsed and
was swallowed by the current. That was the year in which the
redistribution of land took place; it's quite a long time ago now.

The last person to be executed in this parish was the helper
of the innkeeper at Stockfield.

The miller had taken a boy from the poorhouse to help him with the mill. His name was Hans and he was really a stranger to these parts. He didn't stay here long either, for he disappeared. The strange thing was that he had had a dream and the dream came true—or so they say.

It was an ugly story. There was talk about it for years afterward and that was why the miller had to go away. He couldn't stay here any longer.

There was a quagmire in the outer fields of Southern Stockfield, about midway to the town, and the miller tried to throw himself into it many times. In the end they had to take him by force; for he felt that what had happened was, in a way, his fault. He regretted having beaten the boy the last day, though it had to be done if a poorhouse boy like that was to learn to take care of the mill and become a good Christian.

The day it happened the boy must have overslept, for the miller had to go upstairs himself to wake him up. And when the boy came down for breakfast, he was so bewildered and confused that he did everything wrong, and he had no sooner sat down at the table than he put his spoon down and wouldn't eat.

"If you waste your food, you'll go without any," said the miller. "You're to go to town today with thirty dollars for the storekeeper. Now, get ready!"

So saying, he took the money out of the chest and put it on the table. But the boy just sat there and stared at the coins without moving or uttering a word.

Then his master stood up and seized him by the shoulder.

"Can't I escape?" begged the boy.

"Escape? Escape what? Making yourself useful? Are you out of your mind? Or are you ill?"

"No, but I dreamed—I dreamed I was to go to town with thirty dollars, and then you took out the money, and then you got angry, and then you took the whip, and——"

"Then you dreamed the truth," said the man and he took out the whip and used it both well and long.

"I'll go, I'm going, I'm going!" yelled the boy. And he picked up the money and rushed out.

Imagine how he felt when he came out on the road. He was

absolutely frantic and blind with tears, and in this state he set off running—desperate over what he knew would happen, and what he could not evade. He ran like that, right into it, with the silver coins jingling in his pocket.

He had dreamed that too: running so that the money jingled! And the road stretched out ahead with sedge and marshes on both sides, and here and there a grove of spruce. And not a house in sight, nor a single soul to help.

Turn back he could not; his master would only beat him more and send him off again. And if he went off the road, he might get in among the trees—and there, in the shade of a big spruce with drooping branches, a man would bend over him, sneering, with yellow teeth—and there the dream ended!

Then he felt that God must surely help him; dear, good God must let him find another way! And that he did! There lay a road to the left; it was the road to the inn of Stockfield.

The inn was a big, red-painted two-story building with a smaller one beside it, and a storehouse and a cowbarn just opposite. He recognized it! This way he must not go; it was precisely here that he must not go!

He was about to turn and run back again, but there stood the innkeeper himself, an old man, bareheaded with a great silver-gray beard.

"Who are you?" he called.

"Hans from the mill," said the boy. "I'm going to town with thirty dollars for the storekeeper. But someone's following me and wants to take the money away from me, and he takes me under a big spruce——"

"Someone's following you?"

"Yes!"

"Where?"

"Here on the road!"

The innkeeper looked down the hill and smiled: "And then he takes you under a big spruce?"

"Yes!"

"I believe you're dreaming in broad daylight," said the innkeeper and shook his beard.

"No, but I did dream!" said the boy. "I dreamed about you, too, and that you had a great, white beard and shook your head!"

"Let me look at you!" said the innkeeper. "Your name is Hans, is it?"

"Yes. Couldn't you come with me to town?"

"Come with you to town? No, I can't do that."

"Couldn't somebody go with me? Don't let me go alone! I've saved four shillings; they're my own money, and if somebody will come with me, he can have them!"

But as soon as he had said it he knew it was wrong. He heard his own words like an echo; it was as if they had been said once before. It had all happened before, and now it was to happen again.

The innkeeper stood and thought a while. Then he called to the barn: "Jacob!"

Meanwhile, Jacob had come out from the kitchen and was standing right behind them.

"Look here, Jacob," said the innkeeper. "Here's a little lad on his way to town with thirty dollars and he doesn't dare go alone with all that money. You should go with him."

"With pleasure," said Jacob.

Later the innkeeper said that at that moment he felt a little apprehension, for when the boy saw Jacob he handed him his four shillings and said he'd rather go alone. Then he ran off as fast as he could.

The boy ran, stumbling over his own feet—his shoes were far too big for him—he fell and ran without looking where he was going. And the longer he ran, the clearer it became to him that he didn't have much farther to go.

Somebody grabbed him from behind. "Hey, you! What're you running for? You can't be in such a hurry? Take it easy and then I'll come with you. You can't keep flying like that. Let's rest a while here, eh?"

Jacob took him by the hand; he didn't resist. They went across the ditch by the road toward a little grove of spruce on a hillside. Behind them was the quagmire. They sat down beneath the big spruce.

"Now I'll take your money for you; then you won't have to carry it," said Jacob. The boy tried to hold his pocket closed, but it was no use.

"In the name of Jesus, can't I escape?" he asked.

"Jesus? Huh! Is it true that you dreamed about this?" Jacob said.

"Yes."

"You dreamed that we two sat and rested under this spruce, I suppose?"

"Yes."

"And about the quagmire there?"

"Yes."

"And about this knife, eh?" said Jacob, sneering, with yellow teeth in his dark and twisted face. "Rare, how true you dreamed, boy!"

Next day they arrested Jacob at an inn in town. At first he went wild and tried to stab the constable with a knife, but after they took him into the jailhouse and put him in chains, he calmed down.

He confessed to it all, and when the parson came to see him, he repented. When they executed him, his repentance was so great that they buried him in Christian ground.

But the boy was never found, and the parson couldn't pray over a quagmire, so it's hard to know—but it's strange to think about.

As for the miller, he became a little peculiar, so he had to go away. Later they had to put him in an asylum.

Translated by Hallberg Hallmundsson

ICELAND

INTRODUCTION

When King Harald the Fairhaired began his drive for the unification of Norway in the last quarter of the 9th century, he unintentionally touched off a migration which was to have far-reaching consequences. The many petty kings and noble-born farmers who were wont to be their own rulers found his "tyranny" intolerable and, rather than bow under the yoke of the ambitious monarch, left their old country for a new one, recently discovered far west in the Atlantic Ocean.

These were turbulent times. The Viking period was at its height. A century before, seafaring warriors from the North had begun raiding and plundering the British Isles. Subsequently, they had settled on the foreign shores and founded their own kingdoms. In these parts, there was no longer any room for the individualistic Vikings who were seeking new homes to replace the ones they were leaving in Norway. Their choice, therefore, was the remote Atlantic island.

Iceland is considered to have been fully settled in about sixty years. In 930, the Althing, which is the oldest parliament in existence, was established and a state founded. The political structure of this new state closely resembled that of a republic, but it had one serious flaw: no provision was made for an executive power. More than three hundred years later, this lack was one of the main reasons for the fall of this, the first republic of western Europe.

By the time Iceland was settled, poetry was already a well-established art in Norway, as we know from the records of Norse poetry in Old Icelandic books. The emigrants brought with them to their new home the cultural background and the literary tradition of their old country. Indeed, for reasons which have not yet been fully explained, this heritage seems to have been preserved and cultivated only in Iceland. Already in the 10th century, Icelandic poets, called skalds, had become the master craftsmen of their time, and for virtually three hundred years they monopolized the art of poetry in Scandinavia.

Like other medieval poets, the skalds sought to attach themselves to noble households. One after the other they sailed from Iceland in pursuit of honor at foreign courts. Their elaborate recitations, glorifying the heroic deeds and the generosity of Scandinavian kings, brought them both treasured gifts and privileged positions. In the wake of the poets came the saga-tellers whose narrative skill won them similar esteem as royal entertainers.

In the year 1000, the Christian religion was accepted in Iceland by an act of the Althing. Up until that time, the art of writing had been unknown in the country, so that both the poetry and the sagas as well as the law had to be committed to memory. Shortly after 1100, however, Icelandic scribes and authors began to write down the oral literature and to create new works. During the following two hundred years the great bulk of medieval Icelandic literature was put on parchment: scholarly works on history and grammar, laws, legends, sagas, and poetry.

Unlike European scholars of the time, Icelanders did not write in Latin, but in the vernacular. This has been ascribed to the fact that the Church in Iceland was not nearly as powerful as it was in the rest of Christendom. But whatever the reason, it was most fortunate. To the Icelandic writers, we owe not only the sagas, which "can be designated collectively as the sole original contribution of Scandinavia to world literature" (Peter Hallberg in *The Icelandic Saga*, 1962), but also a fairly clear picture of the early literatures of the other Scandinavian nations, whose language was, for all practical purposes, the same.

In 1262, after a long period of intense civil strife, the old republic came to an end, and the Icelanders, for reasons both political and economic, swore fealty to the Norwegian king. This proved to be an unhealthy turn of events for the Icelandic nation. A few decades later, a general decline could be observed in most areas of human activity, a decline that was further accelerated after Iceland, along with Norway, passed to the Danish crown in 1380. In literature, the change was marked. Instead of original saga-writing, scribes turned to mere copying and recopying of previous works, and except for sacred verse, poetry became dominated by *rímur*.

Rímur, a strictly Icelandic creation, were cycles of epic poems, usually based on sagas or translations of foreign romances and most often composed of various types of quatrains. They undoubtedly helped to preserve the Icelandic tongue, for they kept alive the old skaldic circumlocutions, or kennings. Often written with astounding metrical ingenuity, *rímur* (which literally means just "rhymes") tended to become little more than a mere technical feat: in form a skillful arrangement of rhymes and assonances, and in content a compilation of hackneyed phrases, frequently farfetched and obscure in meaning. The genre persisted until the late 19th century.

With the enforced establishment of the Lutheran Reformation in the 16th century, the Danish rulers tightened their hold on Iceland. The economic decline continued, especially after a trade monopoly was imposed by the crown in the early 17th century. Literature remained stagnant. Only occasionally did a good or outstanding poet appear to rise above the general level of mediocrity (see Pétursson, p. 213). Except for the systematic collection of Old Icelandic manuscripts and their removal to Denmark (where they still remain)[1], neither the Renaissance of the 17th century nor the Enlightenment of the 18th had any major effect on literature.

After the sweeping ideological changes following the American and French revolutions, Icelandic literature began to revive. The National-Romantic movement of the 19th century marks the beginning of the modern period. The Icelandic language was freed from the baroque Dano-German influence of the preceding centuries and emerged pure in the works of many distinguished poets (see Hallgrímsson, p. 218). Quite naturally, the works of

[1] In May, 1965, the Danish parliament passed for the second time (with general elections in between) a bill providing for the return to Iceland of a large part of the old manuscripts. The deliverance was to be made in the form of a gift from the Danish nation to the Icelanders. Although the law specified only those manuscripts bearing particularly upon Icelandic culture and national heritage, a group of Danish scholars, who had fiercely fought the bill, decided to place the matter before the Supreme Court in order to test the constitutionality of the law. Until such time as the court may pass a verdict favorable to the Icelanders, the manuscripts remain in Denmark.

the 19th century were largely nationalistic in spirit, concerned with Iceland's cultural and economic upheaval and with the struggle for independence.

Since the end of the last century, change and growth in the national literature has been rapid. To a large degree, it has followed the general European pattern, one modern school succeeding another. In the early part of the 20th century, some Icelandic writers achieved success writing in Danish. Their themes were generally Icelandic and their view Neo-Romantic (see Gunnarsson, p. 238). Others, especially during and after World War I, reacted strongly against the Neo-Romantic outlook and adopted Socialism (see Thórdarson, p. 248). Social satire and class struggle became prominent elements in their works, and during the depression years of the thirties this element became pre-eminent. At the same time, there was a growing awareness of the precarious international scene, the rise of militarism and the danger of a second war (see Laxness, p. 259). Icelandic writers had begun to look beyond their seagirt island to the wide world outside.

ANONYMOUS

(c. 900)

The medieval Icelandic collection called the *Poetic Edda*
does not contain many poems of a humorous nature, but one
of the finest of these is "The Lay of Thrym." The characters, sketched in skillful strokes, are vivid and clear, the
action moves swiftly, and the situation of a man donning
female garments is one which people in all ages have found
laughable. In this myth it is the warrior-god, Thor himself,
who resorts to disguise.

Scholars have widely disagreed about the dating of this
poem, but it seems reasonably safe to assume that it is about
one thousand years old. Like the bulk of medieval Icelandic
literature, the poem is of course anonymous.

In the present translation, no attempt has been made to
preserve the meter, much less the alliteration, of the original.
But it is hoped that this will not diminish the readers' en-
joyment.

The Lay of Thrym

Thor the Hurler   was hot with anger
when he awoke   and missed his hammer.
He shook his beard   and his hair bristled.
The Son of Earth[1]   searched about.

And these were the words   that Thor first spoke:
"Listen well, Loki,[2]   to what I tell you;
no one yet knows it,   neither on earth
nor heaven above: my hammer is stolen."

[1] One of many circumlocutions, or kennings, for Thor (see note 5, p. 43).
Other kennings of the same meaning used in this lay are "Odin's Son" and
"Husband of Sif."

[2] The evil force among the gods (see note 8, p. 43).

187

They went to the fair   Freyja's[3] abode,
And these were the words   that Thor first spoke:
"Will you, Freyja,   lend me your feather-coat
to help me win   my hammer back?"

Freyja said:
"I would give it to you   though it were of gold
and surrender it   though made of silver."

Then Loki flew,   the feather-coat whirring,
until he was out   of Asgard[4]
and arrived   at Jotunheim.

Thrym sat on a mound,   the Lord of Giants,
twisting gold leashes   for his dogs
and trimming the manes   of his horses.

Thrym said:
"What news of the gods?   What news of the elves?
Why have you come alone   to Jotunheim?"

Loki said:
"Bad news of the gods,   bad news of the elves.
Have you hidden   Hlorridi's[5] hammer?"

Thrym said:
"I have hidden   Hlorridi's hammer
eight leagues   below the earth.
No man will   ever regain it
unless he bring me   Freyja for wife."

Then Loki flew,   the feather-coat whirring,
until he was out   of Jotunheim
and arrived   at Asgard.
He met Thor   in the middle of the grounds,
and these were the words   that Thor first spoke:

"Did you harvest   from your hard work?
Tell me the news   while still in the air;
a sitting man often   forgets his story
and the sprawling one   speaks many lies."

[3] In Scandinavian mythology, the goddess of love.
[4] The realm of the gods. The Giants' domain was called Jotunheim.
[5] Another name for Thor.

Loki said:

"I have worked hard   and harvested, too.
Thrym has your hammer,   the Lord of Giants.
No man will   ever regain it
unless he bring him   Freyja for wife."

They went to meet   Freyja the fair,
and these were the words   that Thor first spoke:
"Dress yourself, Freyja,   in the bridal gown.
We two shall drive   to Jotunheim."

Then Freyja was angry   and snorted;
the hall of the gods   around her was shaken
(the great Brising necklace[6]   burst asunder):
"Never shall I be   so mad for men
that I drive with you   to Jotunheim."

Soon the gods were   all assembled
and the goddesses   all talking.
The mighty gods   discussed the means
by which Hlorridi's   hammer could be won.

Then said Heimdal,[7]   the whitest of gods,
and keen of foresight   like other Wanes·
"Let us dress Thor   in the bridal gown
and bedeck him with the great   Brising necklace.

"Let keys dangle   from his belt
and woman's garments   hang to his knees.
Place on his head   a pretty veil
and on his breast   broad stones."

Then said Thor,   the mighty god:
"The gods will call me   unmanly
if I dress   in the bridal gown."

---

[6] A priceless piece of jewelry, fashioned by the dwarfs and owned by Freyja.

[7] The watchman of the gods and the keeper of Bifrost (see note 2, p. 105). He was exceptionally well equipped for his post, for his auditory powers were so keen that he could hear the wool growing on the sheep and the grass upon the ground. Heimdal's genealogy is not clear. Some sources claim that he was the offspring of nine Giant maidens, others state that he was the son of Odin. In this lay, he seems to be regarded as one of the Wanes (see note 6, p. 43).

Then said Loki,   the son of Laufey:
"Be silent, Thor;   say no such words.
The Jotuns[8] will soon   abide in Asgard,
unless you   regain your hammer."

Then they dressed Thor   in the bridal gown
and bedecked him with the great   Brising necklace.

They let keys dangle   from his belt
and woman's garments   hang to his knees.
They placed on his head   a pretty veil
and on his breast   broad stones.

Then said Loki,   the son of Laufey:
"I shall go with you   as your slave-maiden.
We two shall drive   to Jotunheim."

Soon were the bucks[9]   driven home
and hurriedly harnessed   to run briskly.
The rocks splintered,   the earth burned with fire
as Odin's[10] Son drove   to Jotunheim.

Then said Thrym,   the Lord of Giants:
"Rise, Jotuns,   and cover the benches.
Now they are bringing me   Freyja for wife,
the daughter of Njord   from Noatun.[11]

"To my grounds go   gold-horned cows
and oxen all black,   the joy of the Jotun.
I have many treasures   and many jewels.
Freyja alone,   I think, is lacking."

[8] I.e., the Giants.
[9] The team that pulled Thor's chariot (see note 5, p. 43).
[10] Anglo-Saxon: Woden. The principal deity in Scandinavian mythology. He was the giver of victory, the chooser of the slain, and the wisest of all the gods. His palace, Valholl (or Valhalla), was the Paradise of all warriors slain in battle. There they would gather for drinking every night after fighting all day long. Odin's throne was called Hlidskjalf, and from here he could see over the whole world. He rode an eight-footed horse named Sleipnir, accompanied by his two wolves and his two ravens. He was a master of disguise, and his aliases were innumerable. He had two wives, Frigg and Earth. Among his sons were Balder, Thor, and Hod (Hother).
[11] The governor of wind, sea, and fire. He was one of the Wanes, and the father of Freyja. Noatun was his home.

Early in the evening   the guests assembled,
and ale was served   for the Jotuns.

❊ ❊ ❊ ❊ ❊ ❊ ❊ ❊ ❊ ❊ ❊ ❊

Thor alone ate an ox,   eight salmon,
and all the delicacies   that were for the women.
The Husband of Sif[12]   drank three tuns of mead.

Then said Thrym,   the Lord of Giants:
"Where was a bride seen   to bite more sharply?
I never saw a bride   whose bite was broader,
nor a maiden drink   more of the mead."

Sitting near by,   the wise slave-maiden
found the answer   to fit the Jotun:
"Freyja ate nothing   for eight nights,
so eager was she   for Jotunheim."

Wanting to kiss the bride   he bent under the veil,
but he fled back   to the end of the hall:
"Why are Freyja's   eyes so fierce?
Her eyes, it seems,   are like burning fire."

Sitting near by,   the wise slave-maiden
found the answer   to fit the Jotun:
"Freyja had no sleep   for eight nights,
so eager was she   for Jotunheim."

In stepped the Jotuns'   wretched sister,
bold enough to ask   for the bridal fee:
"Take the red rings   from your fingers
if you want   to win my love
(to win my love   and all my favor)."

Then said Thrym,   the Lord of Giants:
"Bring in the hammer   to hallow the bride.
Lay Mjolnir   on the lap of the maiden.
Hallow our bond   with the hand of Var."[13]

Hlorridi's heart   laughed in his breast
as he, the hard-minded,   recognized his hammer.

[12] A goddess, the wife of Thor.
[13] One of the minor goddesses, the protector of marital vows.

First he killed Thrym,   the Lord of Giants,
and he slew all   the Jotun folk.

He killed the Jotuns'   old sister,
who had asked for   the bridal fee.
She got strokes   instead of shillings
and hammer's blows   for abundance of rings.
(So Odin's Son   regained his hammer.)

Translated by Hallberg Hallmundsson

ANONYMOUS

(13th century)

There is ample evidence that the words of the disillusioned preacher of the Ecclesiastes still hold true: "There is no new thing under the sun." Who, for example, would have thought that "modern" psychology had been successfully employed by the belligerent kings of old Scandinavia? Yet, the method used by the 12th-century King Eystein to relieve the mind of his lovelorn skald is, basically, the same as the one to which the occupants of today's leather couches are subjected: the patient talks about his problems.

When measured by modern standards of short story writing, this little vignette by an unknown 13th-century author does not rank among the best. Yet, it is quite well written and its subject matter is unique in medieval Scandinavian literature.

The Lovelorn Skald

What I shall tell now will prove how excellent a man was King Eystein[1] (son of Magnus the Barefoot) in his sagacity, how faithful to his friends, and how imaginatively he sought the cause of their sorrow, if he saw them unhappy.

There was a man with him called Ivar, the son of Ingimund. He was by birth an Icelander of noble family, a wise man and a good poet. The king, as will be seen, held him in high esteem and affection.

Ivar had a brother named Thorfinn. He also went abroad to visit King Eystein and there, with the aid of his brother, secured the favors of many men. But Thorfinn was envious because he was not thought to be his brother's equal, but to be dependent

[1] Ruled Norway with his brothers during the first quarter of the 12th century. He died in 1123. His father, Magnus the Barefoot, had been King of Norway from 1093 to 1103.

upon him. He was, therefore, discontent at court, and prepared
to sail for Iceland. But before the brothers parted, Ivar said to
Thorfinn:

"I would like you, brother, to take a message for me to Iceland. You know a woman named Oddny Joansdottir. Bring her
my compliments and ask her for me not to marry, for she is the
woman whom I most desire."

After that, Thorfinn sailed to Iceland and had a favorable
wind. But he did not carry out his brother's errand, for he resolved to propose to Oddny on his own behalf, and she was
married to him. A little later Ivar came to Iceland and heard the
news. He felt that Thorfinn had behaved basely toward him and,
little content with his lot, he returned to Norway. There he
stayed again with King Eystein, well favored as before, but he
was withdrawn and quite unhappy.

When the king became aware of this, he summoned Ivar for
a private talk and asked him why he was so gloomy—"but when
you stayed with us before, your conversation was always a great
pleasure. Nor do I inquire because I do not know if I have
treated you as favorably as I did before. Besides, you are so wise
a man that you would not imagine what is not. Tell me what
it is that troubles you."

Ivar replied: "Sire, I cannot tell what it is."

The king said: "I will guess, then. Are there any men here
whom you do not like?"

"None, Sire," said Ivar.

The king said: "Do you feel that you are less honored by me
than you would like to be?"

He said that was not so.

The king said: "Have you seen any things in this country
which greatly displease you?"

He said that was not the case.

The king said: "Do you long to go to other courts?"

That had never entered his mind, he said.

"It is becoming difficult for us to guess now," said the king.
"Would you like to manage some property?"

He denied that.

"Are there any women here or in other countries whom you
miss?"

He replied: "That is right, Sire!"

The king said: "Do not distress yourself for that. If the woman is in Iceland, sail there as soon as spring arrives. I will give you both wealth and honor and therewith my sealed letter for the guardians of this woman. I do not expect there is any man who will not grant my friendly request or yield to my threat."

Ivar answered: "This cannot be done."

"That is impossible," said the king. "I will say further, that even if she is another man's wife, still I will get her for you if I want to."

Ivar answered: "The matter is not that easy, Sire. She is my brother's wife now."

"Then let us abandon that thought," said the king, "I see another way out. Immediately after Christmas I will attend many feasts. Come with me. You will meet many genteel women and if you choose one not of royal blood, I will give her to you."

Ivar replied: "Sire, the matter is still more difficult, for whenever I see fair and beautiful women, I am reminded of only one, and so my grief is ever more increased."

The king said: "Then I will give you management over some property as I offered you before, so that you may take pleasure in that."

He replied: "That will not ease my mind."

The king said: "Then I will give you money that you may go and trade in any country you like."

He said he did not want that.

Then the king said: "Now, this is becoming rather difficult. Yet, one never knows what might be best and I have sought as I can for a solution. Now there is only one thing left, and that one is of little worth compared to what I have offered you. But still, I do not know what might be best. From now on, come to me every day when the tables have been cleared, and if I have no important matters to attend, I will chat with you. We shall talk about this woman in every way that you wish and can think of. I will do this because sometimes it happens that one's grief becomes lighter if it is talked about. And let me add that you shall never leave me without a present."

Ivar replied: "This I want, Sire, and thank you kindly for asking me."

And so it came to pass that whenever the king did not have problems of state to deal with, he talked to Ivar about the woman. And this worked. Ivar was relieved of his sorrow sooner than could be hoped for and after a while he was again gay and merry and quite his former self. He remained with King Eystein and was well content.

Translated by Hallberg Hallmundsson

ANONYMOUS
(13th century)

Perhaps no book, save the Bible, has been read more frequently or regarded with more reverence by Icelanders than *Njál's Saga*. Chosen from the rich and multifarious literature of medieval Iceland, it is to them almost a holy book—and for good reasons. No other saga displays a greater variety of characters, a broader scope of dramatic events, or a deeper understanding of psychological complexity. Diverse as life itself, it offers us tragedy and comedy, good and evil, human frailty and firmness of character—and all shadings between. It is a magnificent example of literary genius.

One of the most delightful portraits in the saga is that of Björn of Mörk, the comic, chickenhearted braggart. The character development recalls that of Don Quixote. Like Cervantes, the author begins with sheer mockery. Yet, the character gradually wins our sympathy, for the author, having discovered this comic figure to be universal in his human failings, has grown extremely fond of his creation. In the end, our laughter is considerably dampened, having given way to pathos.

The story of Björn of Mörk constitutes chapters 148–52 of this great saga. When the narrative begins, the burning of Njál and his sons has already taken place, and the complicated legal proceedings that ensued are just about to be settled. The translation is slightly abridged.

Without a Brother Your Back Is Exposed

Thorgeir Skorargeir[1] rode home from the peace meeting, and Kári[2] asked how the reconciliation was coming. Thorgeir said

---

[1] Nephew of Njál.
[2] Njál's son-in-law. He was the only one who escaped from the fire, but his young son perished in the flames. Kári, bent on blood-revenge, refused to be reconciled with the Burners.

that they were fully reconciled. Kári took his horse and started to go.

"You need not ride away," said Thorgeir, "for it was a condition of our settlement that you could stay here whenever you wanted."

Kári said: "That shall not be, kinsman, for as soon as I slay someone, they will say that you are my accomplice and I do not want that to happen. But I should like you to take over my property and hold it in your name and that of my wife, Helga Njálsdóttir, and my three daughters. Then it will not be seized by my enemies."

Thorgeir agreed to Kári's request and lawfully took over his property.

After that Kári rode away. He had two horses, his weapons and his clothes, and some ready gold and silver. He rode west beyond Seljalandsmúli[3] and then up along Mark River,[4] up to Thórsmörk.[5] In those parts there are three farms which all are called Mörk. In the middle one there lived a man by the name of Björn who was nicknamed the White. His grandfather had been a freedman of Ásgerd, the mother of Njál and Holta-Thórir.[6] Björn had a wife called Valgerd Thorbrandsdóttir who was a cousin of Gunnar of Hlídarendi.[7] She had been married to Björn for the sake of his money and did not love him much, but they had children together. They had plenty of everything at the farm.

Björn was a braggart, but his wife did not like that. He was keen of sight and a swift runner.

Kári went there to sleep overnight and was received openhandedly by the couple. The next morning Kári said to Björn:

"I should like your permission to stay here, for I think I shall be well off, being with you. I should also like you to accompany me on my travels, for you are keen of sight and swift, and I think I can also rely on your courage."

---

[3] Mountain in southern Iceland.

[4] Icelandic: Markarfljót. Sometimes translated "Markfleet" (see "Gunnar's Holm," p. 218).

[5] Wooded district in southern Iceland, now uninhabited.

[6] Brother of Burnt Njál and father of Thorgeir Skorargeir.

[7] Principal hero in the first part of *Njál's Saga*. A great warrior, Gunnar incurred the enmity of many men. He was finally exiled for his slayings, but failed to comply with the sentence and was killed shortly afterward.

"Neither do I deny my keen sight nor my courage nor my other manly virtues," said Björn. "And yet, you have probably come here because you have nowhere else to go. But since you ask me, Kári," he added, "I shall not treat you like the common herd. I shall certainly give you whatever aid you ask."

His wife said: "The trolls take your boast and your big talk. You should not deceive yourself and Kári with your vain chatter. As for me, I shall be glad to give Kári food and other good things that may be of use to him. But do not rely on Björn's bravery, for I fear that it will prove different from his talk."

Björn said: "You have often reproached me, but I have such confidence in myself that I shall not yield to anyone. A proof of that is the fact that few men provoke me, because they dare not."

Kári remained there secretly for some time and few people knew of it. Generally, it was thought that Kári had gone to the north to see Gudmund the Mighty,[8] for Kári had made Björn tell his neighbors that he had met Kári heading north over Godaland and Gásasand to Gudmund the Mighty at Mödruvellir. This story was spread all around.

Meanwhile, Flosi[9] spoke to the Burners, his comrades: "It will no longer serve us to remain inactive. We must now think of going abroad and paying our fines and fulfilling the stipulations of the settlement as honorably as we can. Let each of us take a passage where he prefers."

They asked him to arrange it for them.

Flosi said: "We will ride east to Hornafjord,[10] for there is a ship laid up there, owned by a certain Eyjólf Nose from Trondheim.[11] He wants to marry, but cannot have the match made unless he settles here. We will buy the ship from him. It is large and will carry all of us."

That was the end of their talk.

Shortly after, they rode east without a halt until they reached Bjarnaness in Hornafjord. There they found Eyjólf, for he had

[8] Powerful chieftain who lived at Mödruvellir in northern Iceland. His story is treated in *Ljósvetninga Saga*.

[9] Leader of the Burners. He was a chieftain of Svínafell in southeastern Iceland.

[10] Inlet in the southeast whose hinterland is known by the same name.

[11] City in Norway.

stayed there during the winter. Flosi was well received and they all spent the night there. The next morning Flosi made the captain an offer for his ship, and after talking it over for a while they agreed on the terms.

Flosi rode back home to Svínafell and remained there for some time. He sent Kol Thorsteinsson and Gunnar Lambason[12] east to Hornafjord. They were to stay by the ship and prepare it for sailing, set up booths,[13] sack the merchandise, and get provisions.

As for the Sigfússons,[14] they told Flosi that they wanted to ride west to Fljótshlid. They had to see to their farms and bring back their goods and other necessities, they said—"for now we need not be on guard against Kári, if he is in the north."

Flosi replied: "I do not know how true they are, these stories about Kári's journeys. News has often proved to be false even though it has traveled less distance. It is my advice that a number of you go together, separate as little as possible, and guard yourselves as best you can."

After that the Sigfússons and those who were going with them prepared for their journey, eighteen altogether. Before they set off they embraced Flosi. He bid them farewell, predicting that he would never again see some of those who were riding away, but they did not let that dissuade them. They rode on their way to Skapt River Tongue, then over the mountains north of Eyjafjalla Glacier and down to Godaland through the woods to Thórsmörk.

Björn of Mörk saw the flock of riders and immediately went to meet them. They greeted each other amicably. The Sigfússons asked after Kári Sölmundarson.

"I met Kári," said Björn, "but that was a long time ago. He was riding north to Gásasand, bound to see Gudmund the Mighty. I had the feeling that he was rather afraid of you and that he felt himself very much alone."

---

[12] Two of the Burners. Both were later killed by Kári.

[13] Temporary sheds, normally made of turf, but roofed over with canvas. Sheds of this kind were common at trading and assembly places. At Thingvellir, the meeting place of the Althing, each chieftain had his own booth. The turf walls stood for years, and it was easy to put the canvas roof on, whenever the owner arrived for the assembly.

[14] Uncles of Höskuld. He had been slain by the sons of Njál, and it was in revenge for his death that Njál and his sons were burned.

Grani Gunnarsson[15] said: "He will be even more afraid of us later, as he will learn when he comes within striking distance. We do not fear him at all now that he is alone."

Ketil of Mörk[16] told him to keep quiet and stop the big talk. Björn asked when they would be going back.

"We will stay in Fljótshlíd about a week," they said, and they told him when they would be riding back over the mountains.

With that they parted.

The Sigfússons rode to their farms where they had a hearty welcome. They stayed there a week.

Björn went home and told Kári all about the movements and the plans of the Sigfússons. Kári said that he had in this showed him great faithfulness.

Björn said: "I should think that some others would betray you sooner than I, after I had promised you my faith and care."

His wife said: "You can be bad enough without being a traitor."

After this, Kári remained there for six days.

Kári said to Björn: "Let us now ride east over the mountains and down to Skapt River Tongue and travel secretly through Flosi's country, for I am going to get a passage abroad in Álftafjord."[17]

Björn said: "This is an extremely dangerous journey, and few would have the courage to make it but you and I."

His wife said: "If you support Kári badly, let me tell you that you will never come into my bed again, and my kinsmen will divide our property between us."

"It is more likely, woman," said Björn, "that you will have to rely on other grounds for a divorce, for I shall be my own best witness as to what a hero and champion I am in battle."

That day they rode into the mountains avoiding the beaten track. They went down into Skapt River Tongue and kept clear of all farms until they reached Skapt River. There they led their horses into a hollow, remaining always on the alert and camping in such a way that they could not be seen.

[15] Son of Gunnar of Hlídarendi. He was one of the Burners, although the sons of Njál had formerly helped avenge his father.

[16] One of the Sigfússons.

[17] Inlet in the east of Iceland.

Then Kári said to Björn: "What shall we do if they ride down at us from the mountain?"

"Aren't there two alternatives?" said Björn. "Either to ride away north along the slopes and let them ride by, or to wait and see if some of them lag behind and then attack them."

They discussed this at length, and at one moment Björn was all for fleeing as fast as he could, and at the next he wanted to stay and fight them. Kári thought it was all most amusing.

This same day the Sigfússons rode from home, as they had told Björn they would. They stopped at Mörk and knocked at the door, wanting to see Björn. His wife answered the door and greeted them. They asked for Björn at once. She said he had ridden down to Eyjafjöll[18] and east beyond Seljalandsmúli to Holt[19]—"for he has some money to collect there," she said.

They believed this, for they knew that Björn had money coming to him there. Then they rode east over the mountains without a halt until they reached Skapt River Tongue. They rode down along the river and rested where Kári and Björn had expected them to. There they split their forces. Ketil of Mörk rode east to Medalland with eight men, but the others lay down to sleep. Before they knew it, Kári and Björn were coming at them.

There was a little point of land protruding into the river. Kári went out there, asking Björn to stand behind him and not to put himself forward too far—"but be as useful to me as you can."

"I had never planned," said Björn, "to use another man as my shield, but as things stand now, you must have your way. With my wit and my swiftness I can still be of use to you and do no little harm to our foes."

Now all the others jumped up and ran at them. Módólf Ketilsson was the quickest of them, and he thrust a spear at Kári. Kári had his shield before him, and the spear hit it and stuck in it. By a twist of the shield Kári broke off the spear, then drew his sword and hacked at Módólf. At the same time Módólf struck back. Kári's sword hit Módólf's hilt, glanced off it on to his wrist, and cut off his hand which fell down together with the

---

[18] Mountain in southern Iceland. Sometimes translated "Isle Mountain" (see "Gunnar's Holm," p. 218).

[19] The home of Thorgeir Skorargeir.

sword. Then Kári's sword ran on into Módólf's side, in between his ribs. He fell instantly dead to the ground.

Grani Gunnarsson took a spear and hurled it at Kári, but Kári thrust down his shield so hard that it stood in the ground, and then, with his left hand, caught the spear in the air and sent it back at Grani. This done, he quickly caught up his shield again with the same hand. Grani had his shield before him. The spear flew through it, struck Grani in the thigh below the groin, and passed on into the ground, pinning him down. Grani could not rid himself of the spear until his companions pulled him away and laid him down under shields in a hollow.

A man stole up to Kári intending to cut off his leg. He managed to get to his side, but Björn hacked off his hand and then drew back behind Kári, so that they could do him no harm. Kári swept at the man with his sword, cutting him in two at the waist.

Then Lambi Sigurdarson ran at Kári and struck at him with his sword. Kári caught the blow flat on his shield, and the sword did not bite. Then he thrust his sword straight into Lambi's chest, so that it came out between his shoulder blades. That was Lambi's death.

Then Thorstein Gudleifsson ran up to Kári trying to get to his side. Kári caught sight of him and swept at him with his sword across the shoulders, so that he was severed in two. A little later he dealt a fatal blow to Gunnar of Skál, a good farmer.

As for Björn, he had wounded three men who had tried to do away with Kári, and yet he had never put himself forward so far as to be in any danger. Neither he nor Kári had suffered injuries in the encounter, but all the others who got away were wounded. Jumping on their horses they went galloping across Skapt River as fast as they could, while Kári and Björn shouted after them. They were so frightened that they stayed away from all farms and did not dare tell the news anywhere. They rode east to Skógahverfi and did not halt until they reached Svínafell. It was the general opinion that their journey had been a most shameful one.

Flosi was not at home when they arrived, and therefore no search was made for Kári and Björn.

Kári rode to Skál and declared himself responsible for the

slayings. He announced the death of the master of the house and the other four, and he also told of Grani's wound, advising them to bring him indoors if they wanted him to live. Björn let it be known that he had not cared to kill Grani, although he had deserved it, but he got the answer that few men lay rotting on account of him. Björn replied that he was now in a position to make as many of them rot as he chose. If that was the case, they said, things looked bad indeed.

After that Kári and Björn rode away.

Kári asked Björn: "What shall we do now?"

Björn said: "Do you think much depends on our being as wise as we can?"

"Yes," said Kári, "I certainly do."

"Then, to be brief about it," said Björn, "let us fool them all like stupid giants, pretending that we are riding north into the mountains. As soon as we are out of their sight behind the hills, we will turn and go down along Skapt River. If they try to follow us, we will hide wherever we think best while the search is at its height."

Kári said: "That is precisely what we will do and just what I had intended."

"You will find out," said Björn, "that I am no more lacking in wit than in bravery."

After that they rode as planned down along Skapt River to a point where the river branched in three directions. They turned down along the middle branch and did not rest until they reached a mire in Medalland called Kringlumýri. There was lava all around it. Kári asked Björn to watch their horses and stand guard—"for I am very sleepy myself," he said.

So Björn looked after the horses, but Kári lay down. He had slept but a short while when Björn woke him up again, having already brought up the horses.

Björn said: "You are indeed in need of my help. Any other man without my courage would have deserted you already, for here are your enemies coming at you. You had better get up and deal with them."

Kári went up to a projecting crag near by.

Björn said: "Where am I to stand now?"

Kári replied: "There are two alternatives. One is for you to stand behind me and use your shield to protect yourself, if it is of any help to you. The other is that you mount your horse and ride away as fast as you can."

"That I do not want to do," said Björn, "and there are many reasons for it. In the first place, if I ride away, some scathing tongues might say that I deserted you out of cowardice. In the second place, I know what a game they will think me, and so two or three of them will ride in pursuit of me, but I will be of no help to you then. I prefer, therefore, to stand by you and defend myself the same as you do."

Soon, some pack horses went past the mire, driven by three men.

Kári said: "These do not see us."

"Let them pass," said Björn.

Then the three rode by, but the remaining six rode straight at them, leapt from their horses, and attacked at once.

Glúm Hildisson was the first to reach them, and he thrust at Kári with a spear. Kári spun around on his heel, so that Glúm missed him and the thrust hit the rock. Björn saw this and at once hewed the head off the spear. Kári, before fully regaining his balance, hacked at Glúm. The sword hit him in the thigh and took off the leg. Glúm died immediately.

Then the sons of Thorfinn, Vébrand and Ásbrand, ran at Kári. Kári went against Vébrand and ran his sword through him, and then hewed both legs from under Ásbrand. At that moment, both Kári and Björn were wounded.

Ketil of Mörk then ran at Kári and thrust his spear at him, but Kári jerked up his leg and the spear hit the ground. Kári leapt on the shaft and broke it. Then he seized Ketil and held him. Björn came running up and wanted to kill him.

Kári said: "Leave him alone. Ketil shall have peace from me. And even though it may happen again that I have your life in my hands, Ketil, I shall never kill you."[20]

Ketil made no answer, but rode away after his companions, telling the news to those who did not know before. The men of the district were also told what had happened, and they imme-

---

[20] Ketil, like Kári, was married to one of Njál's daughters, so they were kinsmen by marriage.

diately gathered a great force and searched along all the rivers so far north that the trip took them three days. After that they turned back to their homes, but Ketil and his companions rode east to Svínafell and told the news.

Flosi showed no surprise. He said he was not sure whether this would be the end of it—"for of all those who now live in our country no one is the like of Kári."

As for Kári and Björn, they rode down to the sands. They led their horses to a knoll grown with lyme-grass and cut the grass for them to keep them from starving to death. Kári was so clever in his calculations that they rode away just when the others gave up the search for them. They rode up through the district during the night, and then over the mountains, following the same course as when they rode east. They did not rest until they reached Mörk.

Then Björn said to Kári: "Now you must be a real friend to me when I confront my wife, for she will not believe a word I say. As for me, everything depends on this meeting. Now repay me the good support I have given you."

"I will do that," said Kári.

After that they rode home to the farm. Björn's wife greeted them warmly and asked the news.

Björn replied: "Our troubles have rather increased, old girl."

She made no reply and just smiled. Then she said: "How did Björn prove to you, Kári?"

Kári replied: "Without a brother your back is exposed, and Björn proved fine to me. He took care of three men and is wounded himself. He was very helpful to me in every way he could be."

They remained there for three nights. Then they rode to Holt to see Thorgeir. They told him in private what had happened, for the news had not reached there before. Thorgeir thanked Kári, and it was clear that he was pleased at this. Yet, he asked Kári what there still was undone of what he intended to do.

Kári replied: "I intend to kill Gunnar Lambason and Kol Thorsteinsson, if I have the opportunity. Then we shall have killed fifteen men, including the five we two killed together. And now I want to ask a favor of you."

Thorgeir said he would grant him whatever he asked.

"I want you to take this man, Björn, who has been with me at the slayings, under your protection. Exchange his farm for him for a fully stocked one here near you, and keep him under your wing, so that no revenge may be turned upon him. For a chieftain such as you are, this should be easy to arrange."

"I will do that," said Thorgeir.

He gave Björn a fully stocked farm at Ásólfsskáli and himself took over the farm at Mörk. Thorgeir himself moved all of Björn's household and his stock to Ásólfsskáli. He further arranged a settlement for him and fully reconciled him with his enemies.

After that Björn was considered much more of a man than before.

Translated by Hallberg Hallmundsson

ANONYMOUS
(14th century)

Iceland, like the other Scandinavian countries, has her treasure house of medieval ballads. Some of these, it is true, are merely adaptations of foreign works, variations of which may be found in most European tongues. But others, though usually based on imported stories, are purely Icelandic and without corresponding versions in other languages. To this latter group belongs "The Ballad of Tristran," one of the most beautiful of ballads. Written by an anonymous master, probably sometime during the 14th century, it relates the final part of the well-known story in a style which is lucid and sincere, and with an impressive, fatalistic refrain that is typically Icelandic.

The Ballad of Tristran

She is as fair as the sun in morning hour.
Her eyes are like two violets;
never on them a shadow sets.
Happy the one who slumbers in her bower.

Tristran[1] fought the battle with
a heathen hound.
Many in that fray received
a bleeding wound.
—Fate had doomed them only to be parted.

The brave young man was carried home
upon his shield.
Many master-leaches offered
to have him healed.
—Fate had doomed them only to be parted.

[1] The spelling of the original Icelandic is here kept, although a more common form of the name is Tristan. Similarly, Isodd instead of Isolde.

"No healing will I accept"
—so did he swear—
"unless bright Isodd be my leach,
that lady fair."
—Fate had doomed them only to be parted.

Tristran sent his messengers
and vessels three:
"Tell fair Isodd I am wounded
woefully."
—Fate had doomed them only to be parted.

"Let her journey hither be
devised like this:
blue shall be the sails of the ships
on which she is."
—Fate had doomed them only to be parted.

The messengers came forth and spoke
their tidings grim.
"Bold Sir Tristran wishes you
to come to him."
—Fate had doomed them only to be parted.

Isodd went before her king
his grace to win:
"Will you give me leave to heal
Tristran, your kin?"
—Fate had doomed them only to be parted.

But the king right angrily
made this reply:
"What healing would he need, for he
is doomed to die."
—Fate had doomed them only to be parted.

Then fair Isodd gently spoke
his wrath to check,
and both her hands she placed around
her sovereign's neck.
—Fate had doomed them only to be parted.

The second time the king replied
and stroked his chin:
"I would give you leave to heal
Tristran, my kin.
—Fate had doomed them only to be parted.

"I would let you heal his wounds
right willingly,
if I knew you would return
still whole for me."
—Fate had doomed them only to be parted.

"God rules over my return;
His is the power.
I shall not forget my faith
upon this hour."
—Fate had doomed them only to be parted.

She wrapped herself in sable-skin
in sorrow drear,
and forth she went to board the vessels
at the pier.
—Fate had doomed them only to be parted.

"Hoist your sails and turn your prow,"
said the lady fair.
"God grant Tristran be not dead
when I come there."
—Fate had doomed them only to be parted.

"Let my journey thither be
devised so:
blue shall be the sails of the ship
on which I go."
—Fate had doomed them only to be parted.

Isodd the Fair set out to sea;
the sails were blue.
A favorable, steady wind
for three days blew.
—Fate had doomed them only to be parted.

Tristran asked Isodd the Black
—his wounds were sore—
"Do you see the ships come back
I sent before?"
—Fate had doomed them only to be parted.

Isodd the Black, she went without
and this she told:
"Black are the sails upon the ships
which I behold."
—Fate had doomed them only to be parted.

Isodd the Black, she came within
and told again:
"Black are the sails upon the ships
now sailing in."
—Fate had doomed them only to be parted.

Tristran turned to face the wall
in grief immersed.
Three miles' distance men could hear
his stout heart burst.
—Fate had doomed them only to be parted.

They cast the anchors on the shore;
the sand was dark.
First was Isodd, that lady fair,
to disembark.
—Fate had doomed them only to be parted.

The way was long,
but the street was broad;
ever she heard the tolling bells
as on she trod.
—Fate had doomed them only to be parted.

The way was narrow,
the street was long;
ever she heard the tolling bells
and a lovely song.
—Fate had doomed them only to be parted.

Isodd entered in the church
with a crowd of men.
Processionals were being sung
by clergymen.
—Fate had doomed them only to be parted.

The priests were standing, candles lit,
around the dead.
Isodd knelt beside the corpse
and bowed her head.
—Fate had doomed them only to be parted.

Many in this world must yet
with grief abide.
Isodd knelt beside the corpse
and there she died.
—Fate had doomed them only to be parted.

Isodd the Black a heavy breath
in anger drew,
as from the church she saw them bear
the corpses two.
—Fate had doomed them only to be parted.

She spoke the words of spite and woe
and swore on faith:
"You shall have no joy together,
even in death."
—Fate had doomed them only to be parted.

They were buried in the mold
that very day,
and on each side of the church
either lay.
—Fate had doomed them only to be parted.

Up from their graves two slender trees
with green leaves grew.
Over above the church's roof
met the two.
—Fate had doomed them only to be parted.

Translated by Hallberg Hallmundsson

HALLGRÍMUR PÉTURSSON
(1614–74)

The most outstanding hymnist Iceland has produced, Pétursson was in his youth somewhat of a problem child. He is
generally thought to have been expelled from the Cathedral
school at Hólar, whereupon he was sent to Copenhagen and
apprenticed to a blacksmith. Later, he studied theology and
became a minister at Saurbær in southwestern Iceland. Here,
stricken with leprosy, he composed the work upon which
his fame rests: *The Passion Hymns*, a series of fifty hymns re-
lating the passion of Christ. Characterized by a deeply religious and moral feeling, and rendered with utter simplicity,
the cycle soon became a favorite of the Icelandic people.
First published in its entirety in 1666, the work has been
printed more often than any other Icelandic book. The selection below is only a part of the last hymn.

"Just Like the Tender Flower". (1660) is also highly
revered by Icelanders. Even today, this hymn is sung at
every Icelandic funeral, as it has been for the last three hundred years.

Passion-Hymn 50

And so my spirit waits a space,
Lord Jesus, by Thy burial-place;
And as I watch beside Thy grave
    My soul grows brave,
And all death's terrors cease to rave.

Thou hast my dark offenses borne
Thyself, when in deep tortures torn;
Thou didst, dear Lord, endure for me
    Sin's penalty,
And set my heart rejoicing free.

My sins were buried in Thy tomb;
Thy righteousness now takes their room;
In the deep sea my vices vast
    Thy hand has cast
To lie forgot while ages last.

So now my pardon has been sealed,
And my repentant spirit healed:
Behold the dawn of righteousness
    Now breaks to bless
Man's trusting soul with happiness.

Thy death, O Jesus, here has slain
The lusts that in the body reign;
Thy grave has hid my errors quite
    From God's dread sight;
I strengthen in Thy risen might.

Thou seest the rock-tomb of my heart
Won by the Holy Spirit's art;
Faith's linen-cloth I leave to Thee,
    Who set me free,
Sweet with repentance' fragrancy.

In Thee I find all quiet rest.
Come Thou, O Jesus, to my breast,
And seal my life with faith and grace;
    Here show Thy face,
And make my heart Thy dwelling-place!

All glory, praise, and power be Thine!
May honor pure and wisdom shine
O Lord, in Thee, till 'mid the spheres
    Earth disappears—
Yea, down through everlasting years!

Translated by Watson Kirkconnell

Just Like the Tender Flower

Just like the tender flower
That grows beside the way
And greets the morning hour
In nature's bright array
Before the reaper falleth
To earth and withered lies,
So, when the Angel calleth,
Man, young or aged, dies.

All men to higher forces
Must answer soon or late.
On life's uncertain courses
They meet the selfsame fate.
And no one, poor or wealthy,
Can buy a day's reprieve.
When summoned, weak or healthy
Without delay must leave.

To me, as to the sower,
King Death, it seemeth plain,
Is like the tireless mower
Who cuts the standing grain.
And roses, reeds and sedges
Fall victims with the grass
Before the sickle's edges,
Wherever he may pass.

Mankind impatient races,
Nor ever hesitates,
Right into Death's embraces.
Beyond the grave awaits.
The multitudes keep milling
To one predestined goal;
And all, both loath and willing,
Must go—there's no parole.

For neither wealth nor station
Can turn grim Death aside.

No bribe nor supplication
Can buy a single stride.
All human power faileth
His lifted hand to still.
No prayer nor threat availeth
Against his iron will.

Men, ever dazed and fickle
With doubt, are unaware
How Death may swing his sickle,
On whom or when or where.
By one accustomed highway
Into this life we come,
But many a devious byway
Appears to lead therefrom.

Since Death all men arraigneth
And marketh for his own,
No sanguine hope remaineth
He'd spare but me alone.
And as we still inherit
Old Adam's native lust,
I know I truly merit
To be returned to dust.

No right the mind espouseth
Can make this life my own.
The soul my body houseth
Abides there as a loan.
The Lord, whene'er He pleaseth,
May claim His goods in fee;
And Death, His servant, seizeth
What hath been lent to me.

Content in Jesus' keeping
With meekness I obey,
Less worthy than the sleeping,
Whose last remains are clay.
Whene'er the call resoundeth,
No strength nor pleas avail;
But when the night surroundeth,
My courage shall not fail.

My Saviour now resideth
Amongst the pure Above
And in His wisdom guideth
All things with perfect love.
While ending death's fell power
He on the crosstree died,
That I might from that hour
For aye with Him abide.

He conquered death by dying
And set the spirit free.
While on His strength relying
No harm can come to me.
Though deep in earth be hidden
My bones, for timeless rest,
My soul will bide unchidden
In Heaven among the blest.

Christ dwells with me each minute.
In Him my trust I keep,
Outside the house or in it,
Awake or when asleep.
Without Him hope were sterile
And hollow in the strife.
Through Him, in spite of peril,
We gain eternal life.

In Jesus' name I'm biding;
In Jesus' name I'll die.
With Him my footsteps guiding
No fate can terrify.
So, Death, though I be near thee
And foul has been my guilt,
I say: "I do not fear thee.
Come hail whene'er thou wilt!"

Translated by Paul Bjarnason

JÓNAS HALLGRÍMSSON
(1807–45)

Somebody once said: "Nowhere has Iceland been loved better than in Copenhagen." Perhaps Hallgrímsson's life and poetry are the best proof of that statement, for it was in Copenhagen that he spent most of his adult life. While studying natural history at the university, he was caught up in the Romantic movement and the liberalism that swept Europe in the wake of the July revolution. In conjunction with three other young Icelanders, he founded *Fjölnir* (1835), a periodical designed to rouse his countrymen from their continuing lethargy. "Gunnar's Holm" (1838), based on a famous chapter of *Njál's Saga*, and "A Greeting" (1844) were originally both contributions to that periodical.

Hallgrímsson rejuvenated Icelandic poetry. From his pen, the Icelandic language emerged light and flexible after centuries of the heavy rigidity of *rímur* (see Introduction, p. 185). The pre-eminent features of his works are a love of Icelandic nature, a keen sense of beauty, and an impeccable diction. His seat as the best-loved Icelandic poet is uncontested.

Gunnar's Holm

The Sun beamed o'er the land of olden story,
And Isle Mountain peak of silver-gray
Was summit-golden—flushed with sun-set glory.
East towers that mighty shape of white array,
And cools its brow resplendent, which are laving
Cerulean-shining fountains of the day.
On a sheer precipice, a fall is raving
To spirits of the cliff. Beneath are hiding
Frosti and Fialar[1] golden treasures saving.

[1] Dwarfs known from Scandinavian mythology.

Against them Spire Mountains stand bestriding
The land; the sable cloak their limbs enclose
Is girt with green where dales begin dividing.
With helmet glittering like driven snows,
They see blue waters form melodious choirs,
At moot in meads where Crooked River flows,
Where little hearths that burn contented fires
Dot greening fields and lawns alive with flowers.
Northward arises Hecla[2] with her spires;
Above grim frost; below volcanic powers:
In depths unfathomed, fettered and repining,
Death and destruction dwell unnumbered hours.
Above those sable halls flash, mirror-shining,
Their raven-flinted roofs, aloft in air.
Thence smiles prosperity the land entwining;
For Markfleet[3] in the middle valley fair
Booms on the ear; and where its banks are bended,
Lie full-grown fields; and fertile meadows rare
Fling up their filmy tapestries extended,
Glittering, bud-bespangled, golden-spun.
The eagle wheels with yellow talons bended,
For fishes there in all the rivers run.
The birch-thrush, like a flash in air, is flying—
And rowan-tufted woods ring in the sun.
From the rich garth[4] high on the fell-side lying,
Are turned twain steeds unto the distant shore,
Whence breakers' echoes undulate in dying:
Not e'en still days becalm the billows' roar,
On Isle Sand, where mighty Ocean wages
His unremembered, elemental war.
A trusty hawser to the shore engages
A fair-built ship with sails furled to the mast;
A flashing ship's-head 'gainst all danger rages.
Thereon twain brothers are to leave, at last.
Their native shores with yearning they are viewing,
Estranged to be from them till years are past,
In alien countries days of exile ruing,
There never homefelt kindness to abide:

[2] Usually spelled Hekla. A famous volcano in Iceland. It is still active and last erupted in 1947.
[3] River in southern Iceland (see note 4, p. 198).
[4] I.e., farm.

Such is the cruel doom the fates were brewing.
A glorious hero now away doth ride:
Gunnar from lofty Lithend[5] is departed
Armed with his whetted halberd. By his side,
On sorrel steed, the selfsame road has started
One with a saber blue unto him bound;
There all might Coalbeard[6] ken,[7] the noble-hearted.
So both the brothers journey o'er the ground:
Swift-footed coursers hurry to the river.
And Coalbeard gazes out on Isle Sound,
But Gunnar, where the fells in hazes shiver.
The famous hero, then, with spirit glowing,
Neither at foes nor death doth blanch or quiver.
"Ne'er fields grew such unearthly beauty showing;
White flocks cloud meadows green in summer glory;
'Gainst yellow fields the reddened rose is blowing.
Here will I live, e'en should my grave be gory—
Live all days God may send. Now fare thee well
Brother and friend." So runs brave Gunnar's story,
Not e'en grim death could Gunnar's heart compel
To leave his homeland fair for lands asunder,
But ruthless foes, with treachery most fell,
Slew a good man and true in battle-thunder.
And yet his heartfelt story is a spell,
Where on the chilling sands I pace and wonder,
That in the wild surge furiously driving,
Still, Gunnar's Holm is verdantly surviving.
Where there of yore a fertile field was spread,
Cross River rolls in angry perturbation.
Sun-flushed, the olden mountains see, with dread,
The valley meadows suffer mutilation.
The dwarf is flown; the fairy-folk are dead;
Gloom in the land, and droops the weary nation;
A hidden hand still keeps in verdant glory,
The holm, where Gunnar turned in olden story.

Translated by Runólfur Fjeldsted

[5] Icelandic: Hlídarendi (see note 7, p. 198).
[6] Old Icelandic: Kolskeggr. The brother of Gunnar. Both were exiled, but Coalbeard went abroad and never returned to Iceland again.
[7] Archaism for "recognize."

A Greeting

The balmy South a gentle sigh releases—
And countless ocean billows, set in motion,
Breathe to my native shores the South's devotion—
Where strand and hillside feel the kindly breezes.

O give them all at home my fondest greeting,
O'er hill and dale a sacred peace and blessing.
Ye billows, pass the fisher's boat caressing;
And warm each youthful cheek, ye south winds fleeting.

Herald of springtime, thou whose instinct free
Pilots thy shiny wings through trackless spaces
To summer haunts to chant thy poems rare,

O greet most fondly, if you chance to see
An angel whom our native costume graces.
For that, dear throstle, is my sweetheart fair.

Translated by Jakobina Johnson

MATTHÍAS JOCHUMSSON
(1835–1920)

The Icelandic poet laureate of his time, Jochumsson spent most of his adult life in the service of the Lutheran Church. His unswerving faith and trust in God, though occasionally beset by pangs of doubt, found expression in some of the finest hymns in the Icelandic language. Included among his secular works are a vast number of poems that reveal a profound concern for his fellow men, several plays, and some masterful translations of Shakespeare, Byron, Tegnér and Ibsen.

"Millennial Hymn" was written in 1874 for the millennial celebration of the settlement of Iceland. It is now the country's national anthem. "Drift-Ice" (1888), printed here in a slightly abridged form, deals with a traditional enemy of the Icelandic people. "Farewell" was first printed in 1884.

It is worth noticing that Mr. Bjarnason, in his translation of "Millennial Hymn," has retained the alliteration of the original (see also the poems of Einar Benediktsson, pp. 232–237). Iceland is the only nation where old Germanic alliterative forms still survive.

Millennial Hymn
(Iceland's national anthem)

God of our land! Our land's great God!
With lauds we emblazon Thy all-holy name.
Time's legions, the centuries, shaped Thee a crown
From the suns in the heavens aflame.
One day at Thy throne is a thousand years,
A thousand years only a day:
A meek little flower of time with its tears
That trembles and passes away.
 Iceland's thousand years:

A meek little flower of time with its tears
That trembles and passes away.

O God above! On bended knees
We bare Thee, as children, our deep-burning soul.
We tender Thee, Father from age unto age,
As earnest, our holiest toll.
We stammer and thank Thee a thousand years,
And throng to Thy refuge as one.
We stammer and thank Thee with tremulous tears
The trials our destiny spun.
    Iceland's thousand years
Were the morning's deep-icicled measure of tears
That melt in the rays of the sun.

God of our land! Our land's great God!
Our life is a quivering, quivering reed.
Forsaken we perish. For prowess and faith
We pray unto Thee in our need.
O, be Thou each morning the life-giving light
To last through the day of our strife;
Our comfort and guard in the gloom of the night;
Our guide on the highway of life.
    Iceland's thousand years
Shall prosper the nation, repay all our tears
And purchase the kingdom of life.

Translated by Paul Bjarnason

Farewell

Farewell to thee mother. To far distant places
Destiny calls me away from thy side.
Keep me no longer. Thy parting embraces
Fondly detain, when I must not abide.

Cling not, O cling not, 'tis calling, 'tis calling,
Fear and ambition dividing my strength.
Dim grows the way while the darkness is falling,
Gone is my day if I tarry at length.

Fear not, O grieve not, though light be the measure
Valued in gold, which I carry from thee.
Safe in my heart is a limitless treasure—
Truth and devotion I learned at thy knee.

Lord in His mercy a gift has provided:
Undying hope, for the journey begun.
Mother, by cheer and by courage be guided,
Weep not or mourn for thy venturous son.

Translated by Jakobina Johnson

Drift-Ice

Art thou come, our country's ancient foeman?
Thou wert ever first, for no man
Nor the sun nor ship beat thee to shore.
Silver fleet thou sailst for our tormenting.
See the ice-hag, Helja,[1] unrelenting
Grasping for thy prow with dearth-plates hoar!
Mother sea with freezing belly bending
Tugs in terror at her icy chains,
Groans aghast to feel her entrails rending,
Like a monster in its travail-pains.

Where is Ocean? Where her belt of blue,
Bright, brushed with silver hue?
Art thou lost, beloved source of life?
Then from babies' lips the breast is taken,
Bear and fox both scent the snow forsaken,
Hungry gnaw old carrion without strife.
Peace and prowess and fair days are ended;
Valor, strength, and genius lost from sight;
All our darkest dreads are now transcended;
Death comes, and the dead god's night.

Thou, sea-ice, hast all that can dismay us,
All that seeks to hurt and slay us.

[1] I.e., Hel (see note 2, p. 105).

Should we lack the heat of fortitude,
Fornjot's[2] pale and icy wraith would hasten
Fetters of a thousand years to fasten;
Deeply hast thou drunk of Iceland's blood.
Whence art thou? For no one knows thy dwelling;
None knows where thy home and kindred are;
Outer, inner warmth thou art dispelling—
Thou art surely from afar.

Deep within my heart thy breath of hating
Poison-cold is penetrating,
Round life's root the Midgard-serpent[3] gnaws.
Countless thousand shafts of lights are shaking,
Countless thousand rays of radiance quaking,
Frightened at the darkness of thy jaws.
In the sun the lava-fields grow livid;
Mighty birches fear the levin-storm;
But thy savage grows still more vivid,
Nothing can do thee harm.

Lodestone-land, what sprites in thee conspire,
Bright with the flames of heaven's ire,
Round the North's white glacial throne?
Do the grim Gray Sisters[4] wait to shut
Gasping mouths they doom with death to glut?
Bears their wheel our fortune with a groan?
Is a rune there carved upon the rock
In the tongue of gods, a mystic key?
Do vast symbols in that sky unlock
All the riddles of earth's mystery?

No one answers. For thy deeps are clouded,
With death's mantle darkly shrouded,
Hid with life's mysterious veil of grace.

---

[2] In Scandinavian mythology, a nature deity, the father of Lér, Logi, and Kári, i.e., "Sea," "Fire," and "Wind."

[3] Hideous venomous serpent and son of Loki. The gods threw him into the sea where he grew to such an extent that he could encircle the earth and bite his own tail. In Scandinavian mythology, the earth, or the abode of men, was called Midgard.

[4] The norns, or the fates. The three most prominent ones were called Urd ("Past"), Verdandi ("Present"), and Skuld ("Future").

Surely thou hast some great undertaking
Ordered for thy thousand years of waking;
But the ways of God we cannot trace.
Does thy power, perhaps, press toward revealing
Silent life and fire's hidden breath,
Touching sterile foam to health and healing,
Keeper of life and king of death?

Translated by Watson Kirkconnell

STEPHAN G. STEPHANSSON
(1853–1927)

Eminent critics have called Stephansson Canada's finest poet. How much more he could have become if circumstances had been favorable, one cannot say.

He was born into a family of poor Icelandic farmers. At the age of twenty, he immigrated with his parents to the United States, experiencing there the hardships of the pioneer farmer. Having twice broken new land, he left the United States to pioneer for a third time in Canada, where he finally settled.

Stephansson's life was one of the wonders of human endeavor. He never attended school, yet was a widely read man. A farmer all his life, he was nevertheless a cosmopolite in thought. He tilled his land during the day and at night wrote voluminous amounts of poetry, the collection of which he aptly named *Andvökur*, or "Wakeful Nights" (vols. I–VI, 1909–38).

Written exclusively in Icelandic, Stephansson's poetry is always thought-provoking. Typical in this respect are "Protest of the Unknown Soldier" (1921) and "When I Was an Editor" (first printed in 1923). Others, like "From a Speech on 'Icelanders' Day'" (1904), show his reverence for the land of his birth. Aware that his love was divided between Iceland and his adopted country, he came to the wistful conclusion that he "no longer possessed any fatherland."

From a Speech on
"Icelanders' Day"

Though you wayfaring wander
all the world to explore,
yet your mind has been molded
by your motherland's shore,

kin of ice and volcano,
child of stream and defile,
daught'r of lava and ling-moor,
son of inlet and isle.

Over earth, over heaven,
though your heart may aspire,
yet will cascades and mountains
stud the land you desire.
In the ocean eternal
lies your isle, girt with brine:
nightless world of spring's wonders
where the grand vistas shine.

For the land of your wishes
has an Icelandic form,
but the rocks grow with flowers
and the glaciers are warm,
kin of ice and volcano,
child of stream and defile,
daught'r of lava and ling-moor,
son of inlet and isle.

Translated by Hallberg Hallmundsson

Lone Peak

Lone Peak[1] rears his bust to the beautiful sky,
And the bulrushes gaze on astounded.
The copsewood refuses to clamber so high
And the creepers lose footing around it.
And though the cold blasts ever beat without ruth
On his brow, in the strife he engages,
Unconquered he stands, as if courage and truth
Were carved from the rock of the ages.

Translated by Paul Bjarnason

[1] Icelandic: Einbúi. Mountain in Iceland.

When I Was an Editor

So maudlin, with pity and pathos I stood
If someone who erred got the lashes;
If hanged, I'd weep over the ashes.
With vocal dispraise such injustice I viewed.

But somehow as soon as the war-craze ensued,
When slaughter en masse was the popular mood
And corpses all over the planet were strewed,
With dumb indecision I stood.

For there was the problem of friendship and food
—One's sympathies nobody cashes.
To dampen my conscience-clashes
The cracks in my honor I artfully glued
With unctuous lies that I hastily brewed
—And cheered just as loud as I could.

Translated by Paul Bjarnason

Protest of the Unknown Soldier

Nameless, I am unbearably tired
of repeated funeral processions.
If I am or if I ever have been
any Self, it was mislaid entirely
by these endless burials and wanderings.

Heads of states habitually borrow
my remains, one lending to another—
that is to say, if anything except this
namelessness remains, besides the question
who I was and what I really accomplished.

I have had a funeral in Paris,
a funeral in London—now I have been
entombed in Washington with highest honors.
I don't know yet where I'll next be buried—
unlikely my wanderings are over.

Kings with drooping heads, their hats in hand, have
slowly marched behind my hearse, escorted
by distinguished generals, peers, and ladies.
I have been the victim of incessant
flow of words by priests and bishops—and the
eloquence of long-winded orators,
those, you know, who talk best about nothing.

This is also one of many reasons
why I hold the view that I was never
anything at all—except those funerals.
Statesmen, international intriguers,
granddukes pluck their medals and their crosses
off their chests to scatter them all over me.

I am tired—unbearably tired,
stooping, trudging on under their crosses,
eternally on march to my own burial.

And to be subjected to this ever
more, I must refuse. If I am anything.

Translated by Hallberg Hallmundsson

Question and Answer

"Wouldn't you, Stephan, like to travel about
the battlefields in Europe when the war is over?"

Though I traveled free of fare,
it would disgust me to go there
where mankind's greatest follies were
committed—to the world's despair.

Translated by Hallberg Hallmundsson

At Close of Day

When sunny hills are draped in velvet shadows
By summer night
And Lady moon hangs out among the tree tops

Her crescent bright;
And when the welcome evening breeze is cooling
My fevered brow
And all who toil rejoice that blessed night time
Approaches now—

When out among the herds the bells are tinkling
Now clear, now faint,
As in the woods a lonely bird is voicing
His evening plaint;
The wandering breeze with drowsy accent whispers
Its melody,
And from the brook the joyous cries of children
Are borne to me;

When fields of grain have caught a gleam of moonlight
But dark the ground—
A pearl-gray mist has filled to overflowing
The dells around;
Some golden stars are peeping forth to brighten
The eastern wood—
Then I am resting out upon my doorstep
In nature's mood.

My heart reflects the rest and sweet rejoicing
Around, above;
Where beauty is the universal language
And peace and love.
Where all things seem to join in benediction
And prayers for me;
Where at night's loving heart both earth and heaven
At rest I see.

And when the last of all my days is over,
The last page turned—
And, whatsoever shall be deemed in wages
That I have earned,
In such a mood I hope to be composing
My sweetest lay—
And then extend my hand to all the world
And pass away.

Translated by Jakobina Johnson

EINAR BENEDIKTSSON
(1864–1940)

Balancing, if not reconciling, the odd elements of financial speculation and mystic pantheism, Einar Benediktsson had bold dreams concerning his country's physical resources as well as its cultural future. Thus, he spent many years abroad trying to win support and capital for his plans of Icelandic industrialization. Many anecdotes from these years tell of the charming wit and the financial pranks he occasionally employed in his dealings with European capitalists. For example, he was supposed even to have persuaded one of them to buy the aurora borealis!

As a poet Einar Benediktsson was one of the towering figures of modern Icelandic literature. His ponderous, ornate style generally makes his poetry rather heavy reading, but perfectionist that he was, ever polishing his form and diction, he frequently managed to combine beautiful lyricism with a deep-felt pantheistic view of life and the universe.

Of the selections printed here, "The Northern Lights" is from his first volume, *Sögur og kvædi* ("Stories and Poems"), 1897. All the others are from his fourth book, *Vogar* ("Billows"), published in 1921.

The Northern Lights

Has man ever gazed on a grander sight
Than the gods' high realm in a blaze of glory,
Resplendent with torches in tier and story?
—What toper could revel on such a night?
Like a maiden the earth is without a blight
In its alban kirtle of frosted roses.
Each granule of sand is a cinder, bright.
Ensilvered the winding brooklet dozes.
The Arctic at night is aluster with light
That the living aurora imposes.

From the highest plane to the somber sea
The scene is enacted without a shutter.
Each sylph asplutter with flounce aflutter
Is falling and rising in ecstasy.
Some hand with its fingers of filigree
The fiery ocean of ether splashes.
From here below to the life-to-be
We look amazed while the drama flashes.
And the glaciers on high are agaze with each eye
That gleams in their crystal sashes.

In the light of that wonder our problems appear
So petty and mean that they vanish unbidden.
Though roughly I'm chidden my rancor is hidden;
At rest with the masses, no slight can sear,
For the vaulting above is so bright and clear.
Each blazing star is a magic pinion.
It lifts our hopes to a higher sphere,
Where Heaven recharges each lowly minion.
We are sensing tonight and asserting our right
As servants in Light's dominion.

How vast is the infinite ocean of space
And eerie the barks that its waters are plying!
Each skipper on high to a haven is flying,
Whether he veers or goes onward apace.
But blind is the urge that the eye obeys
And the author his light in the dark composes.
With bended knees and a burning face
We bide at the wall the temple encloses.
But into the garden the gateway is barred,
And God in His sanctum reposes.

Translated by Paul Bjarnason

Wave-Life

He lives who created a lay that survives.
He's lost who rose dumb from the Muse's table;
Who knelt at its head with his heart in gyves,
With a hapless mind and a tongue unable.

The soul is akin to the seas we ply.
Each swell resembles a midget ocean:
Dead if it's still; in the storm 'tis high,
And streams along with a sounding motion.

Billowing surge! Thou hast life; and thy lay,
Though lost, from the core of thy heart was streaming.
Thy force on the sands of the silent bay
Subsided, but firstly thy crest was gleaming.
Ocean's songstress, thou drankest deep
The drafts that rose from thy welling fountain.
The land re-echoed thy sounding sweep,
That sank apace, but aimed at the mountain.

The Morning opens her golden gate.
Her gleaming face at the sash is peering.
The grassy liths for her gaze await.
The gloomy brow of the peak is clearing.
In the ocean's shimmering surface-tide
The Sun-steed with gory curb-rein glasses.
The haunts, where of yore I yearned, abide.
Beyond, in a vision, my dreamland passes.

My heart is an ocean of deep desire
For the day of light that has no ending;
That gathered my song—as my soul afire
Absorbs the force that the strand is bending.
My shackled mind is impatient, pent,
Impounded fast by the sea's dominion.
And what is the eagle's high ascent
To a human soul equipped with a pinion?

I feel in the depths of my soul a surge
That seeks away from this life, so hollow.
The soundless tide of my inmost urge
Is an ardent prayer that I long to follow.
To send a strain through the starry zone,
A stilly wave or a mute oration—
To rise at the foot of the Father's throne
And face the hosts, is my aspiration.

Translated by Paul Bjarnason

From "Starkad's Soliloquy"

'Twas dawn and the birds in the branches sang.
From the bitter night to the street I wandered.
A tattered swain from the sewer sprang.
I saw he had slept on a stone, and pondered.
I threw him a coin where he crept in the sand.
He cringed; then smiled through his furtive lashes,
As a gleam illumined the gold in his hand—
Abundance in his; in mine but ashes.

The bit looms large in the realm of grief,
Where Mishap and Luck with the Fates are trading.
For seldom may two hold the same belief,
Though the selfsame mask they are both parading.
And yet, though the world may be hard of heart,
Though the haughty win and the Right must cower,
Misfortune that here played a hapless part
In Heaven amasses a princely dower.

A smile may transmute the dusk into day,
As a drop may change the wine in a beaker.
A cross remark drives kindness away;
So care should govern the tongue of the speaker.
A hidden cord in the breast may break
If bitter words, without cause, are spoken.
You cannot erase the wrongs you make.
No ruing can mend a heart that is broken.

A word, just a move: in a moment's space
Immutable trends in our lives are grounded,
Through an artless pun or a pointed phrase
We pass—by listening walls surrounded.
How wise are we children? A cheerful lay
Or a cup may serve when the mead is waning.
O what says the Master? . . . .
. . . . In mute array
The morning sun his spears is training.

Translated by Paul Bjarnason

My Mother

Mother, I've sailed o'er the seas afoam.
To southward the lands are fading.
A scarf for my isle with the icy dome
The afterglow is braiding.
At last my ship is heading for home.
My heart is the bill of lading.

From stolid crowds that the streets infest
I steer for thy spires so conely.
I find no men where the mobs congest,
Nor music in noises only;
But he is the welcome and willing guest
Who visits himself when lonely.

Abroad in the storm and the times that try
Thy truths with my heart were pleading.
I dreamt of the past, when I played thee nigh,
And peacefully thou wert reading.
If seas were calm or the surf ran high
My soul on the dream was feeding.

At every step along Bifrost[1] burned
A beacon our minds erected.
From thee, with pleasure and love, I learned
The language our isle protected;
For that's where the gods, in trust, interned
Each tone that a thought affected.

We heard in the lilt of her lullabies
The language our fancy teaches
And the ages honed from its hardy guise,
'Mid hills and on sandy reaches.
From nature's morning to reason's rise
It wrote on the manless beaches.

The rhymes I loved and the lullabies,
Though lost, with my dreams are blending.

[1] In Scandinavian mythology, the bridge connecting heaven and earth
(see note 2, p. 105).

A mountain swan, in my fancy, flies
Afar, with his song unending.
And a mother stands by the ocean-ice,
Her arms to her son extending.

Aloft the wings of thy faith have flown
Where the frosted rose was lying.
The swell of thy first young force was thrown
When Fate each heart was trying.
—No keener pain in my soul was sown
Than to see that thy hopes were dying.

Whenever I flee with a fallen crest
Thy faith new courage giveth.
The burdens lift at thy hope's behest.
Thy hardy spirit liveth.
And thine, on the earth, is the only breast
That all my sins forgiveth.

Wherever my ship on the billows swung,
In search of a deeper learning,
Unmarred forever thy image clung
And into my soul was burning.
Thou placed my hand on thy harp, bestrung,
When my heart for the muse was yearning.

Thy life and the songs that my soul regaled
Are seas that the minds are laving.
Mother, my lines that so long had failed
At last on thy shield are graven—
The reason I boarded, the reason I sailed,
The reason I'm back to the haven.

Translated by Paul Bjarnason

GUNNAR GUNNARSSON
(1889–   )

One of many Icelandic writers to seek fame and fortune abroad, Gunnarsson left Iceland before he was twenty to become a novelist in Denmark. Three decades later, one of the best-known Scandinavian writers, he returned to his native country and since 1949 has made his home in Reykjavík.

Gunnarsson has concentrated on Icelandic themes, mostly historic and autobiographical. As a recorder of the strivings of men, and of their futile struggle with fate, he has not many peers. His tremendous vitality and his robust, colorful language combined with a consummate narrative skill have resulted in the creation of some of the most vivid characters in Icelandic literature.

"Father and Son" was originally published (1916) in the Icelandic magazine *Eimreidin,* but the present version, slightly changed, is from Gunnarsson's collected works published in 1951.

Father and Son

The two of them lived just outside the village. They were both called Snjolfur, and they were usually distinguished as old Snjolfur, and little Snjolfur. They themselves, however, addressed each other only as Snjolfur. This was a habit of long standing: it may be that, having the same name, they felt themselves bound still more firmly together by using it unqualified in this way. Old Snjolfur was something over fifty, little Snjolfur only just over twelve.

They were close together, the pair of them—each felt lost without the other. It had been like that ever since little Snjolfur could remember. His father could look further back. He remembered that thirteen years ago he had lived on his farm within easy riding distance of the village; he had a good wife and three sturdy and hopeful children.

Then his luck turned and one disaster after another struck him. His sheep went down with the pest, his cattle died of anthrax and other diseases. Then the children got whooping cough and all three died, close enough together to lie in one grave. To pay his debts Snjolfur had to give up his farm and sell the land. Then he bought the land on the Point just outside the village, knocked up a cabin divided into two by a partition, and a fish-drying shed. When that was done, there was enough left to buy a cockleshell of a boat. This was the sum of his possessions.

It was a poor and dismal life they led there, Snjolfur and his wife. They were both used to hard work, but they had had no experience of privation and constant care for the morrow. Most days it meant putting to sea if they were to eat, and it was not every night they went to bed with a full stomach. There was little enough left over for clothing and comfort.

Snjolfur's wife worked at fish-drying for the factor[1] in the summer months, but good drying days could not be counted on and the money was not much. She lived just long enough to bring little Snjolfur into the world, and the last thing she did was to decide his name. From then on, father and son lived alone in the cabin.

Little Snjolfur had vague memories of times of desperate misery. He had to stay at home through days of unrelieved torment and agony. There had been no one to look after him while he was too small to go off in the boat with his father, and old Snjolfur was forced to tie the boy to the bedpost to keep him out of danger in his absence. Old Snjolfur could not sit at home all the time: he had to get something to put in the pot.

The boy had more vivid memories of happier times, smiling summer days on a sea glittering in the sunshine. He remembered sitting in the stern and watching his father pulling in the gleaming fish. But even those times were mingled with bitterness, for there were days when the sky wept and old Snjolfur rowed out alone.

[1] Agent who transacts business for another. The use of the term in Icelandic originated in the time of the Danish trade monopoly (see Introduction, p. 185).

But in time little Snjolfur grew big enough to go off with his father, whatever the weather. From then on they contentedly shared most days and every night: neither could be without the other for more than a minute. If one of them stirred in his sleep, the other was awake on the instant; and if one could not get to sleep, the other did not close his eyes either.

One might think that it was because they had a lot to talk about that they were so wrapped up in each other. But that was not so. They knew each other so well and their mutual confidence was so complete that words were unnecessary. For days on end no more than scattered phrases fell between them; they were as well content to be silent together as to be talking together. The one need only look at the other to make himself understood.

Among the few words that passed between them, however, was one sentence that came up again and again—when old Snjolfur was talking to his son. His words were:

"The point is to pay your debts to everybody, not to owe anybody anything, and trust in Providence."

In fact, father and son together preferred to live on the edge of starvation rather than buy anything for which they could not pay on the spot. And they tacked together bits of old sacking and patched and patched them so as to cover their nakedness, unburdened by debt.

Most of their neighbors were in debt to some extent; some of them only repaid the factor at odd times, and they never repaid the whole amount. But as far as little Snjolfur knew, he and his father had never owed a penny to anyone. Before his time, his father had been on the factor's books like everyone else, but that was not a thing he spoke much about and little Snjolfur knew nothing of those dealings.

It was essential for the two of them to see they had supplies to last them through the winter, when for many days gales or heavy seas made fishing impossible. The fish that had to last them through the winter was either dried or salted; what they felt they could spare was sold, so that there might be a little ready money in the house against the arrival of winter. There was rarely anything left, and sometimes the cupboard was bare before the end of the winter; whatever was eatable had been eaten by the time spring came on, and most often father and son knew what it was like to go hungry. Whenever the weather was fit, they put off in their boat but often rowed back empty-handed or with one skinny flatfish in the bottom. This did not affect their outlook. They never complained; they bore the burden of distress, heavy as it was, with the same even temper as they showed in the face of good fortune on the rare occasions it smiled on them; in this, as in everything else, they were in harmony. For them there was always comfort enough in the hope that, if they ate nothing today, God would send them a meal tomorrow—or the next day. The advancing spring found them pale and hollow-cheeked, plagued by bad dreams, so that night after night they lay awake together. And one such spring, a spring moreover that had been colder and stormier than usual, with hardly a single day of decent weather, evil chance paid another visit to old Snjolfur's home.

Early one morning a snowslip landed on the cabin on the Point, burying both father and son. By some inexplicable means little Snjolfur managed to scratch his way out of the drift. As soon as he realized that for all his efforts he could not dig his father out single-handed, he raced off to the village and got people out of their beds. Help came too late—the old man was suffocated when they finally reached him through the snow.

For the time being his body was laid on a flat boulder in the shelter of a shallow cave in the cliffside nearby—later they would bring a sledge to fetch him into the village. For a long time little Snjolfur stood by old Snjolfur and stroked his white hair; he murmured something as he did it, but no one heard what he said. But he did not cry and he showed no dismay. The men with the snowshovels agreed that he was a strange lad, with not a tear for his father's death, and they were half-inclined to dislike him for it. "He's a hard one!" they said, but not in admiration. You can carry things too far.

It was perhaps because of this that no one paid any further attention to little Snjolfur. When the rescue party and the people who had come out of mere curiosity made their way back for a bite of breakfast and a sledge for the body, the boy was left alone on the Point.

The snowslip had shifted the cabin and it was all twisted and smashed; posts missing their laths stuck up out of the snow, tools and household gear were visible here and there—when he laid hold of them, they were as if bonded into the snow. Snjolfur wandered down to the shore with the idea of seeing what had become of the boat. When he saw with what cold glee the waves were playing with its shattered fragments amongst the lumpy masses of snow below high-water mark, his frown deepened, but he did not say anything.

He did not stay long on the shore this time. When he got back to the cave, he sat down wearily on the rock beside his dead father. It's a poor lookout, he thought; he might have sold the boat if it hadn't been smashed—somewhere he had to get enough to pay for the funeral. Snjolfur had always said it was essential to have enough to cover your own funeral—there was no greater or more irredeemable disgrace than to be slipped into the ground at the expense of the parish. Fortunately his prospects weren't so bad, he had said. They could both die peacefully whenever the time came—there was the cabin, the boat, the tools and other gear, and finally the land itself—these would surely fetch enough to meet the cost of coffin and funeral service, as well as a cup of coffee for anyone who would put himself out so far as to accept their hospitality on that occasion. But now, contrary to custom, his father had not proved an oracle—he was dead and everything else had gone with him—except the land on the Point. And how was that to be turned into cash when there was no cabin on it? He would probably have to starve to death himself. Wouldn't it be simplest to run down to the shore and throw himself in the sea? But—then both he and his father would have to be buried by the parish. There were only his shoulders to carry the burden. If they both rested in a shameful grave, it would be his fault—he hadn't the heart to do it.

Little Snjolfur's head hurt with all this hard thinking. He felt he wanted to give up and let things slide. But how can a man give up when he has nowhere to live? It would be cold spending the night out here in the open.

The boy thought this out. Then he began to drag posts, pieces of rafter and other wreckage over to the cave. He laid the longest pieces sloping against the cave mouth—he badly wanted his father to be within four walls—covered them over and filled the gaps with bits of sailcloth and anything else handy, and finished by shoveling snow up over the whole structure. Before long it was rather better in the cave than out-of-doors, though the most important thing was to have Snjolfur with him for his last days above ground—it might be a week or more. It was no easy matter to make a coffin and dig out frozen ground. It would certainly be a poor coffin if he had to make it himself.

When little Snjolfur had finished making his shelter, he crept inside and sat down with outstretched legs close to his father. By this time the boy was tired out and sleepy. He was on the point of dropping off, when he remembered that he had still not decided how to pay for the funeral. He was wide awake again at once. That problem had to be solved without more ado —and suddenly he saw a gleam of hope—it wasn't so unattainable after all—he might meet the cost of the funeral and maintain himself into the bargain, at any rate for a start. His drowsiness fell from him, he slipped out of the cave and strode off toward the village.

He went straight along the street in the direction of the store, looking neither to right nor left, heedless of the unfriendly glances of the villagers. "Wretched boy—he didn't even cry when his father died!" were the words of those respectable, generous-hearted and high-minded folk.

When little Snjolfur got to the factor's house, he went straight into the store and asked if he might speak to the master. The storeman stared and lingered before finally shuffling to the door of the office and knocking. In a moment the door was half opened by the factor himself, who, when he caught sight of little Snjolfur and heard that he wanted to speak to him, turned to him again and, after looking him up and down, invited him in.

Little Snjolfur put his cap on the counter and did not wait to be asked twice.

"Well, young man?" said the factor.

The youngster nearly lost heart completely, but he screwed himself up and inquired diffidently whether the factor knew that there were unusually good landing facilities out on the Point.

"It is much worse in your landing place than it is in ours out there."

The factor had to smile at the gravity and spirit of the boy—he confessed that he had heard it spoken of.

Then little Snjolfur came to the heart of the matter—if he let out the use of the landing place in the Point to the factor for the coming summer—how much would he be willing to pay to have his Faroese crew land their catches there? Only for the coming summer, mind!

"Wouldn't it be more straightforward if I bought the Point from you?" asked the factor, doing his best to conceal his amusement.

Little Snjolfur stoutly rejected this suggestion—he didn't want that. "Then I have no home—if I sell the Point, I mean."

The factor tried to get him to see that he could not live there in any case, by himself, destitute, in the open.

"They will not allow it, my boy."

The lad steadfastly refused to accept the notion that he would be in the open out there—he had already built himself a shelter where he could lie snug.

"And as soon as spring comes, I shall build another cabin—it needn't be big and there's a good bit of wood out there. But, as I expect you know, I've lost Snjolfur—and the boat. I don't think there's any hope of putting the bits of her together again. Now that I've no boat, I thought I might let out the landing place, if I could make something out of it. The Faroese would be sure to give me something for the pot if I gave them a hand with launching and unloading. They could row most ways from there—I'm not exaggerating—they had to stay at home time and time again last summer, when it was easy for Snjolfur and me to put off. There's a world of difference between a deep-water landing place and a shallow-water one—that's what Snjolfur said many a time."

The factor asked his visitor what price he had thought of putting on it for the summer.

"I don't know what the funeral will cost yet," replied the orphan in worried tones. "At any rate I should need enough to pay for Snjolfur's funeral. Then I should count myself lucky."

"Then let's say that," struck in the factor, and went on to say that he would see about the coffin and everything—there was no need for little Snjolfur to fret about it any more. Without thinking, he found himself opening the door for his guest, diminutive though he was—but the boy stood there as if he had not seen him do it, and it was written clear on his face that he had not yet finished the business that brought him; the anxious look was still strong on his ruddy face, firm-featured beyond his years.

"When are you expecting the ship with your stores?"

The factor replied that it would hardly come tomorrow, perhaps the day after. It was a puzzle to know why the boy had asked—the pair of them, father and son, did not usually ask about his stores until they brought the cash to buy them.

Little Snjolfur did not take his eyes from the factor's face. The words stuck in his throat, but at last he managed to get his question out: In that case, wouldn't the factor be needing a boy to help in the store?

The factor did not deny it.

"But he ought to be past his confirmation for preference," he added with a smile.

It looked as if little Snjolfur was ready for this answer, and indeed his errand was now at an end, but he asked the factor to come out with him round the corner of the store. They went out, the boy in front, and on to the pebble-bank nearby. The boy stopped at a stone lying there, got a grip of it, lifted it without any obvious exertion and heaved it away from him. Then he turned to the factor.

"We call this stone the Weakling. The boy you had last summer couldn't lift it high enough to let the damp in underneath—much less any further!"

"Oh, well then, seeing you are stronger than he was, it ought to be possible to make use of you in some way, even though you are on the wrong side of confirmation," replied the factor in a milder tone.

"Do I get my keep while I'm with you? And the same wages as he had?" continued the youngster, who was the sort that likes to know where he stands in good time.

"But of course," answered the factor, who for once was in no mood to drive a hard bargain.

"That's good—then I shan't go on the parish," said little Snjolfur, and was easier in his mind. "The man who has got something to put in himself and on himself isn't a pauper—Snjolfur often used to say that," he added, and he straightened himself up proudly and offered his hand to the factor, just as he had seen his father do. "Good-bye," he said. "I shall come then—not to-morrow but the day after."

The factor told him to come in again for a minute, and leading the way to the kitchen door he ushered little Snjolfur into the warmth. He asked the cook if she couldn't give this nipper here a bite of something to eat, preferably something warm—he could do with it.

Little Snjolfur would not accept any food.

"Aren't you hungry?" asked the astonished factor.

The boy could not deny that he was—and for the rest he could hardly get his words out with the sharpness of his hunger whetted still keener by the blessed smell of cooking. But he resisted the temptation:

"I am not a beggar," he said.

The factor was upset and he saw that he had set about it clumsily. He went over to the dogged youngster, patted his head and, with a nod to the cook, led little Snjolfur into the dining room.

"Have you never seen your father give his visitors a drink or offer them a cup of coffee when they came to see him?" he asked, and he gave his words a resentful tone.

Little Snjolfur had to confess that his father had sometimes offered hospitality to a visitor.

"There you are then," said the factor. "It's just ordinary good manners to offer hospitality—and to accept it. Refusing a well-meant invitation for no reason can mean the end of a friendship. You are a visitor here, so naturally I offer you something to eat: we have made an important deal and, what's more, we have come to terms over a job. If you won't accept ordinary hospitality, it's hard to see how the rest is going to work out."

The boy sighed: of course, it must be as the factor said. But he was in a hurry. Snjolfur was by himself out on the Point. His eyes wandered round the room—then he added, very seriously: "The point is to pay your debts, not owe anything to anybody, and trust in Providence."

"There was never a truer word spoken," agreed the factor, and as he said it he pulled his handkerchief out of his pocket. "He's a chip off the old block," he muttered, and putting his hand on little Snjolfur's shoulder, he blessed him.

The boy was astonished to see a grown man with tears in his eyes.

"Snjolfur never cried," he said, and went on: "I haven't cried either since I was little—I nearly did when I knew Snjolfur was dead. But I was afraid he wouldn't like it, and I stopped myself."

A moment later and tears overwhelmed little Snjolfur. It is a consolation, albeit a poor one, to lean for a while on the bosom of a companion.

Translated by Peter Foote

THÓRBERGUR THÓRDARSON
(1889–   )

Long esteemed as a leading stylist and humorist, Thórdarson is a peculiar mixture of paradoxical traits: a clear and keen intellect and a singularly gullible nature. He is an avowed Communist, but inasmuch as he accepts the concept of life after death, he denies materialism. Above all, he is a firm believer in ghosts, which he "feels" everywhere around him. For a time, he became a theosophist, practiced yoga, and even wrote a book on the subject. In addition, he remains one of the most ardent Esperantists in Iceland. Through all his diverse interests can be seen a man who is, basically, an honest seeker after truth, although, politically, he seems to have found it once and for all.

Thórdarson has written essays, biographies, poetry and autobiographical works. His eccentricity, crowned with a brilliant style and an ever present humor, which he frequently points at himself, has resulted in some of the most original and unique works of modern Icelandic literature.

"The Brindled Monster" is the twenty-second chapter of *Bréf til Láru* ("A Letter to Laura") 1924, a series of essays, personal reflections and imaginative sketches, well-suited to the epistolary form in which they appear.

The Brindled Monster

A few years ago I lived in a house facing a busy street. My apartment consisted of a large living room and a small bedroom. The bedroom adjoined a tiny anteroom which had a double door. At night I hooked the outer door to the frame, but the inner one I locked with a key which I always kept with me.

There were two windows in the living room and one in the bedroom. They all faced the street, from which it was less than a man's reach up to the windows. Only one of the living room windows could be opened. When I wasn't at home, I often left it ajar to let in fresh air. My friends sometimes climbed in through it, if they wanted to borrow a book from me. My bed was against the wall in the bedroom. The foot of it faced the door of the anteroom, but the head was at the window, almost at the level of the window sill. In the corner, on the other side, there was a little washstand which I had made myself. There was only about a foot of space between the bed and the washstand.

I have slept at an open window for twelve years. I have never allowed myself to break this rule except in the most severe northern blizzards. But in this apartment it so happened that my bedroom window didn't open. Instead, I kept my living room window ajar at night, and then opened the door between the living room and the bedroom.

As long as I lived in this house I feared for my life. I had heard horrible stories of stone-throwing and shooting through windows and mine were perfectly suited for that kind of artistry. There was also something worse which increased my fear, for I had tangible evidence that all types of villains were seeking my life. I was quite accustomed to being followed on the street at night. And sometimes I was ambushed in dark corners and alleys. Because of my exceptional inventiveness, I nearly always managed to escape unhurt from the traps laid by these murderers. But once, on a New Year's Eve, one of these brutes caught me unaware and immediately knocked me out. The only thing that saved my life was that I rolled in through a basement window as I passed out. My right hand was badly cut by the glass. I'll bear the mark of it to my dying day. But the murderer lost his victim.

After the shock of this incident my fear of the killers became insurmountable, especially after dusk. This fear came over me everywhere. It sprang at me from every shadow and every corner. It clung to every unknown man who crossed my path after dark. It crept in my footsteps on the street. It lay waiting for me in dark alleys. It hid behind my stove. It had a secret place under my bed. It stole under my couch. I wasn't safe anywhere.

But my greatest fear was the windows. I never walked erect past my living room windows after I had put out the lights at night. Whenever I had to pass either one of them, I crept on the floor on all fours.

My desk stood at the wall between the windows. For fear of my life I never dared to sit there at night. Of course, I wasn't so neurotic as to imagine a bullet or a stone coming through the iron-protected wall. But it wouldn't take much imagination to send those murderous instruments through the window at an angle and hit me in the head. Therefore, I crouched up with my work on a dilapidated couch in the corner, although that certainly wasn't without its perils too. While I undressed I sat with outstretched feet on the floor beneath the desk, and then crept to my bed with the utmost care.

Yet, it was precisely then, when I was in bed and had put out the light, that my fright became boundless. Then, it wasn't just the murderers who sought my life. They were joined by half-human devils fluttering around the room in the darkness. A creak of the door, a crack at the window, the rustling of a leaf—all these were forebodings of terrible happenings.

I won't try to describe my sufferings. I can't convey them in words. I desperately wanted to let the light burn all night. It would have decreased my fear of the devils. But it didn't take me long to figure out that it would only attract the attention of the murderers. Besides, my lamp was an old, battered thing. It smoked whenever I took my eyes off it, and the smell of petroleum was quite doing away with me. Of the two evils, I would rather be shot dead by a murderer or hanged by some messenger of the devil than choke in oil smoke and run the risk of being buried alive in a pit of mold, six feet deep.

But the plots of murder below my windows were the worst of all. When I had turned out the light, mysterious whisperings usually began outside the open window. It was as if the scoundrels were waiting near the house—waiting for me to fall asleep in the dark. I listened. I couldn't distinguish the words. There were only muffled whispers and a devilish murmuring. I couldn't bear lying still. I crept out of bed and crawled on my hands and knees into the living room, all the way to the window. I listened. Of course, I didn't risk peeping out; it could have cost me my life. I sat on my heels beneath the window sill, held my breath and listened, listened unceasingly. Every vein in my body was on the verge of bursting. But the villains were so shrewd that I couldn't hear the plan of their scheme, only words out of context: in the small room, the window, shot, hit him, click, sleeping, choked in his quilt. Then everything melted together in a soundless terror. I trembled where I sat on my heels, silent and listening like an open grave. After a long time the villains stole away. The following night they came back again and the plots for my murder were resumed outside the open window. So passed my nights, more terrifying than any torments of hell.

The whole behavior of the murderers bespoke exceptional forethought and carefulness. They had obviously made a very precise plan for the murder, marked down every step, and made a thorough study of all the details, like experienced criminals. They watched every movement in my room, stood peeking in, tiptoed around and spoke in muffled voices. Sometimes they knocked on my bedroom window or tried the knob of the anteroom door. They were obviously testing to see if I was asleep. They didn't intend to make a mess of it when they finally went into action. They were just waiting for the right opportunity. They were probably not yet sufficiently familiar with the layout of my apartment.

My dear Laura! You can imagine what effect this devilish conspiracy had on my health. Often I didn't sleep a wink until dawn. All through the long winter nights I lay awake in a bath of cold sweat. In one of my ears I could hear the murderers' voices; in the other the death knell tolled incessantly, while above and beneath and all around me in the dark, half-human imps in every shape and form fluttered about. These were terrible winter nights. I shudder at the remembrance of them. In the daytime I was stunned and weak. I lost my appetite. My joy in life slowly ebbed away. I dreaded every night like the torments of hell.

I realized that this could not go on much longer. I had to do something to save my life. I tried to get another apartment. I didn't succeed. Then I began to think up some cunning machinations to use against this pack of enemies. During the day I often sat for hours trying to invent traps and schemes which would be of some use to me. But no matter how I beat my brains, I didn't manage to hit upon anything completely workable. First I thought of not sleeping at an open window any more. But I soon saw that this was really no defense. The murderers certainly wouldn't have any scruples about breaking the window and then stealing in. Besides, I knew that people who slept with their windows closed were more prone to influenza and consumption. And consumption had me especially worried at that time.

The only solution that occurred to me was this: I fetched fifteen stones, the size of a fist, from the beach, and systematically placed them under my bed. Before I undressed and put out the light, I put a box of matches on my washstand, leaving a big bunch sticking halfway out, so that I could quickly get at them when the time came. I took the glass off my lamp and put it on the table, and the shade I put on the floor so that I could light the lamp instantly. But my principal weapon of safety was a big pocketknife which I placed open at the head of my bed every night. The chamber pot I left half-full for the ghosts. I knew that to be the traditional way of dealing with them. And my experience had taught me to value popular remedies more than scientific prejudice. After these preparations, I became a little calmer.

Thus a year passed. Then an unexpected thought struck me. Evil spirits of the deceased could make me kill myself in my sleep with the knife. I was greatly ashamed not to have thought of this before. After that I left the knife folded. Half a year passed and the murderers never relinquished their watch. During that time I read much about dreams and sleepwalking. I learned that in their sleep people had often performed sheer miracles: climbed up precipices, waded across impassable streams, opened complicated locks, and many other things. Wasn't it equally conceivable that evil spirits could lure me to open the knife in my sleep and slash myself with it? The following evening I locked the knife in my drawer and asked my landlord to guard the key closely. Then, instead of the knife, I got myself a big cudgel of birch. From then on I put it at the head of my bed every night. In the daytime I practiced using it.

The plotting continued outside the open window. Now it wasn't only men who sought my life. Bloodthirsty females from all over town had joined them. They accused me of having mocked their profession in *Half Soles* and *Wise Man's Garments*.[1]

[1] Two of Thórdarson's early books.

These infamous females certainly did nothing to dissuade the men from bold actions. That was no surprise. I had read much about the fierceness of women in street riots in London. And I myself had experienced their violence and impudence. All my hopes of safety crumbled like childish castles in the air.

At last the hour arrived, shocking and without warning, like all great events. It was the last night of September. I had just gone to bed and put out the light. I lay on my back and let my eyes wander back and forth about the room. Then all of a sudden I saw something gray leaning against the door at the foot of my bed. This had to be something supernatural. I had never noticed anything suspicious there before. What could it be? I stared at it for a while. At first it looked like a gray ghost. Then it gradually became clearer, until I assured myself that it was only a gleam from the window falling on the door. Thus I discovered new wonders of nature every night. And every new bit of knowledge cost me much brainwork and more than minor torments of the soul.

At this time I was in love with a fat nurse. She had dark eyes and dressed in a white robe. This impressed me favorably. I had written her many heartrending love poems. I wrote them all in red ink to make her realize my sacrifice. The next time she saw me she gazed at me, calm like a Stoic, shook my hand and said: "Thank you for the poem." "You're welcome," I said, "do you want some more?" She bowed and said nothing. I kept on writing heartrending love poems in red ink. And nothing more came of it.

Picturing her beauty in my mind, I often forgot myself. Once in a while I even forgot those murderous brutes. Dark eyes, red lips, soft hands, heaving breasts—that was something for me in those days. This night I was singing mad with love because of the especially amusing contempt which she had shown me on the street during the day. It made me glad. Now I was sure of her sincerity in private. Oh, how happy I was! There I lay, pondering how much help she could give me against the murderous brutes. When I grabbed the birch cudgel to do away with the enemy, she would hold the light for me and encourage me: "Strike him dead! I'll take the responsibility!" But what if he knocked me down? Then she would seize the chamber pot and throw it at his head. Only, she had better not hit me in the head by mistake! Or she would pull him off me and strangle him with her hands. Then we would drag the rascal out to the gutter. And after that I would kiss her innumerable burning kisses and the night would pass in blissful harmony and triumph. What a marriage it would be! There it was: a common interest to live for. It was sure to unite us with unbreakable bonds of love. Now I felt that it was a necessity of life to marry a nurse who knew the right way to handle things.

I pictured this in my mind with all the powers of imagination God has given me. Then I heard someone very softly walking around in my living room. I didn't try to listen; I merely became one huge ear. My heart pounded inside me like a twelve-cylinder engine. And I had a weak heart! Christ! The footsteps moved softly and slowly toward the stove. Then someone tiptoed to the window and from there to the middle of the floor again. There he stopped, as if he were peeping in on me through the open door. Doubtless, he intended to take me unawares and murder me in my sleep, before I could utter a sound. He had taken his shoes off lest his footsteps awaken me. I was nearly choking with heartbeat and despair. Tonight I was to die. In a few brief moments I would be a lifeless corpse, dripping with blood. And the soul? Hush, hush! Deliberately, the footsteps moved to and fro in the living room. Why didn't he get it over with? What was he sniffing around there for? Was he looking for my money? I wanted him to finish this deadly game as soon as possible.

Was there nothing I could do? I thought I would lie stock-still, stop breathing and pretend to be dead. I had heard that foxes sometimes saved their lives that way. But I realized that in the dark the rascal wouldn't be able to see my dead face. Then I thought of creeping under the bed. But I saw that I would then have to give up the ghost without being able to move. That, I thought, would be worse than anything. But how about trying to sneak out of the house? To do that I would have to open three locked doors. And my keys were in the pocket of my jacket in the living room! All these years I had never thought of leaving them in the keyholes. What an arch idiot! I tore my hair out in mute frenzy. But what about breaking the window and getting out that way? I felt that would do unforgivable damage to the house. Besides, I would be severely cut by broken glass and then blood poisoning would set in. What was that about the boy who had cut himself on glass? He contracted a terrible case of blood poisoning. His eyes burst out of his head with the pain. Besides, the murderer would have already shot me before I could escape.

I saw no way out. My life hung on a trembling thread. I no longer heard nor saw. All existence had become a pitch-black chaos. Incoherent tatters of thoughts whirled through my brain somewhere out in the blue distance like piles of clouds in a southwesterly blizzard.

Suddenly a bolt of lightning seemed to pass through my body and I was filled with unearthly powers. I jumped out of bed, grasped the box of matches and the birch cudgel and tiptoed to the door of the living room. In an instant I lit a big bunch of matches and peered in through the door with glowering eyes. But there was nothing to see. The shabby chairs stood on the floor as spiritless as I had left them that evening. Had I just heard wrong? I who had never misheard anything in my life! Had I become like the materialists who have hallucinations and hear voices? I had never had any hallucinations. And I had never heard anything that hadn't actually occurred.

With singular care I put my head a little further into the room. There it was! Out of the darkness of the corner by the window two horrible eyes were staring at me. I lost all control. I went charging into the room, striking into the corner with my cudgel with irrepressible fury. At the same moment I heard a fierce hiss come out of the darkness and a huge brindled brute of a cat leapt up on the table. Before I knew it he had vanished through the open window. I struck out after him, but missed.

I was completely dazed. I knew horrible stories of cats that had attacked people in their sleep and scratched out their eyes or torn out their entrails. And in Akureyri a rat ate up a man's cheek from the corner of his mouth all the way back to his ear. In spite of my fear of consumption I closed the window carefully.

For a few moments my fear of the murderers gave way to a dreadful fear of the dark. I felt that there was something mysterious about this confounded cat. I had slept with the window open for four years and never before had a cat come in. Wasn't that strange? What could he be doing here in the dark of night? I was revolted by this weird specimen of a cat.

For a long time I stood and stared into the dark. I couldn't stop thinking about the cat, and felt his behavior was strangely suspicious. Finally, I stumbled into bed, exhausted by palpitations and fright. I wanted very much to leave the light burning, but fear of the murderers overpowered me. So I put out the light, lay down and pulled the quilt up over my head. It was a foolhardy thing to do. And yet I always do it when my fear of the dark overwhelms me. I feel security in seeing nothing. I tried to think of something pretty. I had heard the theosophists say that it worked wonders. But for a long time I couldn't control my thoughts. They raced through my head like express trains. I trembled under the quilt like a beaten dog.

Finally the nurse in her white robe came flying under the quilt to me, fat and healthy-looking like a sheep from Mödrudale. She had vanished from my mind while I was struggling with the cat. I tried to forget myself in her beauty, tried to forget everything but this innocent angel who was going to sacrifice her life in the battle against my murderers. That's what love is like. It follows you even into the valley of death, though it profiteth it nothing. Up to that moment I had thought about my beloved as a beautiful work of art. But now I saw that she also had a practical significance for me. I was glad for that. I had so often been accused of being unpractical.

A long while passed. I was awakened from my meditations on love by a rustling noise. What could it be? I stretched my neck from under the quilt, looked sharply into the darkness and listened. I heard someone moving in the living room, cunningly tiptoeing about. How did the scoundrel get in? I had closed the window carefully. And all the doors were locked. Could he have come in through the wall or penetrated the boards of the floor? Penetrated! It nauseated me. This couldn't be a human murderer. What could he be? An incarnate devil who intended to strangle me in my sleep? I knew from previous experience that that sort are no lambs to play with. They can make one go stark raving mad. They can tear people apart, limb by limb. When you try to get hold of them they slip out of your hands like an eel. Like

an eel! Like an electric eel! That was it. This repugnant simile
touched me like a new revelation, like a dreadful reality that
crushed my heart. I couldn't understand it. I listened. The footsteps moved slowly toward the door, toward me. I became numb
with fear and lay paralyzed in my bed. Ice-cold, invisible paws
grasped me by the throat. Something long and slimy wound
around my nakedness. I tried to roll over, but I was glued to
the bottom of the bed. My eyes snapped shut. The room darted
away from me like a cloud driven by wind somewhere far out
in the dark autumn.

I don't know how long I lay in this frightful nightmare. I was
awakened by a scratch at the living room door. The devil was
testing whether or not I was asleep. Before I knew it, I was out
of bed. I grabbed the birch cudgel and lit the lamp in a flash.
Good Lord! Right there at my toes was the same brute of a cat
as before. He looked at me with his sea-green eyes and hissed
hideously. What ugly eyes! I had never before seen such an
abominable pair of cat eyes. And I thought the beast was much
longer and had shorter legs than ordinary cats. He writhed to
and fro in rhythmical loops. For my life I didn't dare attack this
mysterious enemy. He might change into an awful monster and
make me go mad or tear me apart. It is well known that powerful
ghosts can do such things.

As if by blind instinct, I raced to the window and threw it
wide open. Then I jumped up on the couch and beat my cudgel
on the floor, hissing and cursing. The monster turned toward me
and stared at me with his ghastly eyes. The hair rose on his body.
He frowned at me and squeaked repulsively. Then, still writhing,
he jumped up to the window sill and looked sharply at me. It
grew dark before my eyes. I lost all control. I darted to the
window and with all my might pushed the cudgel into the monster. He slid out into the darkness like an electric eel. I saw him
emit sparks of fire in all directions.

My consternation had become quite unbearable. I shut the
window and dressed hurriedly. Then, for the rest of the night,
I paced the floor in the pitch-black darkness. The following day
I moved out of the house.

Three years have passed since this horrible event occurred. I
have read a number of books on apparitions and on the phenom-

ena of incarnation, and I have collected many remarkable stories on these subjects from honorable men all over the country. Every word in these tales has confirmed my conviction that the brindled monster couldn't have been anything but a devil in the shape of an electric eel which intended to kill me in my sleep that terrible night in September. Since then, I have left my light burning all through the night. If the light goes out, the eyes of the monster haunt me.

Translated by Hallberg Hallmundsson

HALLDÓR LAXNESS

(1902–   )

Few men, if any, have carried the name of modern Iceland
so far and wide as Halldór Laxness. At the same time, few
men have been subjected to as longstanding and severe a
criticism in their own country. An early decision to become a
writer (he published his first novel when only seventeen)
and an iconoclastic bent have gained him the attention of
his countrymen almost all his life. While nobody has denied
his vivid style and wit, brilliant characterization, and an ad-
mirable fusion of tender lyricism with harsh, even cynical,
reality, the frequently scarifying social criticism of his works
has long outraged the more conservative segment of the
population. On the other hand, he has been hailed by the
progressive intelligentsia. Nothing he has ever written has
passed unnoticed.

In spite of an unorthodox approach that is distinctively
different from that of the old saga-writers, Laxness considers
himself primarily a storyteller, a saga-man in close contact
with, and carrying on, the thousand-year-old literary tradition of his native country.

His output includes a number of novels, several volumes
of essays, five plays, and one volume of poetry. He was
awarded the Nobel Prize for literature in 1955, the first
Icelander to be so honored.

The following story was inspired by the visit of Italo
Balbo, the Fascist Air Force ace, who stopped over in Iceland during a group flight to Chicago and New York in 1933.

The Defeat of the Italian Air Force
in Reykjavík 1933

Iceland is the only country in the world which has no army, and therefore this poor insular nation has had to live without the familiar glory uniforms bestow, as well as all the ranks and titles that these peculiar garments express.

But uniforms are not altogether unknown in Iceland. The Salvation Army, which was the first to import trumpets and other brass instruments, also must be credited with having first introduced uniforms to the nation. They were adopted by policemen a little later, and, subsequently, postmen were given the uniforms of Cuban rebels. Finally, when sophisticated hotel management appeared in the country, the office of *piccolo* was established in Iceland, and this Italian title was lent distinction by a beautiful uniform. Yet, this title—or, for that matter, any other title—has never been properly esteemed in this cold nation which always has had to gamble, like sea gulls and whales, on the unstable supply of herring.

It is all quite different in Italy. In that country no one is considered a man among men unless he wears a uniform. And the greatest man of all is he who wears the oddest kind of clothes, the most incredible color and cut, the most peculiar ribbons of gilded brass, together with tufts and tassels and other ornaments —to say nothing of highboots in dry weather. Wise men say that Italy's national wealth has almost completely vanished because of the nation's love of funny costumes covered with trinkets and tinsel, and because of the people's blind passion for fighting in distant deserts. The uninitiated foreigner who strolls for the first time along the Via Nazionale in Rome automatically assumes that every other man he meets must be a *piccolo*. But that isn't so. These are the desert-lovers, the Fascists themselves, and one can't help noticing right away how solemn and important is their mien in spite of their hilarious costumes.

But let us turn our minds again to Iceland—this eccentric insular nation which does not understand the deeper significance of uniforms, much less their distinctions of rank, but prefers the habits of whales and other sea monsters (as is evidenced by its high regard for the most exotic creature of the North, the herring).

The following story occurred the summer the porpoises ran ashore in Nauthólsvík.[1] It so happened that a new bellboy was taken on at the Hotel Geysir in Reykjavík. His name was Stefán Jónsson. The girl behind the buffet counter used to recite a silly poem about him, which went something like this:

"Stebbi stood on the strand, he was treading straw,
   Straw will not be trodden although Stebbi treads on straw,
   Straw trod Stebbi Straw."

Except for the uniform and the Italian title of *piccolo,* he was just an ordinary boy who had been confirmed that spring. He was of average size for his age, and of average intelligence: a very nice boy, as nice as they come in Iceland. He considered everyone his equal, and at the same time was ready to do anything for anyone. He did everything as well as he could and expected the same from others.

But now let us meet the army of the Italian Fascists in their vivid uniforms. In their native country they enjoyed great love and respect, and, besides being handsome and elegant, they were such heroes and patriots that they soon set off with gas machines to induce suffocation among the naked Negroes of the desert. Thus the whole world might see their glory. But just before they embarked on this laudable jaunt to the black barbarians, they felt that they ought also to show the white barbarians what pretty costumes they owned and how handsome they were. In this way they thought to convince the world how natural it was that such men had a vocation for governing deserts. One day, therefore, they climbed into their planes and set off in a large group, choosing various distinguished countries in which to land and show their uniforms; and one of these fortunate countries was Iceland. A whole fleet of Italian Fascist planes landed in Vatnagardar,[2] and in each plane there were at least two newly-

[1] Small inlet, now a beach, within the limits of Reykjavík, capital of Iceland.
[2] Small bay inside the city limits of Reykjavík, where seaplanes used to land in the early days of aviation in Iceland.

tailored uniforms. The visitors arrived when the nights were at their brightest and the buttercups were blossoming in the fields, and no sooner had they climbed out of their planes than they telegraphed to Rome to say that the capital of Iceland had been all floodlit and smothered in flowers in honor of their arrival. An Icelandic historian who lives in Denmark, but loves big nations, then wrote a book in Danish to confirm the contents of these telegrams. As an instance of how well the natives behaved toward the Great Power, he stated that when they heard the roar of the planes overhead, they were seized with such joy and admiration that even total strangers rushed up to each other in the streets and squares of the capital and kissed each other weeping.

Alas, the glory of fame is one thing, reality another.

The truth was that toward evening one could hardly move along the main street for the hordes of strangers all looking like postmen or bellboys. They stood on the sidewalks in their uniforms and talked with their hands. Serious-minded citizens who could barely get through the crowd said in irritation: "What are all these damned dandies doing here?"

That was all.

The Fascist officers were billeted in the hotels of the town. And it so happened that on the very day that Stebbi was hired at the Hotel Geysir and dignified with the title of *piccolo* and put into a uniform, a group of these Italian Fascists booked in at the hotel, all wearing uniforms just like Stebbi.

Self-confident in his own uniform, Stebbi stood in the hotel lobby, critically eyeing theirs. *"Tenente, capitano, maggiore,"* they said to each other. He had an Italian title too.

These people made a beastly lot of noise in the hotel. They bellowed into each other's ears as loudly as though talking to the deaf, and they flapped their limbs in incessant gesticulation. The waiters soon held them in special contempt, for they smacked their lips and sucked their teeth and licked their knives as if they were trying to cut off their tongues. When they had a cigar they did not know which end to bite off and most of them picked the wrong one, so that the waiters thought they must be beggars picked from the gutters and sent on this trip in the hope that they would drown in the Atlantic.

They ate at a long table in the middle of the dining room, and their loud voices reduced the speech of others to a murmur.

Entering the room two by two, they lined up at the table in strict order of rank, so that the absurdity of the uniforms increased proportionately from one end of the table to the other. The last one to appear was a dark-eyed gentleman by the name of Pittigrilli, whose chest stuck out so far that he almost tipped over backward with every step he took. He only lacked the tinsel to be the absolute image of a Christmas tree. When he entered the room, his compatriots rose to their feet, clicked their heels, and stood like dummies until he ordered them to sit down again. Stebbi thought this was great sport.

The waiters took Pittigrilli to be the host, and so began to serve the soup at the other end of the table. Similarly, they brought the meat course first to the man who sat farthest away from Pittigrilli. For some obscure reason this created much commotion among the visitors, and when the waiters did not change their order of serving at the third course, Pittigrilli and those next to him rose to their feet, sent for the headwaiter and talked to him for a while in the most beautiful Italian—up to four hundred words a minute—waving their hands and feet.

"Thank you," said the headwaiter, and bowed.

Then they demanded to speak to the proprietor, and went on with this strange performance for a while, until they sat down again to eat. At the next meal, of course, the waiters, as before, began serving the soup at the other end of the table, intending to end with Pittigrilli as was their custom. Whereupon, Pittigrilli stood up and ordered his men to leave the room. In some amazement, the waiters and other diners present watched the men fall into line, two by two, and march out from the steaming hot soup.

In the evening the Italian consul himself came to the hotel and informed the headwaiter that if they did not give Pittigrilli precedence when serving the soup, ending with the man who sat farthest away from him, the matter would be brought to the attention of the Foreign Ministry.

"Thank you," said the headwaiter, and he bowed and promised to speak to the waiters. But the waiters said they thought Pittigrilli was the one who paid, and it was the custom in restaurants here to serve last the man who was paying.

"It is Mussolini who is paying," said the consul in great agitation.

"Thank you," said the headwaiter, and bowed. "But since the

Italians arrived we have not been able to keep any Englishmen in the hotel. Englishmen cannot bear to hear people smack their lips."

"That is no business of mine," said the consul. "Whoever dishonors Pittigrilli, dishonors Mussolini."

"Thank you," said the headwaiter, and bowed.

That was the end of their conversation.

Next day, Stebbi went off duty at noon. The weather was heavenly and the sun shone on the main door of the hotel and the sidewalk outside. Stebbi stood in the doorway. He didn't want to take off his uniform quite yet, because the sun shone so beautifully on his golden buttons, the gold braid on his trousers, and the golden cap with the strap under his chin looking like a pot set askew. It was so pleasant to be able to stand there like an officer in uniform, while other boys of his age passed by in overalls and knickers. Sometimes young girls walked by, too.

Two Americans came out of the hotel. They said hello to Stebbi, lighted their cigarettes and gave him one as they went by.

No, damn it, he had no desire to go in just yet and change into someone ordinary or even less than ordinary. Moreover, he now had a cigarette, and he felt that if only he could get a light, his prestige would be complete. Who, then, would dare chant "Stebbi Straw" at him? No, he would be Perfection on the Sidewalk, only fourteen years old in the sunshine, the Lord of Life with a cigarette, wearing a uniform.

A man came walking toward the hotel, his steps quick and his shoulders pulled back. He wore a uniform just as Stebbi did, had a cigarette between his fingers just as he did, and a thin bamboo cane in one hand. It was Pittigrilli. He was obviously thinking about himself and his own uniform and consequently did not notice Stebbi and his uniform at all.

"Hello, Pittigrilli," said Stebbi, American style, and he clapped his hand chummily on the Fascist's shoulder, for they were both wearing uniforms; and somehow Stebbi felt they were both great men, considerably improving the look of the street and the whole universe.

"Match?" he said, and pointed to the unlit cigarette between his lips.

But never could Stefán Jónsson have dreamed that a man could

in one moment be so ferociously transformed by a friendly greeting in the midday sun. In an instant the expression on the Italian
Fascist's face turned into a terrifying blend of shock, outrage,
and fury, as though standing before him were a sneak assassin
with his dagger raised. Nor was his answer long in coming. He
ripped the cigarette out of Stebbi's mouth, flung it to the ground,
and then started belaboring the boy about the face with the
bamboo cane.

That was the end of that dream.

It is a commonly held view that few nations have endured
oppression and tyranny with more politeness than the Icelanders.
For centuries up to the present day they have lived in a com-
plaisant understanding of tyranny, without ever trying to revolt.
To no nation was the idea of revolution more alien. The Icelanders were always ready to kiss the whip that hurt the most
and to believe that their most ruthless executioner was their
trustiest helper and their most secure shelter.

But incredible as it may seem with these obedient insular
people, it sometimes happens that they forget everything they
have been taught, forget their politeness, forget their submissive-
ness and their reverence for the executioner; and instead of paus-
ing to contemplate and meditate on the noble and unselfish
reasons that might have inspired the blow, they respond in a
completely instinctive way.

Today was just such a one of those comparatively rare, but
for that the more happy, hours in the life of the nation. No sooner
had General Pittigrilli beaten Stefán Jónsson with his cane than
the boy flew at him and caught him in a wrestling hold. The
general was taken unawares by this response, for it isn't cus-
tomary in Italy for hotel bellboys to fly at the foremost men of
the country. So there ensued a scuffle between the boy and the
general. Soon they were carried into the middle of the street,
and a crowd of people rushed up from all directions to enjoy
this entertainment. And the upshot of the brawl was that Stefán
Jónsson overpowered the friend of the desert.

"*Mamma mia,*" whined the general as he lay in the dusty
street, while the bellboy lay sprawled over him and held him
down.

By this time people had begun to realize that the Fascist was having difficulties, and some good citizens came to his aid, helped him to his feet and brushed the dust from him. They drove the bellboy away and told him to get lost. Icelanders are always on the side of those who lose, ready to help them up and brush them down, probably because they feel, deep down, that they have a common cause with all losers.

But no sooner was the hero of the desert, Pittigrilli, on his feet again, and no sooner brushed and safe from Stefán Jónsson, than he became just as brave as ever before. He stood in the lobby of the hotel, waved his hands and feet, spread his fingers, and spoke with such eloquence that doors and windows were thrown open and a crowd of people gathered round to enjoy his art. Some people even thought Mussolini himself had arrived —except for two Englishmen who put their hands in their pockets and slipped away unobtrusively through the back door. Stefán Jónsson was away long before this, and nobody understood what Pittigrilli was saying. He was brought both cold water and matches in the hope that that might help him, but it did not help him at all.

That evening the Italian consul came by again, still more serious than the first time. Mussolini had been dishonored in Iceland, *la gloria della patria* had been trampled upon in this confounded islet which the holy weapons of Italian Fascism could level to the sea in a few minutes if necessary. The basest of the base and the lowest of the low known to Italy, *un piccolo*, had dared dishonor *la grandissima, eternissima patria della gloria.* This matter would not only be brought to the attention of the Foreign Ministry, but carried to any and all extremes until revenge was done, even if it should cost the King of Denmark his throne.[3]

"Thank you," said the headwaiter, and bowed, while a few Englishmen were seen hurrying away from the hotel with their luggage.

Then began the peace conference.

The General Staff, of course, did not stress the point that the King of Denmark be dethroned, but it demanded an official

---

[3] Iceland was, at this time, a separate, independent kingdom, but it had a personal union with Denmark, i.e., the Danish king was also the king of Iceland. The country became a republic in 1944.

apology to Mussolini from the government because of what had happened. Some mediator remarked that Mussolini might perhaps misconstrue such an apology. Then Pittigrilli demanded that at least the hotel proprietor should apologize to him. A long search was made for the proprietor, but he seemed to be out in the country somewhere shooting curlews. Besides, he did not want to be bothered with the business: it was the headwaiter, not he, who had hired the bellboy. Stebbi was his responsibility.

Then Pittigrilli demanded that the bellboy be dismissed at once.

"Thank you," said the headwaiter, and bowed.

But Stebbi was at home and had the day off. He did not know that anything special had happened. A foreigner had punched his nose, he had fought back, and the foreigner had lost. True, the poor devil had been wearing a uniform. So what? Stebbi had been wearing a uniform, too. He could not imagine that the fellow would bear him a grudge even though he had lost. Stebbi had himself lost many times and had never harbored ill will against his opponent. When people have a fight, it is only natural that one loses and the other wins. That was just as it should be. No, nothing had happened. By evening, he had already forgotten about it.

Next morning the weather was fine, and the Fascists in their uniforms flew away and never returned to Iceland again. And Stefán Jónsson came to work in the morning, put on his uniform, set his cap askew, and everything was as it used to be in the hotel. Nothing had happened. If somebody had told Stebbi that the Italian Air Force had been defeated in Reykjavík the day before, he would not have understood. But one thing he knew: he did not like this Gunna, the girl behind the buffet counter. Stupid girl. She didn't know how to appreciate a young gentleman with gold buttons and a golden pot askew. She never missed a chance to call him Stebbi Straw, and went on chanting that foolish verse, "Straw trod Stebbi Straw," just to tease him whenever he went by.

Translated by Hallberg Hallmundsson

SWEDEN

INTRODUCTION

While the Norsemen were harassing the British Isles and the Danes were sacking France, the Swedes, during the Viking period, turned their prows east. Sailing across the Baltic Sea, they advanced via the great Russian rivers all the way down to the Black and the Caspian seas. There they encountered merchants from such places as Byzantium and Baghdad and traded them furs and slaves for enormous profits in gold, silver, and spices. Where they went in peace they were considered fair traders. But when the opportunity presented itself, they did not hesitate to plunder if that would further increase their gains. In those lands where their Viking greed was aroused, there was no greater terror.

On their way south through the Russian plains, the Swedes subjugated the Slavic populations and founded their own states. One such state had its capital in Novgorod, which the Vikings called Hólmgard. Another was Kiev, or Kænugard, which was founded in the middle of the 9th century by the chieftain Rurik (or Rorik, see note 1, p. 7). His descendants remained on the throne for centuries, their realm eventually growing into the powerful empire of Russia.

At the same time, the Swedes were weak and divided at home. Each district was ruled autonomously, and civil feuds were frequent. Despite some early attempts, unification of the Swedish kingdom was not realized until the 12th century. In all probability there existed, during this period, some oral literature in the form of heroic poetry similar to that of the other Scandinavian countries, but unfortunately none of it has been preserved.

Christianity gained a foothold in Sweden around the year 1000. Although its advance was extremely slow, it gradually made the art of writing familiar to the Swedes, who in the early 13th century wrote down their local law codes in the vernacular. These first books were followed by religious writings in Latin, some historical chronicles, and translations of the most popular Euro-

pean romances. The literary level of these writings was relatively
high.

The 13th century also saw the growth of the powerful Hansa
towns, and their strength in Sweden resulted in an enduring
German influence. As in Denmark, a vast number of German
words were permanently adopted, and German as well as Latin
syntax affected the structure of the Swedish language. Politically,
the 14th century marked the beginning of foreign rule. It cul-
minated in the Kalmar Union, which, established late in the
century, succeeded for the first and only time in uniting all the
Scandinavian countries under one sovereign—the Danish. This
union lasted, at least formally, through the first quarter of the
16th century. But in Sweden its effectiveness remained severely
hindered by native resentment of Danish domination. Continuous strife and rebellion against the power of Copenhagen did
little to encourage literary activities. Consequently, the most vital
genre was folk poetry, especially the ballads.

Simultaneous with the secession of Sweden from the Kalmar
Union was the advent of the Lutheran Reformation. This change
of creed, however, did not bring about much change in literature.
Indeed, the first hundred years following the Reformation are
notable only for their sterility and for the replacement of Latin
by the vernacular as the written language. Didactic and religious
writing remained predominant, and while some attempts were
made at creating a national drama, they proved fumbling and
ineffective.

Sweden's victorious campaigns against Russia and Poland at
the beginning of the 17th century, and her fateful intervention
in the Thirty Years' War, established the country as a formidable
military power. The great surge of national pride became a stim-
ulus for Swedish literature, and a group of outstanding poets
emerged. While some of these wrote in the impressively grand
and classic manner of Europe, others produced simple lyrics,
remarkable not only as poetry, but valuable because of their
generally liberating effect on the poetic language (see Wivallius,
p. 278).

Sweden enjoyed her position unchallenged for one hundred
years. Her power was finally curtailed, however, by military
defeat by Russia in the first quarter of the 18th century. After

the fall of the Swedish empire, currents from the English and French Enlightenment became visible in the literature. The influence of France was further entrenched later in the century when Gustavus III ascended the throne. An enlightened despot and a great admirer of French culture, he vigorously promoted art, theater, and literature. He founded the Swedish Academy and gathered at his court the foremost writers of the time. A general growth in Swedish letters became apparent (see Bellman, p. 284).

Shortly after 1800 Sweden lost Finland to Russia. It was her last possession. A few years later, however, Norway was transferred to the Swedish crown. Both these events coincided, more or less, with the introduction of Romanticism, which became, as it had in Norway, nationalistic in character. Greatly stimulated by this patriotic fervor, the Romantic period became a golden age for Swedish poetry. Never before had so many excellent writers appeared simultaneously on the literary scene. Swedish poetry was translated into the great cultural tongues of Europe, while more use was made of the novel as a medium for literary expression. For the first time, the world became aware of Swedish literature (see Tegnér, p. 290).

Soon after, Sweden began the transformation from an agrarian society to an industrial one. The changed social conditions required new literary norms, and with the steady advance of liberal ideas (see Rydberg, p. 297), Romanticism was finally replaced. The result was similar to that which had already occurred in Denmark and Norway: a preoccupation with social problems and an interest in the life of the working classes. But Realism came later and had a shorter life span in Sweden than in the neighboring countries. Even its leaders and chief exponents were soon pursuing other paths (see Strindberg, p. 302).

Because the reign of Realism was short and weak, the inevitable Neo-Romantic reaction which followed made an easy entry into Swedish literature. Dissatisfied with photographic depiction of reality, young writers denounced the rigid conventions of their predecessors and demanded for literature more freedom, more artistry, and more imagination. While they sang of the joys of life and delighted in exotic themes as well as those of Swedish nature (see Heidenstam, p. 317), they were, at the same time, clearly aware and critical of social conditions (see Fröding, p. 322). Many drew heavily on the regional, rural tradition (see Lagerlöf, p. 309, and Karlfeldt, p. 328). The closing years of the 19th century were one of the most fruitful periods of Swedish poetry.

A trend toward a new or renewed realism became discernible early in the 20th century and grew to maturity during the twenties. Significantly, many of its adherents were recruited from the proletariat, and in the hands of these social critics the novel reached an unprecedented level of artistic sophistication.

Sweden was spared physical destruction in World War I, but her writers did not escape the restlessness and anguish of the postwar period (see Lagerkvist, p. 339). Many adopted a pessimistic and cynical view of life (see Bergman, p. 331), while experimentation in form and in mode of expression became a distinct feature of literary production. Sharing the fears of other Scandinavian writers, Sweden's most prominent authors spoke out boldly against the growing Fascist movements of the thirties. Though Sweden again escaped direct participation when World War II broke out, there was never any doubt where her sympathies lay.

FOLK BALLAD
(probably 14th century)

Throughout the centuries, writers and artists have borrowed material either from the classics or from their native literature and remolded it to their own needs and purposes. An example of this is Ingmar Bergman's use of the medieval folk ballad which is printed below for the film *The Virgin Spring*. The subject matter of this ballad is typical of literature known in the Middle Ages as "Miracles of the Virgin." Although the ballad has earlier analogues in southern Europe, in Swedish tradition it acquired the character of a legend which supposedly occurred in the district of Östergötland, not far from the city of Linköping. Kärna parish has remained in existence and in the surrounding countryside, at least up until the last century, people could still recount a number of tales connected with the tragic events described in the ballad. In the parish churchyard, one may even today see the spring which, according to tradition, welled forth on the spot where the maiden's head was severed from her body.

The Daughter of Töre in Vänge

Töre's daughter of Vänge town,
She sleeps too long in her bed of down.
She oversleeps the morning Mass,
May God have mercy on this churchgoing lass!

Lady Märeta climbs up to the loft
—The forest was wet and cold—
Her daughter Karin she wakens so soft
—And the buds on the trees unfold.

"Rise up my daughter, be not slow;
Thou shalt to church in Kaga go."

Noble Karin sat on her bed,
Binding her locks with a ribbon red.

Noble Karin donned her silken shift,
The work of fifteen maidens' fingers swift.

Noble Karin slipped over her head
The lovely skirts with the golden thread.

Noble Karin donned her cloak of blue,
Now to leave for church she was due.

In the midst of the forest gloom
Three herdsmen in her path did loom.

"Either you serve as our herdsmen's wife
Or thou shalt lose your young life."

"Do not try thy force on me,
Or my father will deal with thee."

"Neither thy father nor kin do we fear,
After we slay thee we shall not be here."

First she became the herdsmen's wife
Then she lost her budding young life.

They led her by her golden hair
Into a grove of birches fair.

By her golden hair so free
They pinned her against a fallen tree.

From her body they cut her golden head,
A spring welled forth where the girl lay dead.

They stripped her body of clothes and gold,
Filled their bags with all they could hold.

In a shallow grave they lay her down
And took her clothes to the nearby town.

By chance they followed the very same way
That noble Karin had taken that day.

They walked so long and the path was the same
That to Vänge the herdsmen came.

They came to the house on Sir Töre's lands.
Waiting at the door Sir Töre stands.

"You look so warm in your coat of fur,
We herdsmen are cold, can you shelter us, sir?"

Into his house of stone he did lead
The herdsmen, and offered wine and mead.

Sir Töre for his daughter yearned.
Why has his Karin not returned?

Before Lady Märeta went up to bed
She turned to look when a herdsman said:

"Do you want to buy a silken shift,
Surely the work of nine maidens swift?"

When the garment he did show
The mother's heart was filled with woe.

Lady Märeta went to her husband's room
To bring him tidings of Karin's doom.

"Wake up my lord, I tell of slaughter,
The herdsmen have slain thy beautiful daughter.

"Her bloodied shift the herdsmen possess,
Anguish upon my heart does press."

Into the hall ran the noble lord,
Under his cloak was a naked sword.

He killed the first, and the second too,
And then the third he also slew.

Then Sir Töre threw down his sword,
"Have mercy on my deed, dear Lord.

"How shall I atone for this deed so gory?
I shall build a church of stone to Thy glory.

"That, we shall willingly do,"
—The forest was wet and cold—
"Let the Kärna church be my penance true."
—And the buds on the trees unfold—

Translated by Lars Malmström
AND *David Kushner*

LARS WIVALLIUS
(1605–69)

Wivallius is one of the most curious figures in the whole of Swedish literature. Of humble origin, he earned a lawyer's degree, but his utterly unscrupulous practices soon got him in trouble with the authorities. He spent most of his early life wandering from one place to another, staying for longer periods only when in prison. His works, written mainly during these enforced "sojourns," reflect much of the same spontaneity and charm that enabled him to lie and cheat his adventurous way through life. But it was precisely these qualities, combined with a certain conscious refinement, that brought Swedish poetry a step forward, freeing it from much of its former stiffness. For this reason, rogue though he was, Wivallius is considered by many to be the first really important poet to appear in Swedish literature.

"Song to Liberty" and "On a Dry and Cold Spring" date from 1632 and 1642 respectively.

Song to Liberty

Ah, Liberty, thou noble thing,
What joy supreme to own thee!
From poverty's cradle shouldst thou spring
Yet no one would disown thee,
E'en though in darkest wilderness
I'd find thee, starved but loyal,
I'd treasure thee, far more, ah yes,
Than any garment royal.

The captive bird with drooping wing
For liberty is aching,
He sings, his nature is to sing,
Though his sad heart be breaking,
Ah, when he hears the birds' sweet song

Which fills the green grove glistening,
Which fills the warm air all day long,
Then mute he sits a-listening.

* * * * * * * * * * * * *

The deer, within the castle walls,
Who feed on clover fragrant,
And those who roam in forest halls,
'Mong thorns and rocks, thus vagrant,
Have not the same fresh look, alas!
One walks by plashing fountain,
The other leaps o'er dewy grass,
On quick limbs, down the mountain.

A deer with golden band around
His neck, by well filled manger,
Another who's compelled to bound
The rocky streams in danger,
Have they the same bold courage? No!
The same heart does not lead them;
Thus freedom's best, sweet freedom, oh!
I would I had my freedom.

Thou star-lit firmament, oh, shed
Hot tears with me, I'm banished!
All happiness from me has fled,
My liberty has vanished,
For two long years, each morning bland,
In iron chains I've risen,
Just for a maid from Denmark's land,
Ah, such is life—a prison!

Of no avail my travels now,
No help for world-wide rover—
What good's the knowledge which my brow
Through long nights sweated over?
What weight has my experience
In foreign land and story?
Much vanity and little sense
This mad world's show and glory.

* * * * * * * * * * * * *

Ye birds that cleave the azure deep,
Ye beasts in woodland bower,

Lament my youthful years, oh, weep
Fair Muse, your tears let shower!
Neptunian hosts in lake and sea,
Oh, mourn my bitter trial,
And all ye people, pity me,
That dwell on land and isle!

Ye youths of Sweden's beauteous land,
In anger break your lances!
Ye Swedish maidens sweet and bland,
Let tears bedim your glances!
Bewail my fate—I feel as though
I ne'er was born of woman:
Disgraced, dishonored, sad I go,
No friends—I feel not human.

My love talk failed; it wove my snare,
How brief the joy I tasted!
For but a maiden sweet and fair
Now everything is wasted.
Hard world, beneath thy blow I moan,
Wish death would come and save me,
I suffer for this girl alone,
And yet, her heart she gave me.

Go all ye zephyrs, your complaint
Sound loud in caves abysmal!
Ye sighing trees break your restraint,
Cry out through forest dismal!
Thou echo, through tears' long night, stay
With me—there dawns no morrow,
Resound my wailing night and day,
Lament and share my sorrow!

Translated by Reinhold Ahléen

On a Dry and Cold Spring

A dry and cold spring makes the summer brief,
And the winter food drives away.
God help us! This spring brings nothing but grief,

The season most lovely and gay—
Sun hear us, come near us!
Expel this thief
Who snatches the beauty of May!

Good May-showers give, let it drizzle all day,
Let warm dew moisten each herb.
The dry weather kill, let no frost-robe gray
The delicate flowers perturb.
Be gracious, be gracious!
For them I pray
Who fear God, and no one disturb.

Let heavenly portals widen ere long,
Tear open the clouds' thick screen.
Let us hear the nightingale's charming song,
Now mute at the cheerless scene.
Let singing be ringing
In young folks' throng,
Let the children play on the green!

❄　❄　❄　❄　❄　❄　❄　❄　❄　❄　❄　❄

Give gladness and hope, let the lark rejoice,
Let the early swallow not die!
Let through Sweden's realm every heart and voice
Sing praises, no more to sigh!
Give flowers, sweet bowers,
Green hay—the noise
From a thousand cuckoos nigh!

❄　❄　❄　❄　❄　❄　❄　❄　❄　❄　❄　❄

O lengthen the day, light the stars at night,
Let the warm rain drench through the mold,
Bid the blackbird warble with all his might,
He's been silent through winter's cold!
Let dancing and glancing
Fill meadows bright
By maidens most fair to behold!

❄　❄　❄　❄　❄　❄　❄　❄　❄　❄　❄　❄

Ay, glorious sun, thou'rt the poor man's friend,
Thy light is for all, shine again
O'er cottage and farm, thy brilliant rays send
To chase the chill breeze to his den!
Now longing and thronging

Are women and men
In thy bright light their way to wend.

Step forth from the clouds, on the farmer smile,
Let verdure drape wood and dale!
See the thirsty, dry fields, mile after mile—
If no rain comes the crops will fail.
Come charmer, grow warmer,
Dispel this guile,
And quickly thy azure heights scale!

Let the groves be green, make the earth content
With fruits; from meadow and glade
Let rise a balmy and glorious scent
That spreads through the woodland shade!
Of roses and posies,
Green leaves anent,
Let beautiful beds be made.

  ✻ ✻ ✻ ✻ ✻ ✻ ✻ ✻ ✻ ✻ ✻ ✻ ✻ ✻

Turn out the cattle to pasture, the ox
Is lowing for greensward and brook!
Let th' stabled beasts jump the mossy rocks,
Let the farmer plow every nook!
Let Autumn allot him
Ripe fruits, and flocks,
Then beam shall his stern, kind look.

  ✻ ✻ ✻ ✻ ✻ ✻ ✻ ✻ ✻ ✻ ✻ ✻ ✻ ✻

From flower and leaf let the bees, in swarms,
Their sweet honey draw; let ring
Their gay hum in place of the martial storms
That howl round our shores! Lord, bring
Peace gracious, most precious
To nations in arms,
Bless all with a prosperous spring!

Thou reigneth, O Lord, and all is Thine!
In the heav'ns is Thy glorious throne,
I praise Thee, Thou'lt hear every prayer of mine
To Thy regions celestial gone!
Restore us, let o'er us
Thy goodness shine,
Our want Thou knowest alone!

We've sinned against Thee, merciful God,
Forgive us! Dispel our dismay!
Inclement weather with rigorous rod
Has frightened the sun away,
Grant flowers, warm showers,
This dry, cold sod
Make fruitful again, we pray!

Translated by Reinhold Ahléen

CARL MICHAEL BELLMAN
(1740–95)

The first writer of unquestionable genius in Swedish letters, Bellman has been now, for two centuries, Sweden's favorite author. He was born in Stockholm, studied for a while at Uppsala University, but left without taking a degree and returned to the capital to lead the life of a Bohemian. Though he had good connections at court, and was in good standing with King Gustavus III, from whom he received a small annual pension, he always felt more at home among the lower circles of society. A popular frequenter of the more dubious taverns of the time, he sang his verses to his own joyous melodies, interweaving poetry and music with such artistry as to make them virtually inseparable. Although most of his poetry celebrates life, it is often set against a dark background of fear of death.

Bellman's poetry was written to be sung. Certainly, it will be, as long as the Swedish language lives.

The selections below are from Bellman's two collections, *Fredmans Epistlar* ("Fredman's Epistles"), 1790, and *Fredmans Sånger* ("Fredman's Songs"), 1791.

To Old Movitz, Ill With Consumption
An Elegy

Empty your glass! Behold where Death is waiting,
Sharp'ning his sword while standing at your door!
Be not afraid; he holds ajar the grating,
Then shuts the tomb and leaves it as before.
Movitz, consumption may spare you a year, man, . . .
       Be of good cheer, man,
Tune up the chords and sing of youth once more!

Thin is your cheek, and yellow-pale its hue is,
Sunken your chest, your shoulders bent—too bad!

Let's see your hand—each vein all swelled and blue is,
Flabby and moist, as if a bath you'd had:
Limp and perspiring your hand is, old fellow, . . .
   Come, strike your 'cello,
Pour out the bottle, sing and drink, be glad!

You're dying fast—so deep your cough is sounding:
Hollow it rings; all's emptiness within.
White is your tongue, your frightened heart is pounding,
Soft as a sponge are muscles, thews, and skin.
Breathe—Lord! the fumes that come out of your throttle . . .
   Hand me the bottle!
Sing of good Bacchus! Here's your health! Begin!

Out of this flask your death by drops is flowing
All unobserved, as laugh and song go by.
Trust me, a troop of maggots fiercely glowing
Pours from yon glass that now you tilt on high.
You are consumed. Into tears you are turning,
   Entrails are burning.
Can you still pledge me one more health? "Ay, ay!"

Well, then, your health! For Bacchus bids farewell now,
From Venus' throne receive your last adieu.
Fondly for her the tide of blood may swell now;
Slight though it be, it warms your body through.
Sing, read, forget, think, or tearfully ponder, . . .
   What, are you fonder
Still of your liquor? Die? No. Here's to you!

Translated by Charles Wharton Stork

To Ulla at a Window in Fishertown, Noon of a Summerday

Ulla, mine Ulla, to thee may I proffer
Reddest of strawberries, milk, and wine,
Or a bright carp from the fen shall I offer,
Or but a bowl from the fountain so fine?

Truly the flood-gates of heaven are broken—
Rich is the scent of flower and tree—
Drizzling, the clouds now the sun but foretoken,
    Thou may'st see.

Chorus

Isn't it delightful, little Fishertown?
    "Delightful! Be it spoken."
Here the rows of tree-trunks stretching proudly down
    In brand-new gown;
    There the quiet reaches
    Of the inlet flow;
    And off yonder mid the ditches
    Ploughed land, lo!
Isn't it delightful—all these meadows, though?
    "Delightful, so
    Delightful, oh!"

Hail, sweet, who there at the window dost hover!
Hark, how the bells from the city sound!
See how with dust-clouds the carriages cover
All the green hue of the country around!
I in my saddle drowsing survey thee.
Hand from the window, cousin mine,
First a dry rusk and a can of, I pray thee,
    Hogland wine.

Isn't it delightful, *etc.*

Off to the stable is led my good charger,
Whinnying, stamping in mad career.
Soon in the doorway he stands. How much larger
Seem now his eyes as he stares at thee here!
Thou dost enkindle all nature with pleasure,
As thy warm eyes enflame now me.
Clang! at thy lattice with heart's fullest measure—
    Here's to thee.

Chorus

Isn't it delightful, little Fishertown?
    "Delightful! Be it spoken."
Here the rows of tree-trunks stretching proudly down
    In brand-new gown;

There the quiet reaches
Of the inlet flow;
And off yonder mid the ditches
Ploughed land, lo!
Isn't it delightful—all these meadows, though?
"Delightful, so
Delightful, oh!"

Translated by Charles Wharton Stork

Of Fishing

Up, Amaryllis! Wake, little sweeting!
Clouds are all fleeting,
Cool the air.
See how the glowing
Rainbow, its flowing
Colors bestowing,
Makes all fair.
Amaryllis, truly I assure thee,
Peace on Neptune's bosom I'll secure thee.
Let the god of sleep no longer lure thee,
Let him no more overmaster thee there!

Let's go a-fishing—nets are all spread now—
Mope not in bed now,
Quickly rise!
Come thou, all bodiced,
Kirtled so modest;
Fish of the oddest
Be our prize!
Amaryllis, little one, awaken—
Lacking thee, of joy I'm quite forsaken;
From our boat the spray will soon be shaken,
As mid the dolphins and sirens it flies.

Bring rods and lines, and spoon for our trolling!
Up the sun's rolling—
Hasten thee!
Sweet, let us revel,
Think thou no evil,
Say no uncivil
Nay to me!

Let us sail into the cove so shallow,
Or to yonder sound thy love did hallow,
Erst, when at my fortune that poor fellow
Thyrsis was angry as angry could be.

Come, then, embark and sing with me sweetly!
    Love rules completely
    In our breast.
    Winds that would harm us
    Cannot alarm us,
    Love still can charm us,
    Make us blest.
Happy on the ocean's fretful billow,
As within thine arms my head I pillow,
Unto death my soul thy soul would follow . . .
Sing, O ye sirens, re-echo the rest!

Translated by Charles Wharton Stork

A Nota Bene

When I have a flask well laden—
Nota bene, with good wine,
And thereto a pretty maiden—
Nota bene, who is mine—
Joy have I in fullest dower—
Nota bene, for an hour.

Gay the time that we inherit—
Nota bene, not all good:
Blows are oft rewards of merit,
Enemies desire our blood.
Many think in bliss to dwell—
Nota bene, bagatelle!

Go your way, life, never falter!
Stop, though—nota bene, there:
Age must never seek to alter
To a witch my sweetheart fair.
Wine and love exalt me high—
Nota bene, till I die.

Translated by Charles Wharton Stork

Of Haga

Butterflies to Haga faring,
When the frosts and fogs are spent,
Find the woods their home preparing,
Flower-enwrought their pleasure-tent.
Insects from their winter trances
Newly wakened by the sun
O'er the marsh hold festal dances
And along the dock-leaves run.

Haga, on thy bosom dozes
Many a plot of verdure brave,
And the snowy swan reposes
Proudly on thy rippling wave.
In the woods a distant clamor
Comes re-echoed faint and fine:
From the quarry sounds the hammer,
Axes ring mid birch and pine.

See the little naiads flashing;
Golden horns they lift in air!
Cool cascades are blithely dashing
O'er the heights of Solna fair.
Statues greet the eyes that gaze there
Down the arching forest aisles;
Wheels go by, a dust they raise there—
Kindly then the peasant smiles.

Ah, what joy beyond repeating
Through that lovely park to rove,
To receive the fair one's greeting
While a monarch's eyes approve!
Each of his most gracious glances
Draws the tear of gratitude—
Ay, that royal look entrances
E'en the surly and the rude.

Translated by Charles Wharton Stork

ESAIAS TEGNÉR
(1782–1846)

In 1809, when Esaias Tegnér was a young docent at the University of Lund, Sweden suffered the loss of Finland to her traditional enemy, Russia. The event inspired the poet to write a long poem called *Svea* ("Sweden"). At once nationalistic and anti-Russian, the piece was awarded the Grand Prize of the Swedish Academy in 1811, and from that time on, Tegnér was recognized as one of Sweden's leading literary talents.

An undeclared Romantic, Tegnér had, since childhood, been a great admirer of the Icelandic sagas. One of them became the basis of his best known work, *Fritiof's Saga* (1825). This beautiful epic, which brought its author world recognition, illustrates Tegnér's forte as a poet: a sure sense of form, clear thought, and magnificent imagery. It is divided into twenty-four cantos of varying length and meter. The first and the ninth cantos are given here in their entirety.

Fritiof and Ingeborg

On Hilding's farm once dwelt a pair
Like plants beneath their guardian's care.
Never our Northern clime had nourished
Such shoots as there waxed green and flourished.

Like the young oak grew one of them:
Straight as a lance that lusty stem,
Whose crown in summer breezes shivering
Seems like a helm with bright plumes quivering.

Folded the other as the rose
At melting-time of April snows,
When Spring, with fruitful promise teeming
Within the rose-bud yet lies dreaming.

But tempests first must rouse their might
And oak contend with them in fight,
And summer suns put forth their power
Ere rose unfold to crimson flower.

Thus grew they, and joy dwelt with them,
And Fritiof was the oak's young stem:
But ah, the rose that green dales water
Was Ingeborg, the King's fair daughter.

Saw you the twain in light of day,
" 'Tis Freja's[1] palace," you would say,
"Where lightly trip her lover-minions
With golden hair and rosy pinions."

Saw you the twain in moonlight's sheen
Dancing beneath the coppice green,
"Was ever vision so entrancing—
The elf-king with his young bride dancing!"

Oh, happy, happy was the day
When his first runes he learnt to say:
No King so proud! but Bele's daughter
Must learn them too, and Fritiof taught her.

How smoothly o'er the waters blue
In their trim vessel sailed the two!
How sweet, as sail he deftly tended,
Her clap of hands with blithe voice blended!

No bird her nest so high could make
But he would seek it for her sake;
E'en that great bird that mocks the thunder
Of eggs and young the boy would plunder.

No stream so swift but he would bear
From shore to shore his playmate fair;
How sweet amid the torrents whirling
To feel white arms around him curling!

[1] More commonly Freyja. The goddess of love.

The first white flower of April's prime,
The first red fruit of Summer-time,
The first gold ear of Autumn's treasure,
All these he gathered for her pleasure.

But childhood's days are swiftly flown;
Behold them now—the youth full-grown,
With hopes and fears, and eyes of fire—
Her, blossomed, ripe for man's desire.

Forever hunting he would fare:
Such hunting his as few would dare—
Who spearless, swordless, all unaided,
The haunts of the wild bear invaded.

There fought they, breast to breast, till sore
Mangled, but still the conqueror,
With shouldered prize behold him faring.
What maid could flout such deeds of daring?

For womankind holds courage dear:
The brave is worthy of the fair;
As helm to forehead fitteth truly,
So brave with fair is wedded duly.

But when in dusk of wintry days
He read beside the firelight's blaze
Tales of high Gods who dwell immortal
Within Valhalla's[2] shining portal—

Thought he: So Freja's locks are gold,
A cornland neath soft breezes rolled;
My Ingeborg's have as fair a seeming—
O'er lily and rose gold network gleaming.

Fair is Iduna's[3] bosom, seen
Beneath her robe of silken green:
A robe I know, that half discloses
Twin elves of day like budding roses.

[2] Palace of Odin (see note 10, p. 190).
[3] Old Icelandic: Idunn. In Scandinavian mythology one of the goddesses. She was the keeper of the apples of youth, without which the gods would have become old and decrepit.

And fair are Frigga's[4] eyes of blue,
As spring-day heaven—so soft in hue;
Blue eyes know I, that as they kindle
Make June's bright day to darkness dwindle.

And Gerda's[5] cheeks are rosy-white—
Fresh snows in hues of Northern Light:
Cheeks have I seen whose blushes tender
Kindle two dawns of crimson splendor.

A heart I know whose gentleness
Nanna[6] might for her own confess:
O "Happy" Balder,[7] Lord of Heaven,
Rightly to thee that name is given!

To win the tears of friend so true,
Even to death, as Balder knew,
Loyal as Nanna's self, and tender—
With joy to Hel[8] would I surrender!"

But Ingeborg would sit and sing
Some chant in praise of hero-king,
And weave his form mid scenes entrancing,
Green groves, and sea with blue waves dancing.

In gold upon a snow-white ground
She wrought the buckler's shining round,
Lances with ruddy pennons streaming,
And, stiff with silver, hauberks gleaming.

Yet howsoe'er she weaveth, lo,
That face doth like to Fritiof's grow!
Crimson with shame she meets his glances,
And yet the heart within her dances.

But Fritiof carves, where'er he be,
An *I*, an *F*, on white-barked tree;
As their own hearts in love combining
So grew those runes together twining.

[4] I.e., Frigg, the wife of Odin.
[5] One of the goddesses.
[6] Wife of Balder (see note 9, p. 43).
[7] God of innocence and piety (see note 4, p. 42).
[8] Goddess of death (see note 2, p. 105).

When Dawn 'gins climb her widening stair—
Light's herald with the golden hair,
And life is stirred to new endeavor,
Their souls through day are parted never.

When Night creeps skyward from her lair—
World's mother with the dusky hair,
And stars through silent heaven are straying,
Each dreams of each, and one is praying—

"O Earth, to whom each new-born Spring
Fresh garlands for thy hair doth bring,
Give me the fairest! let me take them,
Crown for my lover's brow to make them."

"Thou Sea, whose glimmering floor is sown
With pearls in thousands, grant this boon:
Give me the fairest! I will make them
A band of light, so Ingeborg take them."

"Bright jewel in Odin's⁹ shining throne!
Eye of the world, thou glorious one,
Wert thou but mine, thy gold disk glaring
Should serve as shield for Fritiof's wearing."

"Thou lamp in Odin's halls of night!
Pale Moon, arrayed in pearly light!
Wert thou but mine, thine orb white-laden
I'd give to deck that fairest maiden."

But Hilding said, "The gifts of Heaven
Not equally to all are given.
That damsel—vainly hast thou sought her:
How should'st thou wed King Bele's daughter?

"To Odin throned above the earth
Her lineage goes, her scroll of birth.
In vain the son of Torsten striveth;
Like with its like best ever thriveth."

⁹ Supreme deity in Scandinavian mythology (see note 10, p. 190).

But Fritiof laughed, "*My* roll of birth
Goes down to graves beneath the earth!
Wood-king I slew—his skin, I wear it:
His forbears too by right inherit.

"A man freeborn will never yield:
The world lies in his hand to wield:
Fate may atone her past transgression:
A kingly crown is Hope's possession.

"High-born is Might—for dwells not Thor[10]
In Thrudvang yet, Might's ancestor?
Not birth he weigheth, but the doer,
And sword-blade maketh a mighty wooer.

"So fight I for my bride to be
Though Thor himself contend with me.
Live happy, my white rose, for ever,
And woe to him who us would sever!"

Translated by C. D. Locock

Ingeborg's Lament

Autumn is come:
Storm-winds are lashing the seas to foam.
Hurry they never so madly,
There I'd be gladly.

Long in the West
Watched I his sail as he flew on his quest:
Happy thou sail spreading over
Fritiof my lover!

Curl not so high,
Billows, your crests—swift enough doth he fly!
Shine on him, guard him from straying,
Stars, with your raying!

10 Chief warrior against the Giants (see note 5, p. 43).

When the Spring winds blow
Comes he again—but his loved one shall go
Ne'er thro' the palace to meet him—
Nowhere shall greet him.

Pallid and chill
For her love's sake lieth she there on the hill:
Or worse yet, lives, by her brother
Bound to another.

Thee will I tend,
Falcon he loved and hath left in the end;
Beautiful bird, I will feed thee
Here till he need thee.

Perched on his hand,
Weave I thy form with my silken strand:
Silver thy wings shall be gleaming—
Talons gold-seeming.

Hawk-wings they say
Freja once borrowed and flew on her way,
Seeking the wide world over
Öder[11] her lover.

Even tho' thine own
Pinions thou lent'st me, in vain were the loan:
Not till Death's shroud shall enwind me
Wings may I find me.

Hunter, with thee
Perched on my shoulder we'll gaze o'er the sea:
Never, for all your yearning,
See him returning.

When I am dead
Surely he cometh: then tell him I said,
"Fritiof, in tears tho' we sever,
Hail thee, for ever!"

Translated by C. D. Locock

---

[11] Also spelled Od. Freyja's husband who left her. At one time she set out
to seek for him all over the world.

VIKTOR RYDBERG

(1828–95)

Although Rydberg had written several novels, he did not attract much attention until he published his controversial pamphlet on *The Teaching of the Bible Concerning Christ*. After the stir caused by this publication, his fame steadily increased until, in the seventies and eighties, this former journalist became one of the central figures of Swedish cultural life.

An idealistic opponent of intolerance and narrow-mindedness, Rydberg wrote a number of pamphlets on church matters and was gradually drawn into politics, sitting for two years in the Swedish parliament. In 1884 he was made a professor at the newly founded University of Stockholm.

Although Rydberg occupies a prominent place in the evolution of the Swedish novel, he is now better remembered for his poetry. He brought the philosophical poem to polished perfection, and his influence upon later Swedish poetry has been immeasurable.

Of the following poems "The Bathing Children" and "A Flower" are both taken from *Dikter* ("Poems"), Vol. I, published in 1882; "Vain Quest of Beauty" is from *Vapensmeden* ("The Swordsmith"), 1891; "Longing" was written shortly before Rydberg's death in 1895.

Vain Quest of Beauty

Exhaustless, Nature, is thy patient mood,
Yea, as the Deep from which thou art renewed.
May not thy hand grow weary at the last
Of imitating on this isle of Time
The patterns of a region more sublime,
When all that loveliness will soon be past?
Will thy hand never falter or grow weak
Strewing soft color on an infant's cheek

Or in a flower's cup, when thou dost know
The hues must perish like the sunset's glow?
The tender ones, with beauty as of heaven,
Bear to their grave the gifts that thou hast given.

Under Death's garland hast thou ever seen
On any furrowed brow the light serene
Of innocence thou pouredest on it? Never,
Neither on man's nor yet on woman's ever.
Thou bearest bud on bud in endless troup,
Whose promise is but born to fade and droop.
Thou weavest; then the web, for all thy skill,
Is rent, but never stands thy shuttle still.
Strange, that thy strength has lasted till today,
Thou from thy work-bench hast not shrunk away
Despairing at the grim, unending play!

Translated by Charles Wharton Stork

The Bathing Children

Clumps of lilies-of-the-valley, daisies too on either hand
Fringe a small transparent brooklet gliding o'er its bed of sand;
Hedges clad in snowy blossoms breathe their perfume manifold,
Maples o'er the water-lilies lean their boughs of green and gold.

Two small children, boy and girl, are sitting there amid the flowers,
Hawk-and-dove they've been a-playing all the warm long morning
    hours.
Says the boy, "I'm going bathing, it's so hot here in the sun."
"Yes, the water's cool," the girl says; "I'll go bathing too. What fun!"

Soon the boy has cast his stockings and his other clothes aside,
Scattered on the grass about him, though the dew is scarcely dried.
Pantaloons with bright suspenders which his mother made for him,
Though discarded, show the roundness of each little chubby limb.

By this careless heap the maiden, far more orderly than he,
Lays her kerchief, skirt, and bodice, with her linen, daintily;
Lays on top her summer bonnet with its ribbons all agleam,
And with shouts of joy the two then jump into the limpid stream.

Look! to meet the merry children how the brook's clear waters leap,
Round their fresh and lovely bodies cuddling wavelets kiss and creep;
Pearly drops fly all around them high above the streamlet's brim
Where the boy with glad endeavor shows his playmate how to swim.

If she learn, he'll fill her basket full of nuts, a princely treat.
How she sprawls and kicks and splashes with her plump and dainty
   feet!
How she stretches out first one arm, then the other, while she rests
With the boy's firm hands upholding underneath her tender breasts!

Meanwhile from her new-built dwelling in a bending maple tree,
Twittering, a sparrow-mother spies the two, and thus thinks she:
"Though they have no wings to fly with, yet their antics are the same
As when I and sparrow-father played in youth the splashing game."

So too when the lark above them, poising on his out-stretched wing,
Sees the innocents at play there, loud his throbbing quavers ring,
Like an echo of the gladness that resounded to the skies
When the first lark sang his rapture o'er the groves of Paradise.

Translated by Charles Wharton Stork

Longing

He longs with a tireless yearning,
Still seeking, wandering, turning
At all times and everywhere,
The sought-for goal receding,
Flitting, enticing, leading
With shifting likeness fair.

A nodding flower of azure
Above the field's ripe treasure
First lures the wanderer on,
But when he would stoop to pick it,
It sinks in the billowy thicket
Of rye-blades and is gone.

A banner all golden-rifted,
That spirit hands have lifted,
On sunset towers upborne,
An echo resounding faintly,
That's blown from an old and quaintly
Wrought silver legend-horn.

An organ-rapture outpouring
From some great cathedral soaring
Mid streets where visions dwell.
The blow of a hammer thund'rous
When angels rear a wondrous
Dream-lovely citadel.

A sighing of ocean surges
When dawn's first wave emerges
On night's pale galaxy.
He listens and looks with yearning,
Still this way and that way turning
To find what it may be.

A sea to which years run lightly,
A river that mirrors brightly
The spring and its beauties rare,
Beside whose waters haunted
Two mortals languish enchanted
And see but each other there.

The river hastes from the flowers
To autumn's golden bowers,
And whirls the dry leaves they wore
To ocean, the dark Unbounded.
The wanderer, staring astounded,
Asks: "What of the farther shore?"

Perhaps his desire is bended
On something uncomprehended,
Which no man may comprehend;
But he must ever be yearning,
Must ever be wandering, turning,
And seeking it without end.

And should he reach World's Ending,
With no road further tending,
The border of Nothingness,
He'd bend him over the steep there
And gaze into the deep there
With straining-eyed distress.

And leaning over the steep there,
He'd cry into the deep there—
That echoless, vast Untrod—
And onward the shout should go where
Is naught but the voice of Nowhere,
Go ringing through Chaos: "God!"

Translated by Charles Wharton Stork

A Flower

It grew up by the cross' foot
on a lonely grave;
a broken heart to the flower's root
its nurture gave.

It gently blinked while bowing down
for the breeze of night, tear-stained and weak.
The fading scarlet on its gown
before adorned a maiden's cheek.

A riddle was in her eyes concealed;
but what it meant
to a youth at the graveside was revealed
by the flower's scent.

Translated by Hallberg Hallmundsson

AUGUST STRINDBERG
(1849–1912)

One of the most influential and ingenious of modern drama-
tists, Strindberg vies with Henrik Ibsen alone for the title of
Scandinavia's foremost playwright. Yet the two are very different. While Ibsen was a Realist who debated problems with
a clear, logical mind, Strindberg said about himself: "I am
not a Realist. I write best when I hallucinate." Ibsen's approach is that of the sober observer. Strindberg's plays are
filled with subjective intensity that constantly verges on
explosion.

Strindberg was an odd mixture of contrasting traits. Although extremely impressionable, he often rebelled fiercely
against the very people who had impressed him. Unsure of
what he should believe and anxious about what he should
think, Strindberg nevertheless could express deep, if unstable, convictions. In society he appeared to be quiet and
composed, but when writing he became as one possessed by
a demon. In view of all this, it is not surprising to learn that
his lack of emotional equilibrium resulted in several mental
crises, one of which developed into actual insanity. Uncanny
as it may seem, part of his self possessed the power to remain
outside the vortex, reporting with clinical precision on the
depths to which his mind had plunged. Indeed, it is precisely
this tension in Strindberg's mind between control and com-
bustibility that makes his drama such a powerful theatrical
experience.

The Stronger was written in 1889.

The Stronger
A scene

CHARACTERS
Mrs. X, *actress, married*
Miss Y, *actress, unmarried*

THE STAGE. *A corner in a ladies' café; two small tables of wrought iron, a red, plush-covered settee and a few chairs.*

Mrs. X (*enters, dressed in a winter coat and a hat, carrying a pretty Japanese basket on her arm.*)

Miss Y (*is sitting with a half-emptied bottle of beer in front of her, reading an illustrated magazine which she later exchanges for others.*)

Mrs. X. Hello, Amelie dear! Here you sit on Christmas Eve all alone like a poor bachelor.

Miss Y (*looks up from her magazine, nods, and continues reading.*)

Mrs. X. You know, I really feel sorry to see you like this all alone in a café—and on Christmas Eve, too. I feel as sorry as that time in Paris when I saw a wedding party in a restaurant, and the bride was reading the comics while the bridegroom was playing billiards with the witnesses. Ugh, I thought, with a beginning like that, what will the aftermath be like, and the end? Imagine! Playing billiards on his wedding night! I know, you'll say she was reading the comics, but that's quite different!

A Waitress (*enters, places a cup of chocolate in front of Mrs. X and leaves.*)

Mrs. X. You know what, Amelie! *Now* I think you should have held on to him! Remember that I was the first one to tell you to leave him? Do you remember that? You could have been married now and had a home. Remember last Christmas, how happy you felt when you were in the country with your fiancé's parents? How you praised domestic bliss and really wanted to get away from the theater! Yes, Amelie dear, a home is the best thing—next to the theater—and the kids, you know—well, you wouldn't understand that!

Miss Y (*looks disdainful.*)

Mrs. X (*sips a few spoonfuls from the cup, then opens the basket and exhibits some Christmas presents.*) Now I'll show you what I bought for the kids. (*Takes out a doll.*) Look at this one! This is for Lisa! See how she can roll her eyes and turn her neck? See? And here's a cork pistol for Maja. (*Loads and fires at Miss Y.*)

Miss Y (*appears frightened.*)

Mrs. X. Were you frightened? You didn't think I was going to shoot you, did you? Upon my soul, I believe you did! I wouldn't be surprised if *you* wanted to shoot *me,* since I got in your way—and that I know you can never forget—even though I was quite innocent. You still believe that I plotted to get you out of the Grand Theater, but I didn't! I didn't do it, though you think so! Well, it doesn't matter what I say, because you still believe it was me! (*Takes out a pair of embroidered slippers.*) And these are for my husband—with tulips that I embroidered myself. I detest tulips, understand, but he wants them on everything.

Miss Y (*looks up from the magazine with a mixed expression of irony and curiosity on her face.*)

Mrs. X (*puts one hand in each slipper.*) See what small feet Bob has? And what an elegant walk! You've never seen him in slippers, have you?

Miss Y (*laughs aloud.*)

Mrs. X. Such mincing steps, like this, see? (*She makes the slippers walk on the table.*)

Miss Y (*laughs aloud.*)

Mrs. X. And then, when he's angry, he stamps his foot like this: "Won't those damned maids ever learn to make coffee?" or "The morons haven't cut the lampwick properly!" And when there's a draft along the floor and his feet are freezing: "It's cold, dammit! Why can't those blasted idiots keep a fire going?" (*She rubs the sole of one slipper against the instep of the other.*)

Miss Y (*roars with laughter.*)

Mrs. X. And then he comes home and has to search for his slippers which Mary has shoved under the bureau . . . oh, but it's not right to sit and make fun of one's husband like this. He's a dear, anyway, a real little darling. You should have a man like him, Amelie, you really should! What are you laughing at? And then, you see, I know he's faithful to me; yes, that I know! For he's told me himself—what are you grinning at?— that when I was on tour in Norway, that rotten Frédérique tried to seduce him—can you imagine anything so beastly? (*Pause.*) I'd have scratched her eyes out if she'd come near him when I was home! (*Pause.*) It was fortunate that Bob told me himself, so I didn't hear it first as gossip. (*Pause.*) But you can be sure that Frédérique wasn't the only one! I don't know why, but all those women are just crazy about *my* husband. They must think he has something to say about jobs at the theater just because he's in the department. Maybe you've been trying with him too! I didn't quite trust you, but now I *know* that he didn't care about you, and it always seemed to me as if you had some grudge against him! (*Pause. They observe each other discomfited.*)

Mrs. X. Come over tonight, Amelie, and show us you're not angry—not at me, in any case. I don't know why, but it feels especially uncomfortable not being friends with you. Maybe it's because I got in your way that time—(*more slowly*)—or I really don't know why—at all! (*Pause.*)

Miss Y (*gazes curiously at Mrs. X.*)

Mrs. X (*thoughtfully.*) It was so strange about our relationship. The first time I saw you I was afraid of you—so afraid that I didn't dare let you out of my sight. No matter what, I always found myself around you. I didn't dare be your enemy; therefore I became your friend. But whenever you came to our house there was always a feeling of awkwardness, because I saw my husband didn't like you, and I was conscious of it just as I am of ill-fitting clothes. And I did everything I could to make him be nice to you, but without result—until you became engaged! Then you two became so friendly that for a while it looked as if, for the first time, you dared show your real feelings—when you were on the safe side. And afterward— how was it afterward? I wasn't jealous—that's strange! And I remember at the baptism, when you were godmother, that I

forced him to kiss you—and he did—but you were so abashed—
that is, I didn't notice it then—didn't think about it afterward
either—haven't thought about it until—now! (*Rises vehe-
mently.*) Why don't you say something? All this time you
haven't said a word; you've just let me talk! You have drawn
me out with your eyes and got out of me all these thoughts,
which were lying there like raw silk in a cocoon—thoughts—
suspicions, perhaps—let me think. Why did you break off your
engagement? Why didn't you ever come to our house after
that? Why don't you want to come to us tonight?

Miss Y (*looks as if she wants to speak.*)

Mrs. X. Hush! You needn't say a word, for now I understand
everything myself! Oh, yes, that was the reason! Now it all fits
together! That's how it is! For shame, I won't sit at the same
table as you! (*Moves her things to the other table.*) That's
why I had to embroider those hateful tulips on his slippers,
because you liked tulips. That's why—(*throws the slippers on
the floor*)—we had to live on the lake during the summer,
because you couldn't stand the seashore. That's why my boy
had to be named Eskil, because that was your father's name.
That's why I had to wear your colors, read your authors, eat
your favorite dishes, drink your beverages—your chocolate, for
example. That's why—oh, my God—it's ghastly when I think
about it, ghastly! Everything, everything was forced on me
by you, even your passions! Your soul burrowed into mine like
a worm into an apple, and ate and ate, and dug and dug, till
only the peel was left, and a little black powder! I wanted to
escape you, but I couldn't. You lay like a snake with your
black eyes and hypnotized me. I felt how my wings beat the
air only to drag me down; I lay in the water with my feet
bound together, and the more I tried to swim, the deeper down
I worked myself—down, down, till I sank to the bottom. And
there you lay waiting like a giant crab, ready to grab me with
your claws—and now I lie there!

Oh, how I hate you, hate you, hate you! But you—you only
sit and remain silent, calm, indifferent—indifferent to everything and everybody—whether others are happy or unhappy—
incapable of hating or loving—immovable like a stork at a

rat-hole. You couldn't go in after your prey yourself, you couldn't pursue it, but you could outwait it! Here you sit in your corner—do you know it's called the rat-trap—after you?—and you read your papers to see if anybody's doing badly, if anybody's got into trouble, if anybody's been fired from the theater. You sit here and watch your victims, calculate your chances like a pilot appraising shipwrecks for salvage, and receive your tributes.

Poor Amelie! You know, I still feel sorry for you, because I know you're unhappy. You're unhappy like one who's wounded, and malicious because you're wounded! I can't feel angry at you even though I want to, for in spite of it all you are the smaller one. Yes, that thing with Bob I don't care about! What harm does it do me? And whether you or someone else taught me to drink chocolate doesn't make any difference! (*Sips a spoonful out of the cup. Smugly.*) Chocolate is very good for you, anyway! And if I learned from you how to dress—*tant mieux*—it's only brought my husband closer to me—and there's where you lost while I gained. Yes, judging from certain signs, I believe you've already lost him! Surely you meant me to break it off as you did. You regret that now—but, you see, I don't. We mustn't be small-minded, you know. And why should I take only what nobody else wants?

Perhaps, when all is said and done, I'm really at this moment the stronger. You never got anything from me, you only gave away—and now it's with me as with the thief: when you woke up, I possessed what you had lost.

Why else was it that everything you touched turned worthless, sterile? You couldn't keep the love of any man with your tulips and your passions—as I could. You didn't manage to learn the art of life from your authors, but I did. You didn't have any little Eskil even if that was your father's name! And why are you always and ever so silent, silent, silent? Yes, I thought it was strength; but perhaps it was only that you had nothing to say! Because you couldn't think of anything! (*Rises and picks up the slippers.*)

Now I'll go home and take the tulips with me—your tulips! You couldn't learn anything from others, you couldn't bend—

and therefore you broke like a dry reed—but I didn't do that! Thanks, Amelie, for all your good lessons, thanks for teaching my husband how to love! Now I'll go home and love him! (*Leaves.*)

Translated by Hallberg Hallmundsson

SELMA LAGERLÖF

(1858–1940)

Selma Lagerlöf had been a schoolteacher for a number of years when she made her debut as a novelist. The reception of her first book, *Gösta Berling's Saga*, was such that it enabled her to devote all her time to writing, though it may very well have been her juvenile book *The Wonderful Adventures of Nils* which first carried her name around the world.

Miss Lagerlöf was first and foremost a storyteller of captivating charm. Her form was that of the legend or saga; her style Romantic, pathetic, truthful, and even naive. Her work is permeated by a spirit of casuistry, and the virtues which she glorifies are, above all, self-denial and self-sacrifice. She was awarded the Nobel Prize for literature in 1909, the first Swedish writer to be so honored. Five years later she was elected to the Swedish Academy.

"The Bird's Nest" is from *Osynliga länkar* ("Invisible Links"), published in 1894.

The Bird's Nest

Hatto the hermit was standing still in the waste and praying to God. A storm was blowing, and his long beard and disheveled hair fluttered around him like the wind-tossed grass that crowns an old ruin. But he did not brush his hair out of his eyes or push his beard into his girdle, for he held his arms uplifted in prayer. Ever since the sun rose he had kept his sinewy, hairy arms raised toward the sky as steadfastly as a tree stretches out its branches, and purposed to remain in that attitude until the evening. He had a serious matter to pray about. He was a man who had experienced much of the world's evil. He had himself persecuted and pained others, and persecution and pain inflicted by others had fallen to his share to a degree that he found intolerable.

So he had gone out into the great wilderness, dug out for himself an underground dwelling by the riverside, and became a saint whose prayers were heard at God's throne.

Hatto the hermit stood there by the riverside, outside his grotto, and prayed the great prayer of his life. He prayed God to let the Day of Judgment break upon this evil world. He invoked the angels with the trumpets who should announce the overthrow of the power of sin. He called on the waves of the sea of blood which should drown the unrighteous, and the plague which should fill the churchyards with heaps of corpses.

Round about him stretched the barren moor. But a little higher up on the riverbank stood an old willow tree with a short trunk, which swelled out into a great head-shaped protuberance from which fresh green clusters of branches continually grew. Every autumn it was stripped of the year's fresh growth by the scattered dwellers in the plain where there was very little fuel. Every spring the tree put forth new pliant shoots, and on stormy days these could be seen waving about it, like Hatto the hermit's hair and beard about him.

A pair of wagtails who were accustomed to build their nest on the upper part of the willow's trunk among the sprouting twigs had intended to begin their building enterprise that very day, but the branches were lashing about so furiously that the birds could find no peace. They came flying with rush stalks and root fibers and sedge, but had to go back with their errand unaccomplished. Just then they observed the aged Hatto, who was praying God that a storm might come seven times more violent than one which could only sweep away a small bird's nest or wreck an eagle's aerie.

Of course no one alive now can understand how moss-grown and dried-up and gnarled and black and unlike anything human such an old man dwelling in the wilderness might become. The skin was drawn so tightly over his forehead and cheeks that he very nearly resembled a death's-head, and only a little glimmer at the bottom of his eye sockets showed that he was alive. There was no curve in his body on which the dried muscles stood out stiffly, and his upstretched bare arms consisted merely of some bones clothed with creased, hardened, barklike skin. He wore an old tight-fitting black mantle. He was burnt brown by the sun, and black with dirt. Finally his hair and beard were light-colored, showing the effects of the rain and the sun, and had assumed the same gray-green color as the underside of the willow leaves.

The birds which flew about, seeking for a place to build in, took Hatto the hermit for another old willow, cut short in its upward strivings by axe and saw, as the real one was. They circled around him many times, went away and returned, made careful observations of the paths which led to him, remarked his situation with regard to birds of prey and storms, found it highly unfavorable, but determined nevertheless to choose him because of his nearness to the river, and the knolls of sedge, and easy access to the necessary provisions. One of them shot swift as an arrow down into his outstretched hand, and deposited his root fiber in it.

There was a pause in the storm, so that the root fiber was not at once carried out of his hand, but there was no pause in the hermit's prayers. "Oh Lord, come soon and destroy this world of corruption so that men may not succeed in piling more guilt on themselves! Save the unborn children from life—the living are past salvation!"

The storm recommenced, and the little root fiber fluttered out of the hermit's great sinewy hand, but the birds came again and tried to fasten the foundations of their new home between his fingers. Suddenly a clumsy and dirty thumb closed over the stalks and held them fast, and four fingers curved themselves over the palm of the hand so as to form a quiet nook to build in.

But the hermit continued his prayers. "Lord, where are the skies of fire which destroyed Sodom? When wilt Thou open the fountains of heaven which lifted the ark to the top of Ararat? Is not the store of Thy patience exhausted, and are not the vessels of Thy grace empty? Lord, when wilt Thou descend from the cloven skies?"

And then Hatto the hermit beheld feverish visions of the Day of Judgment. The earth quaked and the heavens glowed with fire. Under the red sky he saw black clouds of flying birds; over the ground there rolled, roaring and bellowing, herds of frightened animals.

But at the same time that he was engrossed in these fiery visions his eyes began to follow the flight of the small birds as they sped

to and fro with lightning-like celerity, and with a little cheep of
satisfaction fitted a new stalk into the nest. The old man never
thought of moving. He had made a vow to pray standing still with
outstretched hands the whole day in order to compel the Lord
in this manner to listen to his prayers. The more exhausted his
body became, the more vivid were the apparitions that filled his
brain. He saw the walls of towns fall in ruin and the dwellings
of men collapse. Crowds of shrieking, panic-stricken people
rushed past him, pursued by angels of vengeance and destruction, lofty shapes with severe, beautiful faces, wearing silver
armor, riding black horses, and brandishing scourges woven of
white lightnings.

The two small wagtails built and carpentered diligently the
whole day, and the work made great progress. On this knolly
heath with its stiff sedge, and by this river with its reed and
rushes, there was no want of building material. They had no
pause for rest all day long. Glowing with fervor and delight they
sped to and fro, and before evening came they had nearly finished
the roof to their nest.

But before the evening came the hermit had fastened his eyes
on them more and more. He followed them in their flight, he
scolded them when they behaved stupidly, he was indignant
when the wind blew them about, and was most impatient of all
if they made a pause. So the sun sank and the birds went to rest
in their accustomed sleeping place among the reeds.

Anyone who stoops down as twilight deepens on the waste so
that his head is not much higher than the ground can see wonderful sights outlined against the glowing west. Owls with great
round wings sweep over the plain, invisible to anyone who stands
upright. Vipers wriggle about lithe and quick, their small heads
supported by swanlike crooked necks. Great toads crawl forward
lazily, hares and water rats fly from beasts of prey, and a fox
makes a spring after a bat who is chasing midges above the
river. Every hillock seems to be teeming with life. But amid all
this the small birds slept on the swaying stems of the reeds, secure from all harm in their place of rest, which no enemies could
approach without making a splash in the water or shaking the
reeds and awaking them.

When morning came the wagtails at first believed that the

doings of the previous day had been a beautiful dream. They had
carefully observed the way and flew straight to their nest, but
it was gone. They hunted about the plain seeking for it, and flew
straight up in the air to reconnoiter. Not a trace of nest or tree
was to be seen. At last they settled on a couple of stones by the
riverside and pondered the matter. They wagged their long tails
and turned their heads about. Where had the tree and the nest
gone?

But scarcely had the sun risen a hand's breadth above the belt
of the woods before their tree came walking, and planted itself
in the same place which it had occupied the previous day. It was
as dark and gnarled as before, and carried the nest on the top
of a dry, straight branch. The wagtails immediately resumed their
nest-building without worrying their heads about nature's many
wonders.

Hatto the hermit, who used to drive small children away from
his grotto, telling them that it would have been best for them if
they had never seen the daylight, he who rushed out to hurl
curses after the merry young people who rowed in boats decked
with streamers, he from whose evil eye shepherds on the waste
guarded their flocks, returned to his post by the river for the
sake of the small birds. But he knew that not only every letter
in the Holy Scriptures has its hidden mystic significance, but also
everything which God allows to happen in the sphere of nature.
He had now discovered what was signified by the wagtails building their nest in his hand. God wished that he should remain
standing, praying with his arms uplifted till these birds had reared
their young, and if he could do that his prayer would be heard.

But during that day he certainly saw fewer visions of the Day
of Judgment. In place of that he followed the birds all the more
eagerly with his eyes, and saw the nest quickly completed. The
two small architects fluttered round it and inspected it. They
fetched some scraps of moss from the real willow tree and fastened them carefully on the outside of the nest to serve as plas-
tering and coloring. They fetched the finest cotton grass, and the
female wagtail took down from her own breast and lined the
inside of the nest by way of furnishing it.

The peasants who feared the terrible power which the hermit's
prayers might have with God were accustomed to bring him

bread and milk to propitiate his wrath. They happened to come just at this juncture, and found him standing motionless with a bird's nest in his hand. "See how the holy man loves the small creatures!" they said, and feared him no more, but lifted the milk pail to his mouth and put bread between his lips. When he had eaten and drunk he drove them away with hard words, but they only smiled at his curses.

His body had for a long time been the slave of his will. By fasting and scourging, by day-long kneeling and week-long waking it had been taught to obey. Now his muscles, as hard as iron, sustained his uplifted arms for days and weeks, and when the hen-bird laid her eggs and no longer left the nest he did not go to his grotto even at night. He taught himself to sleep sitting with his arms uplifted. Many hermits of the desert have done equally strange things.

He grew accustomed to the two tiny restless birds' eyes which looked down at him over the edge of the nest. He watched against hail and rain, and protected the nest as well as he could.

One day the hen-bird left her post. Both birds sat on the edge of the nest, jerked their tails, consulted with each other and looked delighted, although the whole nest seemed full of an anxious cheeping. After a little they set off on an energetic hunt after gnats.

Gnat after gnat was caught and brought to the creatures cheeping in his hand, and when the night came the cheeping was worse than ever, and disturbed the holy man in his prayers. Very softly he lowered his arm, although his muscles had almost lost the power to move, and his small, fiery eyes stared down into the nest. Never had he seen anything so helpless, ugly, and wretched —small naked bodies with a little thin down on them, no eyes, no power to fly, really nothing but six great gaping mouths. They seemed to him very strange, but he liked them just as they were. He had never exempted their parents from the great destruction that was coming, but after this when he prayed to God to bring about the deliverance of the world through destruction, he silently excepted these half-dozen defenseless creatures.

When the peasant women now brought him food he thanked them without wishing for their destruction. Since he was necessary for the little things up there he was glad that they did not let him die of hunger. Soon six round heads appeared all day long, stretching themselves over the edge of the nest. Old Hatto let his arm sink more and more frequently in order to watch them. He saw feathers projecting from their red skins, their eyes opening, and their bodies becoming rounder. Fortunate heirs of the beauty which nature has bestowed on the denizens of the air, they developed rapidly.

And all the while the prayers for the great destruction rose more hesitatingly from old Hatto's lips. He believed he had God's promise that it would come when the young birds were able to fly. Now he stood, and, as it were, tried to make a bargain on their behalf with God the Father, for he could not make up his mind to sacrifice these six small things which he had protected and nursed. It had been a different matter altogether when he possessed nothing of his own. Love to the small and helpless, which it has been every little child's mission to teach its formidable elders, came over him and made him hesitate.

Sometimes he felt inclined to throw the whole nest into the river, for he thought it would be good for them if they died without sin or sorrow. Should he not save the little creatures from birds of prey and cold, from hunger and the many trials of life? But just as he was thinking this a hawk swooped down with a rush on the nest to destroy the young ones. Hatto seized the daredevil with his left hand, swung him round over his head, and hurled him wrathfully into the river.

The day came when the young ones were ready for flight. One of the wagtails got into the nest in order to push them over the edge, while the other flew around to show them how easy it was if they would only try. But when the young ones were obstinate in their fears the two parent birds began to exhibit all their best arts of flying. Starting suddenly, they flew forward in long curves, or rose straight up like larks and kept themselves suspended in the air, with their wings vibrating vigorously.

But as the young ones still remained obstinate Hatto the hermit could not resist mixing in the affair. He gave them a real push with his finger and settled the matter. Out they came, fluttering and insecure, beating the air like bats. They sank, but rose again, doing their best to get back into the nest as soon as possible. Their parents flew down to them, proud and rejoicing, and old Hatto smiled. It was he who had decided the matter anyhow. He now set his wits seriously at work to see whether he could not beg them off from the coming destruction. Perhaps after all God the Father held this world in His right hand like a great bird's nest, and perhaps He had come to feel affection for all those who build and dwell in it, for all the defenseless children of earth. Perhaps He pities those whom He had vowed to destroy, like the hermit pitied the young birds. Certainly the hermit's birds were much better than the men whom God the Father had created, but yet it was believable that He had a heart for them also.

The next day the bird's nest was empty, and the bitterness of solitude weighed heavily upon the hermit. Slowly his arm sank down to his side, and it seemed to him as though all nature were holding its breath to listen for the trump of doom. But at that very moment all the wagtails came back and settled on his head and shoulders, for they were not at all afraid of him. Then a ray of light shot through old Hatto's bewildered brain. He had lowered his arm every day to look at the birds.

As he stood there with all the six young birds fluttering and playing about him he nodded contentedly at Someone Whom he did not see. "You let them off," he said. "You let them off. I have not kept my word, so You need not keep Yours."

And it seemed to him as though the rocks ceased to tremble, and the river, subsiding, flowed quietly on its course.

Translated by C. Field

VERNER von HEIDENSTAM
(1859–1940)

As a young man Heidenstam aspired to become a painter and went to Paris to study. But he soon gave up pictorial art to wander around Europe and the Near East and write poetry. On his return to Sweden he published a first volume of poems, *Vallfart och vandringsår* ("Pilgrimage and Wander-Years"), 1888, which brought him immediate recognition. A stanch opponent of the Realist school, he glorified the joy of life and the glimmering colors of the Swedish countryside. Later, however, a feeling of resignation to the insoluble mystery of life and death took hold of him, and the tone of his poetry became more subdued and nostalgic.

Among Heidenstam's best-known works is *The Charles Men* (1897–98), a series of short stories describing life and fate in the army of Sweden's great military hero-king, Charles XII. One of these is printed below.

Heidenstam was elected to the Swedish Academy in 1912 and was awarded the Nobel Prize for literature in 1916, but wrote very little during the last twenty-five years of his life.

Gunnel the Stewardess

In a vault of the fortress at Riga, Gunnel the stewardess, an old woman of eighty, sat and spun. Her long arms were veinous and sinewy, her breast was lean and flat like an old man's. Some thin white wisps of hair hung down over her eyes, and she had a cloth knotted about her head like a round cap.

The spinning wheel whirred, and a trumpeter lad lay on the stone floor in front of the fire.

"Grandma," said he, "can't you sing something while you are spinning? I've never heard you do otherwise than nag and scold."

For a brief moment she turned toward him her tired and wickedly chilling eyes.

"Sing? Perhaps of your mother, who was set on a wagon and carried to the Muscovites? Perhaps of your father, whom they hanged at the chimney of the house on the bridge? Curse will I the night when I was born, and myself will I curse and every human being I have met. Name me a single one who is not even worse than his repute."

"If you sing a song, you'll be cheerful, grandma, and I should be so glad to have you cheerful, this evening."

"He whom you see playing or laughing is only a master of deception. Misery and shame is all, and it is for the sake of our sins and our baseness that now the Saxons have come and besieged our city. Why don't you go in the evening and do your duty on the wall as at otherwhiles, instead of lying here in your laziness?"

"Grandma, can't you say a single pleasant word to me as I go?"

"Thrash you I should, if I were not so infirm and bent with my years that I no more can lift my countenance to heaven. Do you not want me to tell your fortune? Do they not call me the Sibyl? Shall I tell you that the crooked line over your eyebrows signifies on early death? I see years ahead into the future, but as far as I see I find only evil and low purposes. You are worse than I, and I am worse than my mother, and all that which is born is worse than that which dies."

He arose from the floor and stirred the logs.

"I will tell you, grandma, wherefore I sat myself by you this evening, and wherefore I asked of you a kindly word. The old governor-general has ordered today that before the following night all women, young and aged, sound and sick, shall go their way, so as not to consume the bread of the men. Those who refuse shall be punished with death. How can you, who in ten years have never gone further than across the castle courtyard to the storehouse, now be able to range about in wood and waste in the midst of the winter cold?"

She laughed and trod the spinning wheel faster and faster.

"Haha! I have been waiting for this after I tended so faithfully the noble lord's storeroom and all that was his. And you, Jan? Aren't you worried at having no one any longer to bake for you at the oven and make your bed on the folding-bench? What other feeling is there in children? Praised be God, be God, Who at the end casts us all under the scourge of His wrath!"

Jan clasped his hands about his curly brown hair.

"Grandma, grandma!"

"Go, I tell you, and let me sit in peace and spin my tow, till I open the door myself and go out of it to be quit of this earthly life!"

He took a few steps forward toward the spinning wheel, but thereupon turned about and went out of the vault.

The spinning wheel whirred and whirred, until the fire burned out. Next morning, when Jan the trumpeter came back, the vault stood empty.

The siege was long and severe. After divine service had been held, all the women went out of the city in the snowy days of February, and the feeble or sick were set upon litters and wagons. All Riga became a cloister for men, who had nothing to give to the flocks of begging women that now and then stole out in front of the wall. The men had scarcely bread for their own necessities, and the starved horses tore each other to pieces in the stalls, or devoured the mangers, and gnawed great holes in the wooden walls. Smoke hung over the burned suburbs, and at night the soldiers were often wakened by warning tocsins, and took down their broadswords from the ceiling.

In the evening, however, when Jan the trumpeter came home to the vault which he and his grandmother had had as a living room, he almost always found the folding-bench made up as a bed, and a bowl with moldy meat beside it on a chair. He was ashamed of saying anything about it to the others, but he was really terrified. He believed that his grandmother had perished in the snowdrifts, and that now, remorseful over her former hardness, she went about again without rest. In his fright he shook as with ague, and many a night he preferred to sleep hungry in the snow on the wall. After he had strengthened himself with prayer, however, he became easier, and finally he felt himself more surprised and anxious when he now and then found the folding-bench untouched and the chair empty. Then he would seat himself at the spinning wheel and, treading it very softly, would listen to the familiar whirring which he had heard day after day since his birth.

Now it happened one morning that the governor-general, the celebrated Erik Dahlberg, a man of seventy-five, heard violent shooting. He rose with impatient anger from his sketches and fortification models of wax. As a reminder of his bright youthful excursions in the service of beauty, splendid etchings of Roman ruins hung on the wall, but his formerly mild countenance had become wrinkled with melancholy, and an expression of harshness stiffened around the narrow, compressed, almost white lips. He adjusted his great spliced wig, and tremblingly ran his nails over his thin mustache. When he went down the stairs, he struck heavily on the stones with his cane, and said:

"Ah, we Swedes, we blood-kindred to the Vasa kings, who in their old age could only find fault and quarrel and at the last sat in their own rooms afraid of the dark—we have in our soul a black seed, from which with the years is raised a branching tree filled with the bitterest gall-apples."

He became bitterer and harsher in spirit the farther he went, and when he finally stood at the wall, he spoke to no one.

Several battalions had been drawn up with flags and music, but afterward the shooting had quieted, and through the gate returned scattered bands of weary and bleeding men who had just repulsed the enemy's attack. Last of them all came a thin and feeble old man, who had himself a red saber wound on the breast, but who painfully carried in his arms in front of him a wounded boy.

Erik Dahlberg raised his hand over his brows to look. Was not the fallen boy Jan the trumpeter, the lad from the castle? He recognized him by his curly brown hair.

At the arch of the gate the exhausted bearer sank down against the stone pillar, and remained there sitting with his wound and with the dead boy on his knee. Some soldiers, bending down to examine the wound, slit up the bloody shirt above the breast.

"What!" they shouted, and stepped back. "It's a woman."

Wondering, they bent down still lower to look at her face. She had sunk her head sidewise against the wall, and the fur cap slid down, so that the white locks of her hair fell forward.

"It's Gunnel the stewardess, the Sibyl!"

She breathed heavily and opened her dulling eyes.

"I didn't want to leave the boy alone in this world of evil, but after I had put on men's clothes and served night and day among the others on the wall, I thought that I was eating a man's bread without wrong."

Soldiers and officers looked dubiously at Erik Dahlberg, whose commands she had transgressed. He continued to stand there, reversed and harshly gloomy, while the stick in his hand trembled and tapped on the stone paving.

Slowly he turned to the battalion and the thin lips moved. "Lower your colors!" he said.

Translated by Charles Wharton Stork

GUSTAF FRÖDING
(1860–1911)

Fröding began to write poetry after suffering a nervous breakdown in 1889. The subsequent, productive period of his life lasted only about seven or eight years, but the influence of those few years' work was such that Swedish poetry has never since been the same. Fröding combined deep, sincere emotions and a variety of moods with an ingenious mastery of form. But his most pervasive characteristic is, perhaps, a sympathy with the unhappy, the miserable, the outcasts of society. His poetry spans a wide range of themes and tones, from social satires to humoristic descriptions of rural life, from lyric nature poems to Biblical fantasies.

After the publication of his third volume of poems in 1896, he was indicted as an offender of moral and common decency for the poem "A Morning Dream," in which he described the sexual act. Although Fröding was acquitted, the public censure to which he was subjected during the trial probably contributed to the deterioration of his frail mental health. In 1898 he was committed to an asylum where he remained until 1905.

Because of the difficulty of translating sensitive lyric poetry, Fröding is not widely known in the English-speaking world. Nevertheless, he was undoubtedly one of the truly great masters of lyric poetry in 19th-century European literature.

The poems below are from the volumes *Gitarr och dragharmonika* ("Guitar and Concertina"), 1891, and *Stänk och flikar* ("Splashes and Rags"), 1896.

Methinks Upon Thy Forehead

Methinks upon thy forehead should the stars have been shining,
Like garlands entwining
Their diadems of light in thy hair,

Where clear and bright as silver and gold pale-raying
Are thin bands playing,
Like streamers of the North-sheen in winter's air.

Lonely I see thee: thy wrists and feet were slender,
So fine and so tender,
And delicate and shy was thy gait;
I see thee as some fairy shape all shining and swaying,
With starlight arraying
Her tresses—such a phantom as in dreams we create.

In the shimmer on thy brow beheld I grief and music blended,
But frozen, suspended,
The melody lay voiceless on thy lips divine;
Thy form was fair and gracious, yet lacked it free expression
Of the soul's confession
In the spacious-curving harmonics of every rippling line.

Thy head thou heldest low, like the reed wind-shaken,
Life's hues had forsaken
Thy cheeks more pale than the wood's pale flowers;
But dark as skies of twilight was thine eyes' dull burning,
For far lands yearning,
Too dim in their remoteness for eyes like ours.

In torment ever seemedst thou—the wan light dying,
The half-quenched sighing
Of the godhead fading in thy glance, in thy breast;
Like a young muse singing, one too frail in her weakness,
Too mild in her meekness
To vie with all those great ones of the wide-arched chest.

Do I think, Thou art rich in thy loves and thy dreaming,
In the bright rays beaming
With all love, all beauty that thy soul must conceal—
What boots it? cometh shaming for thy wealths undoing,
Down-trampled in ruin
As violet in forest by the footpad's heel.

Thy neck I see it bended in thralldom: thy meekness,
Thy love and thy weakness
To harlotry shall bring thee—a slave shalt thou toil;

For ever 'tis the sweetest soul—that dreams the brightest vision—
Whom lust and derision
Shall break against the earth and befoul with its soil.

Yet haply hast thou nobler, more splendidly borne thee—
Tho' earth-folk may scorn thee,
Yet haply thy good fairies preserved thee from wrong!
For me thou wert a shape of light, of night's uprearing,
At dawn disappearing—
Who think of thee as starlight, a saga, a song.

Translated by C. D. Locock

Sigh, Sigh, Sedges

Sigh, sigh, sedges,
Flow, wave, flow!
Now tell me of young Ingalill,
What way may she go?

Like the wing-shattered gull's was her cry as she sunk in the mere:
'Twas when spring was in green last year.

They were wroth with her, the good folk of Östanalid,
And it made her young heart bleed.

They were wroth with her, the neighbors, for her goods and her gold,
And the love that her heart did hold.

Stabbed with thorns is an eye's pure blue,
Black mud they cast on a lily's dew.

Then sing, oh sing your grief-song,
Ye little waves and low:
Sigh, sigh, sedges,
Flow, waves, flow!

Translated by C. D. Locock

Little Inga

Inga, little Inga, now sing the song for me:
My soul feels so lonely on life's dull sea,
And Sorrow has filled for me the chalice.
Inga, little Inga, now sing the song for me:
Like tidings of comfort and delight shall it be
As it rings through my desolate palace.

Inga, little Inga, now sing the song for me,
And the half of my kingdom I swear I'll give to thee,
And all the gold and silver in my palace.
My love is all the silver and gold I can show,
And the half of my kingdom is the half of my woe:
O Inga, wilt thou drink of that chalice?

Translated by C. D. Locock

King Eric's Song to Karin
(After her dancing)

Of noblest flowers will I fashion
This garland for thy glorious hair:
Be memories of our love and passion
A wreath for thine old age to wear!

Thus with mine own hands do I place it
Around thy head, O child most dear—
This crown for thy lone years, to grace it
Thro' days when I no more am here.

How fairly in the dance she glideth,
So young, so fresh, yet never gay!
Thus in my wreath a rose-thorn hideth,
And poison in the blossomed spray.

I see a red drop start and quiver,
Oozing adown her sunny hair;
How torment hides in all I give her—
My gifts work ill, my wreath's a snare!

Translated by C. D. Locock

Poet Wennerbom

June's soft whispers, thro' the warm park stealing,
Greet the Poet Wennerbom, slow reeling
From the Workhouse—bottle tight in hand,
Tacking warily along the sand,
Smiling, feeling grand,
Mumbling happy in his mellow feeling.

Bees about the pathway he is treading
Droning circle: chestnut boughs are shedding
Tumbling larvae from each scented bloom:
All the air is filled with rich perfume—
Poet Wennerbom
Sits him down beneath the branches spreading.

Wild with joy the birds of heaven twitter,
Grasshoppers in hundreds twang the zither;
Wennerbom, he hears with bitter mien,
Takes another swill of wretched wine,
Guzzling like a swine;
Bright upon his flask the sunrays glitter.

Bard and Bottle thus converse demurely;
"Gin it is that holds our wits securely,
Comfort giving when all hope is fled.
Drink we to our youth and days long dead,
Just a drop," he said;
"Otherwise we'll get the staggers surely.

"Full of faith was I, of lofty thinking,
Till I drowned myself in all this drinking—
Fifteen years I've struggled in its grip.

Come, old comrade, here's good fellowship!
Just another sip!
Beauty flies—let's face it without blinking!"

Drowsy is he now: soon sleep is calling:
Kindly treetops filter the light falling
On the head of Poet Wennerbom,
Tenderly the chestnut rains its bloom,
Empty, neath the gloom,
Lies the flask, mid caterpillars crawling.

Rich and deep the glow that o'er him creeping
Floods his soul—into far limbos sweeping
Stings of conscience, thoughts of crime and ruth;
Gone into the dreamland of his youth,
Sleeps he well in sooth:
Good it is when Poets can lie sleeping.

Translated by C. D. Locock

ERIK AXEL KARLFELDT

(1864–1931)

A native of the beautiful Dalarna district, Karlfeldt was
always deeply attracted to the earth and the old farming
tradition. He was himself a farmer's son, and no other Swedish poet so identified himself with the soil. He knew from
experience the changes of the seasons, the plants and animals
of the countryside, every aspect of its nature and population.
And he wrote about it in colorful verses, filled with his own
peculiarly musical rhythm and broad humor. Next to Fröding
he is probably the greatest of modern Swedish poets.

Karlfeldt was to receive the Nobel Prize in 1918, but be-
cause he was at the time the secretary of the Swedish
Academy, which awards the prize, he would not accept it.
The prize was awarded him posthumously in 1931.

"The Virgin Mary" is taken from *Fridolins lustgård*
("Fridolin's Pleasure Garden"), 1901, "A Vagrant" from
Fridolins visor ("Fridolin's Verses"), 1898.

The Virgin Mary

She's coming down the meadow from the hall of Sjugareby,
A little maid with cheeks as fair as almond flowers to see,
As almond flowers and wild-rose flowers where town may never be,
Or road where dust of traffic soils and smothers.
What pathway have you followed, that your cheek was never burned?
What have you dreamed, O Mary, what has your bosom learned,
That your blood burneth not as that of others?
Around your hair uncovered a strange effulgence glows,
Your brow is like the crescent moon that beameth,
When over Meadow Mountain all white and bent it goes
And through the leafy blackthorn stems it gleameth.

The cooling winds of even set the columbine asway,
The lilies' yellow bells ring in the peaceful holy day;
The kids are hardly bleating, the colts will hardly neigh,
From nest and grove come faintest chirpings only.
And now the young Dalecarlian lads and girls go pair by pair;
But you, the flower of them all, whom each lad longs to wear,
Why have you come to ponder here so lonely?
You look as would a virgin, by her first communion stirred,
Who on Whitsunday night her watch is keeping,
While thinking of the Bread of Life and all that she has heard
Until her heart with ecstasy is leaping.

Turn back, turn back, O Mary, for dark is evening's brow,
Your mother must be anxious that alone you wander now;
For you are slight and fragile as a slender willow bough,
And in yon wood the grim bear prowleth surely.
The rose you hold as token, though, will keep you even there,
'Twas brought you by an angel from a sacred garden fair:
And you can tread on snake or thorn securely.
Yea, that long sunbeam stretching down so radiantly bright
O'er Silja Lake from glowing towers of even—
In truth you might be passing on your bridal way tonight
Along that narrow trembling bridge to heaven.

Translated by Charles Wharton Stork

A Vagrant

"Who are you and whence do you come?"
    I will not and cannot reply,
I am no man's son and I have no home,
    No son shall I have when I die.
    A stranger from far am I.

"What's your religion, what is your creed?"
    I only know this: I know naught.
And if I have missed the right path, indeed
    My error I've never been taught.
    But God first and last I have sought.

"How is your life?" It is storm and pain,
   A hard, endless battle-drive;
A glow that is quenched, a hope made vain,
   And clouds that with sunbeams strive.
   But still I am glad I'm alive.

Translated by Charles Wharton Stork

HJALMAR BERGMAN

(1883–1931)

Though practically unknown outside Scandinavia, Hjalmar Bergman is nevertheless considered one of the greatest Swedish writers of the 20th century. Prolific and versatile, his production includes novels, short stories, fairy tales, and dramas.

Bergman had an unusually keen insight into the human mind and an uncanny ability for penetrating the most complex psychology. Most of all, he was fascinated by people who wreck their lives through obstinacy, thoughtlessness, or self-delusion, and in his large gallery of characters these are the ones who appear most frequently. Writing in an original, fluent, and highly imaginative style, he had a unique way of affecting warm sympathy without suspending his keen satirical powers.

The following selection is from the short story collection *Labyrinten* ("The Labyrinth"), 1931.

Judith

The old man sat on a folding stool outside the gate. To anyone who approached he called out:

"Leave my house in peace!"

There were only three rooms and a kitchen in his house, plus two rooms in the attic. In the orchard the trees stood bare, the mats of grass were frostbitten, so that they were not even good for grazing. There was, in fact, not much to watch over. But the old man did not leave his post. He was still sitting there at dusk and to anyone who passed by he called out: "Leave my house in peace!"

If any of the foreign soldiers stopped at his gate, he got up from the stool, took off his greasy, green cap and told them that he had death in the house.

"Mr. Soldier, I'm telling you for your own good. I have death in my house. If you don't believe me, then come with me. I'll show you. But it's contagious, Mr. Soldier."

And Mr. Soldier took him at his word. He looked like death himself.

This house, where death was lodging, was the last one in town. When twilight had darkened into night, a young soldier came, asking to be let in. He had knocked at every door and found all the beds occupied. To grope around for the next house or the next town was impossible in the dark. And death he feared as little as it becomes a soldier to do. The old man repeated what he told every passer-by. But this one was young and rather overbearing. He laughed and said:

"I've heard that tune before. Look here, just let me in now. I won't steal or murder. I just want to sleep."

And when the old man informed him that death was in the house, he still wasn't frightened. He pushed the old man aside and stepped into the garden. It was so dark that he couldn't make out the door of the house, but he walked toward a light in a window. The old man followed him. When they came to the window, the old man said:

"See now, Mr. Soldier. I'm not lying. My son-in-law is in there. He's dead."

In the middle of the room stood a bed, the foot of it facing the window. A dead man lay upon it. He was young like the soldier, but dead. He was wrapped in a sheet all the way up to his chin. Near the head of the bed sat a woman or a girl. She sat before a table on which four candles were burning. The soldier looked more at the girl than at the dead man. He found her pretty, although far too dark and not at all as pretty as his own girl back home. Anyhow, that was none of his business. He just wanted to sleep. He turned toward the old man and said:

"Surely there must be a bed in the house or at least a mattress or something to lie on?"

"Yes, there is," said the old man. "The room in the attic has a bed where my son-in-law used to sleep before they were mar-

ried. But, Mr. Soldier, I'm telling you for your own good. You
can see with your own eyes that I have death in my house. It's
contagious. I ask you to leave my house in peace. I'm an old man
and I have grief enough already."

The soldier said:

"Look, pop, I don't intend to let that bed in the loft go unused.
No one will get hurt if I lie there, and it sure will feel good to
crawl in between the sheets."

He was deaf to the old man's protests and groped around for
the door. The anteroom was completely dark. The soldier was
obliged to open the door to the room where the four candles were
burning. But having opened the door it would have been impo-
lite not to step in and explain what he wanted. He clicked his
heels inside the threshold. The young woman straightened her
back slowly and nodded.

The soldier said:

"Excuse me, ma'am. I'm just looking for a bed for the night.
Would you or somebody else be kind enough to show me to the
room where your fiancé used to sleep?"

She said:

"The bed is already made and I will bring you water and light.
It's cold. Perhaps you'd like a fire? This time of year we always
used to light a fire when my fiancé was to sleep up there. Actually,
he was my husband; we were married last summer."

The soldier took off his cap and tiptoed toward the bed. He
felt he had to say something and asked:

"From what illness?"

"Oh," she said, and for the first time she looked him straight
in the eyes. "My husband died in the war. He fell the day before
yesterday. According to what they told me, it happened in a
bayonet fight. His throat was cut."

"Your father——" began the soldier.

She interrupted him:

"Yes, I know—he says we have a contagious disease in the
house. You didn't let that trick frighten you? It's too common.
Father's afraid that I'll lose my head if I see any of you. But I'm
not that stupid. Who murdered him? No one in particular. It's
the war."

"That's true," said the soldier. "One can't be angry at anyone in particular. It's the war, that's all."

He took a few more steps toward the head of the bed and looked at the dead man. The wife bent forward and pointed out how the bayonet had cut his throat from ear to ear. "It was a wound that just wouldn't stop bleeding. A whole day after he died, it was still bleeding." The soldier shook his head:

"Yes, it isn't pleasant to see them like this," he said. "When it happens, one thinks it's as it should be. But to see them afterward, and then here at home—that's hard. Yes, they fought damned well, your men. I was in that bayonet fight too."

"I know," said the woman. "Father claimed that our men got reinforcements and that you would take another road. But I knew you'd come. We heard your signals at noon. Father wanted us to hide. But what good would that do?"

"That's true!" exclaimed the soldier. He blushed with joy and enthusiasm. "We don't harm anybody. Just leave us in peace, then—it's very nice of you not to be afraid——"

He stopped suddenly, embarrassed over his enthusiasm. He felt miserably homeless here in enemy country, but that was a feeling which shouldn't be betrayed to just anybody. Fortunately, her thoughts seemed to be elsewhere. She had bent down over the dead man. She stroked his hair and his forehead in the same soft, comforting way as the soldier's own girl used to do, but now she said:

"We mustn't be standing here. I'm sure you're hungry."

She led him out to the dining room, lit a lamp hanging from the ceiling, and put a cloth on the table. She took his cap and his coat and hung them in the anteroom. His rifle she didn't touch. He preferred keeping it by him. When she went out to the kitchen, he took care to place it under the table. He kept his foot on the butt end. She made him a real feast. The soldier took out his purse and counted his coins. They weren't very many. "Thanks, thanks," he murmured, embarrassed. "Madame takes too much trouble."

And when she brought out two bottles of wine, he couldn't restrain himself.

"No, this is too much. I don't need anything so fine. And for the moment I don't have cash . . ."

She smiled.

"Now look, put that back in your pocket. It's high treason to sell food to the enemy. But to feed someone who's hungry can't be wrong. Not even in wartime."

She poured a glass of wine.

"Drink! Drink to anyone you like. Perhaps you have a fiancée at home? Yes, I can see you have. Now eat and drink. Meanwhile, I'll ready your room."

The soldier ate and drank. He thought: I'll just eat until I'm full, no more. She's terribly nice to me and it would be taking advantage of her kindness if I ate everything. But it's very tasty. If she or her old man would keep me company, it'd be different. But I can't ask that.

In a little while she came back. "Why don't you eat? Don't scorn the little our house can offer. Do you think, perhaps, that I've poisoned the wine? Look here!"

She poured a glassful and half-emptied it. Then she gave it to the soldier. He laughed and drank.

"Oh," he said. "It's not that I'm afraid. You're so kind. But why won't your father keep me company?"

She shrugged her shoulders.

"Father has old-fashioned ideas. He won't share his bread with an enemy. But it doesn't make sense to be so narrow-minded in our times. When one's own are gone, one has to make the best of the company that's offered. Right? I'm really hungry. Just think, I haven't eaten since I sat at the table with my husband the last time. And it's four days since then."

She took a chair and sat down opposite him. The soldier cut the roast and gave her some. They drank together. They began talking about this and that, about the weather, the bad roads, about the harvest that was interrupted. They avoided the war, but the soldier told humorous stories about home. First he told her about his parents and his childhood. He wanted most of all to talk about his fiancée, but he didn't dare. She listened attentively and smiled when he laughed. Suddenly she asked: "But your fiancée? Aren't you going to tell me anything about her?" He blushed. There wasn't anything to tell. Vague plans for the future. She agreed with him.

"Perhaps you'll never see her again."

The soldier sighed. He thought: Why does she torment me with this? I wish she'd sit here beside me. I'd like to hold her hand in mine. I'm so lonesome.

Just then she stood up and went to the front door. She listened. The soldier moved uneasily in his chair; he bent down and carefully drew up his rifle. The woman returned to the table and moved her chair nearer to the soldier. She said she felt terribly lonesome. "Just think, Mr. Soldier. I've been married four months and now I'm a widow. Can you understand that kind of emptiness? It's as if the whole world had come to an end. I've nothing more to think about, nothing to hope for, nothing to fear. It's dreadful not to have anybody to be fond of . . ."

The soldier asked:

"Were you very fond of your husband?"

She didn't answer. Her head sank down. Her bare neck bent in a pretty, touching, shy curve. The soldier thought: Ah, poor little girl, how pretty she is! And think how lonesome! Just like me. What shall I do now? I don't want to fall in love with her. I don't want to; no, I don't want to. Maybe I've had too much to drink. In there lies the husband. Ugh. Ah, she's never cared for him. Why else would she be sitting here? I'd better go up to my room.

He asked:

"What is your name?"

She looked up and stared at him with a surprised expression.

"What's my name? You mean my Christian one? My name is Judith."

"Judith," he repeated and smiled sleepily. "It sounds biblical, but it's a pretty name."

She nodded and suddenly she said:

"What a nice neck you have, Mr. Soldier."

He laughed embarrassed and asked her pardon. Without thinking, he had undone a few buttons of his uniform. Field manners! He started buttoning again. But she wouldn't let him. No, no, he should make himself at home. At least for tonight he should have a home. In unbuttoning him again she touched his bare neck. He took her by the arms and pulled her to him. She resisted but slightly. Then their feet touched the gun. The bayonet hit the leg of the table with a ringing sound of steel. They were startled.

The soldier burst out laughing.

"There you see!" he said. "Here we sit almost like man and wife at the dinner table in our home. But we keep a bayonet under the table. *C'est la guerre.*"

She stood up quickly and went out to the kitchen. Now you have offended her, he thought. How clumsy and stupid you are. Did you think she'd throw herself into your arms. Oh no, this is a respectable woman. And you didn't want anything of her. You've had too much to drink, that's all there is to it. Now go to sleep without saying good night. She won't see you.

He prepared to go and took up the gun. But just as he was getting up she came back. She had fetched dessert and a bottle of sherry. The soldier was on his guard. He behaved as correctly as he possibly could. He talked about inconsequential things and forced himself to keep his eyes and thoughts away from the woman. For the last time he drank to her.

"Are you going to sleep now too?" he asked.

She said:

"No, I'll go in to my husband."

He detected reproach in her words, and it irritated him. He felt an irrepressible desire to say something bitter to her. Why are you sitting here if you really cared for your husband? But he controlled himself and only said when he raised his glass:

"I'm sorry for you, my pretty enemy. But—*c'est la guerre.*"

He bowed as he left and took his gun. The old man held a light for him when he went up the stairs. The soldier closed the door behind him and put the latch on. He began to undress. The room was quite small, and the ceiling was low. The bed stood in the middle of the floor, nicely made with white sheets. Ah, that would feel good! On the nighttable four candles were burning. What a waste! He put out two of the lights. He kicked off his boots. Suddenly he crept toward the door and listened. The staircase creaked. He opened the door and whispered into the darkness: "Judith . . . Judith . . ."

Silence. He closed the door slowly but didn't latch it. He crept into bed and put out the lights. He said to himself: I'll just think about my own back home. . . .

In a few moments he was asleep.

He woke up. The room was bright with light; he saw the four candles. Judith stood bent over him. His heart began to beat and beat and beat. Ah, it was almost painful. He stretched up his arms and with trembling hands took her head.

"Judith . . . Judith . . ."

She said: "To you my name is Judith. To him down there I had another name. Who shall now name my name?"

"Judith . . . Judith . . ."

He pulled her head down.

Then he felt that she was cutting his throat.

"Judith!" he shrieked.

She said: "I'm sorry for you, my pretty enemy——"

He began to gurgle. She left him alone. The whole house was dark except for the two rooms where the candles burned. All the town lay quiet in the dark of night, where strangers slept among foes.

Translated by Hallberg Hallmundsson

PÄR LAGERKVIST
(1891–   )

When Pär Lagerkvist published his first volume of poetry in 1913, he called it *Ångest* ("Anguish"). It was typical of the poet, because anguish, resulting from the conflict between man's demand for a meaning in his existence and the inaccessibility of any interpretation of life has ever since been the recurrent theme of his works. While this feeling was at first strong, it figures less potently in his later works. Concurrently, Lagerkvist's faith has grown in man's ability to conquer evil and in the power of love to redeem the world.

A writer of poetry, novels, and dramas, Lagerkvist is a master of all three genres. Known in the English-speaking world mainly as a novelist, he is nevertheless regarded, by some critics, to be at his best in dramatic works. But in whatever form he may choose to communicate, the lyrical strain in his nature is always predominant.

Lagerkvist received the Nobel Prize for literature in 1951.

The story appearing below is from *Onda sagor* ("Evil Tales"), 1943.

The Lift That Went Down Into Hell

Mr. Smith, a prosperous businessman, opened the elegant hotel lift and amorously handed in a gracile creature smelling of furs and powder. They nestled together on the soft seat and the lift started downward. The little lady extended her half-open mouth, which was moist with wine, and they kissed. They had dined up on the terrace, under the stars; now they were going out to amuse themselves.

"Darling, how divine it was up there," she whispered. "So poetic sitting there with you, like being up among the stars. That's when you really know what love is. You do love me, don't you?"

Mr. Smith answered with a kiss that lasted still longer; the lift went down.

"A good thing you came, my darling," he said; "otherwise I'd have been in an awful state."

"Yes, but you can just imagine how insufferable he was. The second I started getting ready he asked where I was going. 'I'll go where I please,' I said. 'I'm no prisoner.' Then he deliberately sat and stared at me the whole time I was changing, putting on my new beige—do you think it's becoming? What do you think looks best, by the way, perhaps pink after all?"

"Everything becomes you, darling," the man said, "but I've never seen you so lovely as this evening."

She opened her fur coat with a gratified smile, they kissed for a long time; the lift went down.

"Then when I was ready to go he took my hand and squeezed it so that it still hurts, and didn't say a word. He's so brutal, you've no idea! 'Well, good-bye,' I said. But not a word from him. He's so unreasonable, so frightfully, I can't stand it."

"Poor little thing," said Mr. Smith.

"As though I can't go out for a bit and enjoy myself. But then he's so deadly serious, you've no idea. He can't take anything simply and naturally. It's as though it were a matter of life and death the whole time."

"Poor pet, what you must have gone through."

"Oh, I've suffered terribly. No one has suffered as I have. Not until I met you did I know what love is."

"Sweetheart," Smith said, hugging her; the lift went down.

"Fancy," she said, when she had got her breath after the embrace, "sitting with you up there gazing at the stars and dreaming—oh, I'll never forget it. You see, the thing is—Arvid is impossible, he's so everlastingly solemn, he hasn't a scrap of poetry in him, he has no feeling for it."

"Darling, it's intolerable."

"Yes, isn't it—intolerable. But," she went on, giving him her hand with a smile, "let's not sit thinking of all that. We're out to enjoy ourselves. You do really love me?"

"Do I!" he said, bending her back so that she gasped; the lift went down. Leaning over her he fondled her; she blushed.

"Let us make love tonight—as never before. Hm?" he whispered.

She pressed him to her and closed her eyes; the lift went down. Down and down it went.

At last Smith got to his feet, his face flushed.

"But what's the matter with the lift?" he exclaimed. "Why doesn't it stop? We've been sitting here for ever so long talking, haven't we?"

"Yes, darling, I suppose we have, time goes so quickly."

"Good Heavens, we've been sitting here for ages! What's the idea?"

He glanced out through the grill. Nothing but pitch darkness. And the lift went on and on at a good, even pace, deeper and deeper down.

"Heavens alive, what's the idea? It's like dropping down into an empty pit. And we've been doing this for God knows how long."

They tried to peep down into the abyss. It was pitch dark. They just sank and sank down into it.

"This is all going to hell," Smith said.

"Oh dear," the woman wailed, clinging to his arm, "I'm so nervous. You'll have to pull the emergency brake."

Smith pulled for all he was worth. It was no good. The lift merely plunged down and down interminably.

"It's frightful," she cried. "What are we going to do!"

"Yes, what the devil is one to do?" Smith said. "This is crazy."

The little lady was in despair and burst into tears.

"There, there, my sweet, don't cry, we must be sensible. There's nothing we can do. There now, sit down. That's right, now we'll sit here quietly both of us, close together, and see what happens. It must stop sometime or there'll be the devil to pay."

They sat and waited.

"Just think of something like this happening," the woman said. "And we were going out to have fun."

"Yes, it's the very devil," Smith said.

"You do love me, don't you?"

"Darling," Smith said, putting his arms around her; the lift went down.

At last it stopped abruptly. There was such a bright light all around that it hurt the eyes. They were in hell. The Devil slid the grill aside politely.

"Good evening," he said with a deep bow. He was stylishly dressed in tails that hung on the hairy top vertebra as on a rusty nail.

Smith and the woman tottered out in a daze. "Where in God's name are we?" they exclaimed, terrified by the weird apparition. The Devil, a shade embarrassed, enlightened them.

"But it's not as bad as it sounds," he hastened to add. "I hope you will have quite a pleasant time, I gather it's just for the night?"

"Yes, yes!" Smith asserted eagerly, "it's just for the night. We're not going to stay, oh no!"

The little lady clung tremblingly to his arm. The light was so corrosive and yellow-green that they could hardly see, and there was a hot smell, they thought. When they had grown a little more used to it they discovered they were standing as it were in a square, around which houses with glowing doorways towered up in the darkness; the curtains were drawn but they could see through the chinks that something was burning inside.

"You are the two who love each other?" the Devil inquired.

"Yes, madly," the lady answered, giving him a look with her lovely eyes.

"Then this is the way," he said, and asked them to follow please. They slunk into a murky side street leading out of the square. An old cracked lantern was hanging outside a filthy, grease-stained doorway.

"Here it is." He opened the door and retired discreetly.

They went in. A new devil, fat, fawning, with large breasts and purple powder caked on the mustache around her mouth, received them. She smiled wheezily, a good-natured, knowing look in her beady eyes; around the horns in her forehead she had twined tufts of hair and fastened them with small blue silk ribbons.

"Oh, is it Mr. Smith and the little lady?" she said. "It's in number eight then." And she gave them a large key.

They climbed the dim, greasy staircase. The stairs were slippery with fat; it was two flights up. Smith found number eight and went in. It was a fairly large, musty room. In the middle was a table with a grubby cloth; by the wall a bed with smoothed-down sheets. They thought it all very nice. They took off their coats and kissed for a long time.

A man came in unobtrusively from another door. He was dressed like a waiter but his dinner jacket was well cut and his shirtfront so clean that it gleamed ghostlike in the semidarkness. He walked silently, his feet making no sound, and his movements were mechanical, unconscious almost. His features were stern, the eyes looking fixedly straight ahead. He was deathly pale; in one temple he had a bullet wound. He got the room ready, wiped the dressing table, brought in a chamber pot and a slop pail.

They didn't take much notice of him, but as he was about to go, Smith said, "I think we'll have some wine. Bring us half a bottle of Madeira." The man bowed and disappeared.

Smith started getting undressed. The woman hesitated.

"He's coming back," she said.

"Pshaw, in a place like this you needn't mind. Just take your things off." She got out of her dress, pulled up her panties coquettishly and sat on his knee. It was lovely.

"Just think," she whispered, "sitting here together, you and I, alone, in such a queer, romantic place. So poetic, I'll never forget it."

"Sweetheart," he said. They kissed for a long time.

The man came in again, soundlessly. Softly, mechanically, he put down the glasses, poured out the wine. The light from the table lamp fell on his face. There was nothing special about him except that he was deathly pale and had a bullet wound in his temple.

The woman leaped up with a scream.

"Oh my God! Arvid! Is it you? Is it you? Oh God in Heaven, he's dead! He's shot himself!"

The man stood motionless, just staring in front of him. His face showed no suffering; it was merely stern, very grave.

"But Arvid, what have you done, what have you done! How could you! My dear, if I'd suspected anything like that, you know I'd have stayed at home. But you never tell me anything. You never said anything about it, not a word! How was I to know when you never told me! Oh my God. . . ."

Her whole body was shaking. The man looked at her as at a

stranger; his gaze was icy and gray, just went straight through everything. The sallow face gleamed, no blood came from the wound, there was just a hole there.

"Oh, it's ghastly, ghastly!" she cried. "I won't stay here! Let's go at once. I can't stand it."

She grabbed her dress, hat and fur coat and rushed out, followed by Smith. They slipped going down the stairs, she sat down, got spittle and cigarette ash on her behind. Downstairs the woman with the mustache was standing, smiling good-naturedly and knowingly and nodding her horns.

Out in the street they calmed down a little. The woman put on her clothes, straightened herself, powdered her nose. Smith put his arm protectingly round her waist, kissed away the tears that were on the point of falling—he was so good. They walked up into the square.

The head devil was walking about there, they ran into him again. "You *have* been quick," he said. "I hope you've been comfortable."

"Oh, it was dreadful," the lady said.

"No, don't say that, you can't think that. You should have been here in the old days, it was different then. Hell is nothing to complain of now. We do all we can not to make it too obvious, on the contrary to make it enjoyable."

"Yes," Mr. Smith said, "I must say it's a little more humane anyway, that's true."

"Oh," the Devil said, "we've had everything modernized, completely rearranged, as it should be."

"Yes, of course, you must keep up with the times."

"Yes, it's only the soul that suffers nowadays."

"Thank God for that," said the lady.

The Devil conducted them politely to the lift. "Good evening," he said with a deep bow, "welcome back." He shut the grill after them; the lift went up.

"Thank God that's over," they both said, relieved, and nestled up to one another on the seat.

"I should never have got through it without you," she whispered. He drew her to him, they kissed for a long time. "Fancy," she said, when she had got her breath after the embrace, "his doing such a thing! But he's always had such queer notions. He's never been able to take things simply and naturally, as they are. It's as though it were a matter of life and death the whole time."

"It's absurd," Smith said.

"He might have *told* me! Then I'd have stayed. We could have gone out another evening instead."

"Yes, of course," Smith said, "of course we could."

"But, darling, let's not sit and think of that," she whispered, putting her arms around his neck. "It's over now."

"Yes, little darling, it's over now." He clasped her in his arms; the lift went up.

Translated by Alan Blair

EPILOGUE

The apprehension felt by writers of the late thirties was well founded. Sooner than they had expected, the holocaust swept across the world, leaving none of the Scandinavian countries untouched. Denmark and Norway were occupied by the Nazi armies, Iceland by the British. Sweden, though not invaded, was forced to submit to German requests for transportation facilities over her territory.

The occupation of Denmark and Norway was responsible for a certain amount of typical wartime literature. Some of it was boldly patriotic in tone and served to unite the people against the Nazi tyranny. Such literature had to be distributed by underground channels. Those writers who openly published their work, on the other hand, had to clothe their ideas in subtle symbols in order to slip through the German censorship. After the war, memoirs of these trying years comprised the substance of innumerable publications.

In Iceland, occupation by Allied troops brought an end to the country's isolation. After centuries of poverty, overemployment and sudden economic prosperity caused serious dislocations, both social and moral. The effect on literature was marked. Icelandic writers were faced with hitherto unfamiliar problems, which in turn demanded fresh approaches in form and style. Moreover, the strong foreign influence created a broader international outlook. Contrarily, the continued presence after the war of American military personnel has resulted in a partial return to more nationalistic views.

Despite the upheaval caused by World War II, there was little real change in Scandinavian letters. In most respects, contemporary literature is either a direct continuation or a development of prewar trends. Generally—it may be argued—the writers have become more skeptical, more reluctant to take any "truth" at face value. Thus, for example, the idealistic Marxism of the period between the wars has been tempered by a more pragmatic political outlook, while the soul-searchings of serious writers, though more profound, are now less conclusive.

On the whole, Scandinavian writers of the younger generation have not yet given us literature of a quality comparable to its bulk. But this should not surprise us. Their fumbling steps, their incessant experimentations, their *avant garde* anger—in short, their search for new values—is merely indicative of the general insecurity of our time. As long as mankind is threatened by total destruction, a troubled note is bound to be heard in literature, not only in Scandinavia, but throughout the world.

BIBLIOGRAPHY

GENERAL SCANDINAVIAN LITERATURE

LITERARY HISTORY AND CRITICISM

Bredsdorff, Elias, B. Mortensen, and R. Popperwell. *An Intro-duction to Scandinavian Literature* from the earliest time to our day. Copenhagen, 1951.

Gustafson, Alrik. *Six Scandinavian Novelists*. Lie, Jacobsen, Hei-denstam, Selma Lagerlöf, Hamsun, Sigrid Undset. Princeton and New York, 1940.

COLLECTIONS

A Pageant of Old Scandinavia, ed. by Henry Goddard Leach. Princeton and New York, 1946.

Scandinavian Plays of the Twentieth Century. Introductions by Alrik Gustafson. 3 vols. Princeton and New York, 1944–51.

20th Century Scandinavian Poetry, 1900–1950. General editor, Martin S. Allwood. Copenhagen, 1950.

DENMARK

BIBLIOGRAPHY

Bredsdorff, Elias. *Danish Literature in English Translation*, with a special Hans Christian Andersen supplement. Copenhagen, 1950.

Mitchell, P. M. *A Bibliographical Guide to Danish Literature*. Copenhagen, 1951.

LITERARY HISTORY AND CRITICISM

Claudi, Jørgen. *Contemporary Danish Authors*. Copenhagen, 1952.

Mitchell, P. M. *A History of Danish Literature*, with an introduc-tory chapter by Mogens Haugsted. New York, 1958.

COLLECTIONS

A Book of Danish Ballads, selected and with an introduction by Axel Olrik. Translated by E. M. Smith-Dampier. Princeton and New York, 1939.

A Book of Danish Verse, translated into the original meters by S. Foster Damon and Robert Silliman Hillyer. Selected and annotated by Oluf Friis. New York, 1922.

Denmark's Best Stories: An Introduction to Danish Fiction, ed. by Hanna Astrup Larsen. New York, 1928.

The Hymns of Denmark, translated by Gilbert Tait (pseud.). London, 1868.

In Denmark I Was Born. A Little Book of Danish Verse, selected and translated by R. P. Keigwin with contributions by other hands. Copenhagen, 1948.

The Jutland Wind and Other Verse from the Danish Peninsula, done into English by R. P. Keigwin. Oxford, 1944.

Modern Danish Poems, selected by Knud K. Mogensen. Copenhagen, 1949.

A Second Book of Danish Verse, with a foreword by Johannes V. Jensen. Princeton, 1947.

INDIVIDUAL WORKS

Saxo Grammaticus. *The Nine Books of the Danish History of Saxo Grammaticus*, translated by Oliver Elton. London and New York, 1907.

Holberg, Ludvig. *Comedies* [*Jeppe of the Hill, The Political Tinker, Erasmus Montanus*], translated by O. J. Campbell and Frederic Schenck. New York, 1914.

———. *Four Plays* [*The Fussy Man, The Masked Ladies, The Weather Cock, Masquerade*], translated by Henry Alexander. New York, 1946.

———. *Journey of Niels Klim to the World Underground*, ed. by James I. McNelis, Jr. Lincoln, Nebr., 1960.

———. *Peder Paars*, translated by Bergliot Stromsoe. Introduction by Børge Gedsø Madsen. Lincoln, Nebr., 1962.

———. *Seven One-Act Plays* [*The Talkative Barber* (*Gert Westphaler*), *The Arabian Powder, The Christmas Party, Diderich the Terrible, The Peasant in Pawn, Sganarel's Journey to the*

Land of the Philosophers, The Changed Bridegroom], translated by Henry Alexander. New York, 1950.

Ewald, Johannes. *The Death of Balder*, translated by George Barrow. London, 1889.

Oehlenschläger, Adam. *Axel and Valborg. An Historical Tragedy in Five Acts*, translated by Frederick Strange Kolle. New York, 1906.

———. *Correggio: A Tragedy*, with a sketch of the autobiography of Oehlenschläger. Boston, 1846.

———. *An English Version of Oehlenschläger's Hakon Jarl*, by J. C. Lindberg (*University of Nebraska Studies*, Vol. V). Lincoln, 1905.

———. *The Gods of the North. An Epic Poem*, translated into English verse. London, 1845.

———. *Palnatoke. A Tragedy*, translated by John Chapman. London, 1855.

Andersen, Hans Christian. *Andersen's Fairy Tales*, translated by Jean Hersholt and illustrated in color by Fritz Kredel. New York, 1947.

———. *Fairy Tales, I-IV*, ed. by Svend Larsen. Translated by R. P. Keigwin. Illustrations by Vilhelm Pedersen and Lorenz Frølich. Odense, 1950.

———. *Hans Christian Andersen's Longer Stories*, translated by Jean Hersholt and illustrated in color by Fritz Kredel. New York, 1948.

———. *Hans Christian Andersen's Shorter Tales*, translated by Jean Hersholt and illustrated in color by Fritz Kredel. New York, 1948.

———. *It's Perfectly True and Other Stories*, translated by Paul Leyssac. Illustrated by Richard Bennet. New York, 1944.

———. *The True Story of My Life*, translated by Mary Howitt. New York, 1926.

———. *The Tumble-Bug and Other Tales*, translated by Paul Leyssac. Illustrated by Hertha List. New York, 1940.

Jacobsen, J. P. *Marie Grubbe: A Lady of the Seventeenth Century*, translated with an introduction by Hanna Astrup Larsen. New York, 1962.

———. *Mogens and Other Stories*, translated by Anna Grabow. New York, 1921.

——. *Niels Lyhne,* translated by Hanna Astrup Larsen. New York, 1930.

——. *The Plague in Bergamo,* translated by Else Ellefsen. Edinburgh, 1923.

——. *Poems,* translated by P. Selver. Oxford, 1920.

Pontoppidan, Henrik. *The Apothecary's Daughter,* translated by G. Nielsen. London, 1890.

——. *Emanuel, or Children of the Soil,* translated by Mrs. Edgar Lucas. Illustrated by Nelly Erichsen. London, 1896.

——. *The Promised Land,* translated by Mrs. Edgar Lucas. Illustrated by Nelly Erichsen. London, 1896.

Andersen-Nexø, Martin. *Days in the Sun.* Authorized translation by Jacob Wittmer Hartmann. New York, 1927.

——. *Ditte, I–III,* translated by A. G. Chater and Richard Thirsk. New York, 1931.

——. *In God's Land.* Authorized translation by Thomas Seltzer. New York, 1933.

——. *Pelle the Conqueror, I–II,* translated by Jessie Muir and Bernard Miall. New York, 1930.

——. *Under the Open Sky; My Early Years,* translated by J. B. C. Watkins. New York, 1938.

Jensen, Johannes V. *The Fall of the King,* translated by P. T. Federspiel and Patrick Kirwan. New York, 1933.

——. *The Long Journey,* translated by A. G. Chater, with an introduction by Francis Hackett. Nobel Prize edition. New York, 1945.

——. *The Waving Rye.* Copenhagen and New York, 1959.

Hansen, Martin A. *The Liar [Løgneren],* translated by John Jepson Egglishaw. London, 1954.

NORWAY

LITERARY HISTORY AND CRITICISM

Beyer, Harald. *A History of Norwegian Literature,* translated and edited by Einar Haugen. New York, 1956.

Jorgenson, Theodore. *Norwegian Literature in Medieval and Early Modern Times.* Northfield, Minn., 1952.

McFarlane, J. W. *Ibsen and the Temper of Norwegian Literature.* London, 1960.

COLLECTIONS

Anthology of Norwegian Lyrics, translated in the original meters by C. W. Stork, with an introduction by C. J. Hambro. Princeton, 1942.

Told in Norway. An Introduction to Modern Norwegian Fiction, ed. by Hanna Astrup Larsen. New York, 1927.

INDIVIDUAL WORKS

Dass, Petter. *The Trumpet of Nordland*, translated by Theodore Jorgenson. Northfield, Minn., 1954.

Wergeland, Henrik. *Poems*, translated by G. M. Gathorne-Hardy, J. Bithell, and I. Grøndahl. London, 1929.

Asbjørnsen, P. Chr., and Jørgen Moe. *East o' the Sun and West o' the Moon, and Other Norse Fairy Tales*, translated by G. W. Dasent. New York and London, 1917.

——. *Fairy Tales from the Far North*, translated from the Norwegian by H. L. Brækstad. New York, 1897.

——. *Folk and Fairy Tales*, translated by H. L. Brækstad. New York, 1886.

——. *Norwegian Fairy Tales*, translated by Helen and John Gade. New York, 1924.

——. *Norwegian Folk Tales*, illustrated by Erik Werenskiold and Theodor Kittelsen. Translated by Pat Shaw Iversen and Carl Norman. New York, 1960.

——. *A Time for Trolls. Fairy Tales from Norway*, selected and translated with an introduction by Joan Roll-Hansen. Illustrated by Kai Ovre. Oslo, 1962.

Ibsen, Henrik. *Brand*, translated by Michael Meyer. New York, 1960.

——. *The Collected Works of Henrik Ibsen*. Copyright edition, ed. by William Archer. 12 vols. New York, 1929.

——. *A Doll's House*. English version by Norman Gainsbury. London, 1950.

——. *Early Plays* [*Catiline, The Warrior's Barrow, Olaf Liljekrans*], translated by Anders Orbeck. New York, 1921.

——. *An Enemy of the People*. An adaptation by Arthur Miller. New York, 1951.

——. *Ghosts*, translated by Bjorn Kofoed. New York, 1952.

——. *Hedda Gabler and Three Other Plays* [*The Pillars of Society, The Wild Duck, Little Eyolf*], translated by Michael Meyer. New York, 1961.

——. *In the Mountain Wilderness and Other Poems*, translated by Theodore Jorgenson. Northfield, Minn., 1957.

——. *Ibsen Letters and Speeches*, ed. by Evert Sprinchorn. New York, 1964.

——. *The Last Plays of Henrik Ibsen* [*Rosmersholm, Hedda Gabler, The Master Builder, John Gabriel Borkman, When We Dead Awaken*], translated by Arvid Paulsen with an introduction by John Gassner. New York, 1961.

——. *Lyrics and Poems from Ibsen*, translated by F. E. Garret. London, 1912.

——. *Peer Gynt*, translated by Michael Meyer. New York, 1963.

——. *When We Dead Awaken and Three Other Plays* [*The Master Builder, John Gabriel Borkman, The Lady from the Sea*], translated by Michael Meyer. New York, 1960.

Bjørnson, Bjørnstjerne. *Mary, Queen of Scots*, translated by A. Sahlberg. Chicago, 1910.

——. *The Novels of Bjørnstjerne Bjørnson*, ed. by Edmund Gosse, 13 vols. [1. *Synnøve Solbakken*, 2. *Arne*, 3. *A Happy Boy*, 4. *The Fisher Lass*, 5. *The Bridal March, One Day*, 6. *Magnhild, Dust*, 7. *Captain Mansana, Mother's Hands*, 8. *Absalom's Hair, A Painful Memory*, 9–10. *In God's Way*, 11–12. *The Heritage of the Kurts*, 13. *Mary*]. London, 1895–1909.

——. *Paul Lange and Tora Parsberg*, translated by H. L. Brækstad. London, 1899.

——. *Plays*. Two series. [I. *The Gauntlet, Beyond Our Power, The New System*, II. *Love and Geography, Beyond Human Might, Laboremus*], translated by Edwin Björkman. New York, 1913–14.

——. *Poems and Songs*, translated in the original meters by Arthur Hubbell Palmer. New York, 1915.

——. *Sigurd Slembe*, translated by William Morton Payne, Chicago, 1910.

——. *Three Comedies* [*The Newly-married Couple, Leonarda, A Gauntlet*], translated by R. Farquharson Sharp. New York, 1914.

——. *Three Dramas* [*The Editor, The Bankrupt, The King*], translated by R. Farquharson Sharp. New York, 1914.

Hamsun, Knut. *August,* translated by Eugene Gay-Tifft. New York, 1931.

——. *Dreamers,* translated by W. W. Worster. New York, 1921.

——. *Growth of the Soil,* translated by W. W. Worster. New York, 1921.

——. *Hunger,* translated by George Egerton (pseud.). New York, 1920.

——. *Look Back on Happiness,* translated by Paula Wiking. New York, 1940.

——. *Mysteries,* translated by A. G. Chater. New York, 1927.

——. *Pan,* translated by J. W. McFarlane. London, 1955.

——. *The Road Leads On,* translated by Eugene Gay-Tifft. New York, 1934.

——. *Segelfoss Town,* translated by J. S. Scott. New York, 1925.

——. *Vagabonds,* translated by Eugene Gay-Tifft. New York, 1930.

——. *Victoria,* translated by A. G. Chater. New York, 1923.

——. *Wanderers,* translated by W. W. Worster. New York, 1922.

Duun, Olav. *Good Conscience,* translated by Edwin Björkman. New York, 1928.

——. *Floodtide of Fate,* translated by R. G. Popperwell. London, 1960.

——. *The People of Juvik,* translated by A. G. Chater, 6 vols. [I. *The Trough of the Wave,* II. *The Blind Man,* III. *The Big Wedding,* IV. *Odin in Fairyland,* V. *Odin Grows Up,* VI. *The Storm*]. New York, 1930–35.

Undset, Sigrid. *The Burning Bush,* translated by A. G. Chater. New York, 1932.

——. *The Faithful Wife,* translated by A. G. Chater. New York, 1937.

——. *Gunnar's Daughter,* translated by A. G. Chater. New York, 1936.

——. *Ida Elisabeth,* translated by A. G. Chater. New York, 1933.

——. *Images in a Mirror,* translated by A. G. Chater. New York, 1938.

——. *Jenny,* translated by W. Emmé. New York, 1921.

———. *Kristin Lavransdatter*, translated by C. Archer and J. S. Scott, 3 vols. [I. *The Bridal Wreath*, II. *The Mistress of Husaby*, III. *The Cross*]. New York, 1923–27.

———. *The Master of Hestviken*, translated by A. G. Chater, 4 vols. New York, 1928–30.

———. *Return to the Future*, translated by Henriette C. K. Næseth. New York, 1942.

———. *The Wild Orchid*, translated by A. G. Chater. New York, 1931.

ICELAND

LITERARY HISTORY AND CRITICISM

Andersson, Theodore M. *The Problem of Icelandic Saga Origins: A Historical Survey* (*Yale Germanic Studies*, No. 1). New Haven, Conn., and London, 1964.

Beck, Richard. *History of Icelandic Poets 1800–1940* (*Islandica*, Vol. XXXIV). Ithaca, N.Y., 1950.

Einarsson, Stefán. *History of Icelandic Prose Writers 1800–1940* (*Islandica*, Vols. XXXII and XXXIII). Ithaca, N.Y., 1948.

———. *A History of Icelandic Literature*. New York, 1957.

Hallberg, Peter. *The Icelandic Saga*, translated with introduction and notes by Paul Schach. Lincoln, Nebr., 1962.

Liestøl, Knut. *The Origin of the Icelandic Family Sagas*. Oslo, 1930.

Turville-Petre, G. *Origins of Icelandic Literature*. Oxford, 1953.

COLLECTIONS

Bjarnason, Paul. *More Echoes*. Vancouver, Canada, 1962.

———. *Odes and Echoes*. Vancouver, Canada, 1954.

Eirik the Red and Other Icelandic Sagas, selected and translated with an introduction by Gwyn Jones. London, 1961.

Four Icelandic Sagas [*Hrafnkel Freysgodi's Saga, Thorstein the White's Saga, The Weaponfirther's Saga, The Saga of the Men of Keelness*], translated with introduction and notes by Gwyn Jones. Princeton and New York, 1935.

Icelandic Christian Classics, translated in whole or part with introduction by C. V. Pilcher. Melbourne, 1950.

Icelandic Lyrics. Originals and translations selected and edited by Richard Beck. Reykjavík, 1930.

Icelandic Poems and Stories, ed. by Richard Beck. New York, 1943.

The North-American Book of Icelandic Verse, by Watson Kirkconnell. New York and Montreal, 1930.

Northern Lights. Icelandic poems translated by Jakobina Johnson. Reykjavík, 1959.

Old Norse Poems. The Most Important Non-Skaldic Verse, translated by Lee M. Hollander. New York, 1936.

Seven Icelandic Short Stories, ed. by Ásgeir Pétursson and Steingrímur J. Thorsteinsson. New York, 1961.

The Skalds. A selection by Lee M. Hollander. New York, 1945.

Three Icelandic Sagas [*Gunnlaugs saga Ormstungu, Bandamanna saga*, (and) *Droplaugarsona saga*], translated by M. H. Scargill and Margaret Schlauch. Illustrated by H. G. Glyde. Princeton and New York, 1950.

INDIVIDUAL WORKS

Egil's Saga, translated with introduction and notes by Gwyn Jones. Syracuse, N.Y., 1960.

Eyrbyggja Saga, translated by Paul Schach. Introduction and verse translations by Lee M. Hollander. Lincoln, Nebr., 1959.

Heimskringla. History of the Kings of Norway, by Snorri Sturluson. Translated with introduction and notes by Lee M. Hollander. Austin, Tex., 1964.

The Laxdoela Saga, translated with introduction and notes by A. Margaret Arent. Seattle and New York, 1964.

Njál's Saga, translated by Carl F. Bayerschmidt and Lee M. Hollander. New York, 1955.

The Poetic Edda, translated with an introduction and notes by Henry Adams Bellows. New York, 1957.

The Prose Edda, translated by Jean I. Young. Introduction by Sigurdur Nordal. Cambridge, 1954.

The Saga of Gísli, translated by George Johnston, with notes and an essay on "The Saga of Gísli" by Peter Foote. London and Toronto, 1963.

The Saga of Grettir the Strong, translated by George A. Hight. London, 1914.

The Vatnsdalers' Saga, translated by Gwyn Jones. New York, 1944.

Pétursson, Hallgrímur. *Icelandic Meditations on the Passion*, selected and translated by C. V. Pilcher. New York, 1923.

Benediktsson, Einar. *Harp of the North. Poems*, selected and translated by Frederic T. Wood. Charlottesville, Va., 1955.

Gunnarsson, Gunnar. *The Good Shepherd*, translated by Kenneth C. Kaufman. Illustrated by Masha Simkovitch. Indianapolis, 1940.

———. *Guest the One-Eyed*. London, 1920.

———. *The Night and the Dream*, translated by Evelyn Ramsden. Indianapolis, 1938.

———. *Seven Days' Darkness*, translated by Roberts Tapley. New York, 1930.

———. *Ships in the Sky*, translated by Evelyn Ramsden. Indianapolis, 1938.

———. *The Sworn Brothers*, translated by C. Field and W. Emmé. New York, 1921.

Thórdarson, Thórbergur. *In Search of My Beloved*, translated by Kenneth G. Chapman. Reykjavík, 1961.

Laxness, Halldór. *The Atom Station*, translated by Magnus Magnusson. London, 1961.

———. *The Happy Warriors*, translated by Katherine John. London, 1958.

———. *The Honor of the House*, translated by Kenneth G. Chapman. Reykjavík, 1959.

———. *Independent People*, translated by J. A. Thompson. New York, 1946.

———. *Paradise Reclaimed*, translated by Magnus Magnusson. New York, 1962.

———. *Salka Valka*, translated by F. H. Lyon. London, 1964.

SWEDEN

BIBLIOGRAPHY AND LITERARY HISTORY

Afzelius, Nils. *Books in English on Sweden*. Stockholm, 1951.

Gustafson, Alrik. *A History of Swedish Literature*. Minneapolis, 1961.

COLLECTIONS

Anthology of Swedish Lyrics from 1750 to 1925, translated with an introduction by C. W. Stork. New York, 1930.

Modern Swedish Masterpieces. Short stories selected and translated by C. W. Stork. New York, 1923.

Modern Swedish Short Stories. London, 1934.

A Selection from Modern Swedish Poetry, translated by C. D. Locock. London and New York, 1929.

Sweden's Best Stories, translated by C. W. Stork with an introduction by Hanna Astrup Larsen. New York, 1928.

Swedish Poets of the Seventeenth Century. Some Gleanings from the Swedish Parnassus. Translations from the Swedish and biographical notes by Reinhold Ahléen. San Francisco, 1932.

INDIVIDUAL WORKS

Bellman, Carl Michael. *The Last of the Troubadours: The Life and Music of Carl Michael Bellman,* by Hendrik Willem van Loon and Grace Castagnetta. New York, 1939.

Tegnér, Esaias. *Frithiof's Saga,* translated in the original meters by C. D. Locock. London and New York, 1924.

——. *Poems by Tegnér: The Children of the Lord's Supper and Frithiof's Saga,* translated by Henry Wadsworth Longfellow and W. Lewery Blackley with an introduction by Paul R. Lieder. New York, 1914.

Rydberg, Viktor. *The Freebooter of the Baltic,* translated by Caroline L. Broomall. Media, Pa., 1891.

——. *The Last Athenian,* translated by William W. Thomas, Jr. Philadelphia, 1879.

——. *Singoalla,* translated by Aksel Josephson. Illustrated by Carl Larsson. New York, 1903.

——. *Teutonic Mythology,* translated by R. B. Anderson. London, Stockholm, and New York, 1906.

Strindberg, August. *Eight Famous Plays by Strindberg [The Link, The Father, Miss Julie, The Stronger, There Are Crimes and Crimes, Gustavus Vasa, The Dance of Death, The Spook Sonata],* translated by Edwin Björkman and N. Erichsen. New York and London, 1949.

——. *Five Plays of Strindberg [Creditors, Crime and Crime, The Dance of Death, Swanwhite, The Great Highway],* translated by Elizabeth Sprigge. Garden City, N.Y., 1960.

——. *The Growth of a Soul,* translated by C. Field. New York and London, 1914.

——. *The Inferno,* translated by C. Field. London and New York, 1913.

——. *Married: Twenty Stories of Married Life,* translated by Ellie Schleussner. New York, 1917.

——. *The People of Hemsö,* translated by Elspeth Harley Schubert. London, 1959.

——. *Plays by August Strindberg.* Five series [I. *The Dream Play, The Link, The Dance of Death, I and II,* II. *There Are Crimes and Crimes, Miss Julia, The Stronger, Creditors, Pariah,* III. *Swanwhite, Simoon, Debit and Credit, Advent, The Thunderstorm, After the Fire,* IV. *The Bridal Gown, The Spook Sonata, The First Warning, Gustavus Vasa,* V. *The Father, The Black Glove, The Pelican, Moses*], translated with introduction by Edwin Björkman. New York, 1912–16.

——. *The Red Room,* translated by Ellie Schleussner. London and New York, 1913.

——. *Seven Plays by August Strindberg* [*The Father, Miss Julie, Comrades, The Stronger, The Bond, Crimes and Crimes, Easter*], translated by Arvid Paulson with an introduction by John Gassner. New York, 1960.

——. *Six Plays of Strindberg* [*The Father, Miss Julie, The Stronger, Easter, A Dream Play, The Ghost Sonata*], translated by Elizabeth Sprigge. Garden City, N.Y., 1955.

——. *The Son of the Servant,* translated by C. Field. With an introduction by H. Vacher-Burch. New York and London, 1913.

——. *Three Plays by August Strindberg* [*The Father, Miss Julie, Easter*], translated by Peter Watts. London, 1958.

Lagerlöf, Selma. *The Emperor of Portugallia,* translated by Velma S. Howard. New York and London, 1926.

——. *The Girl from the Marshcroft,* translated by Velma S. Howard. Garden City, N.Y., 1924.

——. *The Holy City. Jerusalem II,* translated by Velma S. Howard. New York, 1918.

——. *Jerusalem,* translated by Velma S. Howard. New York, 1915.

——. *Mårbacka,* translated by Velma S. Howard. New York, 1931.

——. *The Queens of Kungahälla and Other Sketches,* translated by C. Field. London, 1917.

——. *The Ring of the Löwenskölds.* A trilogy including *The General's Ring, Charlotte Löwensköld,* and *Anna Svärd,* translated by Francesca Martin and Velma S. Howard. New York, 1931.

——. *The Story of Gösta Berling,* translated and with an afterword by Robert Bly. New York, 1962.

——. *The Tale of a Manor and Other Sketches,* translated by C. Field. London, 1923.

——. *The Wonderful Adventures of Nils,* translated by Velma S. Howard. New York, 1907.

Heidenstam, Verner von. *The Charles Men, I–II,* translated by C. W. Stork with an introduction by Fredrik Böök. New York, 1920.

——. *Sweden's Laureate. Selected Poems of Verner von Heidenstam,* translated with an introduction by C. W. Stork. New Haven, Conn., 1919.

——. *The Swedes and Their Chieftains,* translated by C. W. Stork. New York, 1925.

——. *The Tree of the Folkungs,* translated by A. G. Chater. New York, 1925.

Fröding, Gustaf. *Gustaf Fröding. Selected Poems,* translated with an introduction by C. W. Stork. New York, 1916.

——. *Guitar and Concertina. A Century of Poems by Gustaf Fröding,* translated in the original meters by C. D. Locock. London, 1925.

Karlfeldt, Erik Axel. *Arcadia Borealis. Selected Poems of Erik Axel Karlfeldt,* translated with an introduction by C. W. Stork. Minneapolis, 1938.

Bergman, Hjalmar. *God's Orchid [Markurells i Wadköping],* translated by E. Classen. New York, 1924.

——. *The Head of the Firm,* translated by Elizabeth Sprigge and C. Napier with an introduction by R. G: son Berg. London, 1936.

——. *Thy Rod and Thy Staff [Farmor och Vår Herre],* translated by C. Napier. London, 1937.

Lagerkvist, Pär. *Barabbas,* translated by Alan Blair with a preface by Lucien Maury and a letter by André Gide. New York, 1951.

——. *The Death of Ahasuerus,* translated by Naomi Walford. Drawings by Emil Antonucci. New York, 1962.

——. *The Dwarf,* translated by Alexander Dick. New York, 1945.

———. *The Eternal Smile and Other Stories,* translations by Alan Blair, Erik Mesterton, Denys W. Harding, and Carl Eric Lindin. With an introduction by Richard B. Vowles. New York, 1954.

———. *Midsummer Dream in the Workhouse. A Play in Three Acts,* translated by Alan Blair. London, 1953.

———. *The Sibyl,* translated by Naomi Walford. New York, 1958.